China in Transition

Hohenheimer Volkswirtschaftliche Schriften

Band 68

PETER LANG
Frankfurt am Main · Berlin · Bern · Bruxelles · New York · Oxford · Wien

Christian Böber

China in Transition

Poverty, Income Decomposition and Labor Allocation of Agricultural Households in Hebei Province

PETER LANG
Frankfurt am Main · Berlin · Bern · Bruxelles · New York · Oxford · Wien

Bibliographic Information published by the Deutsche Nationalbibliothek
The Deutsche Nationalbibliothek lists this publication in the Deutsche Nationalbibliografie; detailed bibliographic data is available in the internet at http://dnb.d-nb.de.

Zugl.: Hohenheim, Univ., Diss., 2011

D 100
ISSN 0721-3085
ISBN 978-3-631-63328-1

www.peterlang.de

To Anne and Simone

Acknowledgements

The present work was approved by the Faculty of Business, Economics and Social Sciences at the University of Hohenheim as a dissertation in June 2011.

I am especially grateful to my supervisors and referees Professor Dr. Michael Ahlheim and Professor Dr. Manfred Zeller for their advice and support, their encouragement and for the freedom I was granted during my time as doctoral student and the experiences I could make while working with them. Furthermore, I want to thank Professor Dr. Harald Hagemann for his interest and participation in the oral doctoral examination.

I am thankful to Professor Dr. Reiner Doluschitz for his support in the International Research Training Group (IRTG) "Sustainable Resource Use in the North China Plain". The administrative support of Miss Bayer is highly appreciated. I am also thankful to Dr. Diana Ebersberger for helping me organizing the research stays in China and making my participation at international Ph.D. courses and conferences possible. I am grateful to my Chinese friends, colleagues, interviewers and translators who enabled me to conduct my data collection and provided me with many positive insights into the Chinese culture.

During my research within the IRTG and at the Department of Rural Development Policy and Theory I benefited from fruitful discussions with my friends and colleagues during seminars, excursions and coffee breaks. They have also cheered me up in times of difficulties and trouble. Therefore, I say thanks to Stephan, Xiangping, Martin, Gabriela, Mercedes, Abera, Alwin, Steffen, Tina Heike, Til, Thilo, Yannick, Alexander, Christian, Camille, Nazaire, Tim, Florence, and Yoshiko. I am especially thankful to Miss Contag and Katharina Mayer for helping me with organizing office life and traveling and to Coni Schumacher for providing me accommodation during my last months in Stuttgart.

Without the love and support of my parents my studies would never have been successful. I am greatly indebted to them.

I am most grateful to my wife Simone for her patience and mental support.

Anne, you make me happy and our life more joyful.

Neuss, January 2012 Christian Böber

Table of contents

List of tables

List of figures

List of abbreviations and acronyms

ACMR	All China Marketing Research Co., Ltd
CCP	Chinese Communist Party
CPI	Consumer price index
CV	Coefficient of variation
DASP	Distributive Analysis Stata Package
EDE	Equally-distributed equivalent
ELS	Elasticity of poverty with respect to inequality
FGT	Class of poverty indices developed by Foster, Greer and Thorbecke (1984)
GDP	Gross domestic product
H	Headcount index
hh	Household
HRS	Household responsibility system
ID	Identification number for observations
IIA	Irrelevant alternatives assumption
IRTG	International Research Training Group
JR	or JR approach, referring to Jalan and Ravallion (1998)
MII	Marginal impact on inequality
MIP	Marginal impact on poverty
MLD	Mean logarithmic deviation
MoA	Ministry of Agriculture of the People's Republic of China
NBS	National Bureau of Statistics of the People's Republic of China
NCP	North China Plain
NCT	Nordchinesische Tiefebene
PG	Poverty gap index
RCRE	Research Center for the Rural Economy of the Ministry of Agriculture of the People's Republic of China
RLCL	Rural Land Contract Law of the People's Republic of China

SDM	Social Decision Maker
S-Gini	Single parameter Gini
SPG	Squared poverty gap index
SWF	Social welfare function
WDR	World Development Report
WTO	World Trade Organization

Max.	Maximum
Min.	Minimum
SD	Standard deviation
ha	Hectare
km^2	Square kilometers
ln	Natural logarithm
mu	1 mu = 1/15 ha, (Chinese measure for square)
yrs	Years
Yuan	1 Yuan (Chinese currency unit) = 0.149 US$ or 0.113 EUR (2010-09-22)

List of Chinese terms and expressions

gai ge kai fang	"change the system, open the door"
guomai	Expression for "purchase"
huabei pingyuan	Huang-Huai-Hai Plain (equivalent North China Plain)
hukou	Household registration system
liangshi butie	Grain subsidy
nongmin jiti	Farmer's collective
nongzi zonghe butie	Input subsidy
san-nong	"Three-Problems" related to three issues: agriculture, peasants and rural areas
zhichu	Expression for "expenses"

Zusammenfassung

Die vorliegende Arbeit betrachtet die Hebei Provinz in der Nordchinesischen Tiefebene (NCT). Sie wurde im Rahmen des internationalen Graduiertenkollegs „Sustainable Ressource in North China“ erstellt. Aufgabe dieses interdisziplinären Projektes ist die Erforschung von landwirtschaftlichen Anbau- und Betriebsführungsmethoden in der NCT und die Formulierung von Empfehlungen, wie die landwirtschaftliche Produktion der Region nachhaltiger organisiert werden kann.

Die institutionellen Rahmenbedingungen im ländlichen China haben sich seit dem Beginn der Reformen im Jahre 1978 stark verändert. Von den Kollektiven übertrug man die Verantwortung für die landwirtschaftliche Produktion an einzelne Haushalte. Diesen Haushalten wurden auf Basis der Anzahl der Haushaltsmitglieder Landnutzungsrechte zugewiesen. Da die Bevölkerung in Hebei über die letzten 30 Jahre kontinuierlich wuchs, schrumpfte die landwirtschaftliche Betriebsgröße und ist nun gemessen am internationalen sowie am chinesischen Durchschnitt verhältnismäßig klein. Als ein Hauptanbaugebiet für Getreide in der Volksrepublik China kommt der Hebei Provinz eine zentrale Rolle bei der politisch sehr relevanten Frage der Sicherung der Versorgung Chinas mit Grundnahrungsmitteln zu. Um die Erträge zu steigern, wurden in den letzten 20 Jahren vor allem mehr chemischer Dünger und Pestizide eingesetzt. Eine Mechanisierung landwirtschaftlicher Arbeitsschritte fand hingegen kaum statt. Ein Hauptgrund hierfür liegt darin, dass landwirtschaftliche Arbeitskräfte auf dem Land gebunden werden sollten, um die Abwanderung in städtische Ballungsräume zu verhindern oder zumindest zu reduzieren. Durch das „System der staatlichen Haushaltsregistrierung“ (hukou) sind die Migrationsmöglichkeiten der ländlichen Bevölkerung, insbesondere der Arbeitskräfte, stark eingeschränkt. Aus dieser und anderen administrativen Beschränkungen ergibt sich ein Überangebot an landwirtschaftlicher Arbeitskraft. Andererseits sorgt die wachsende Bedeutung der industriellen Produktion und des Servicesektors im Zuge der dynamischen Entwicklung der chinesischen Volkswirtschaft seit Beginn der 1980er Jahre dafür, dass mehr Möglichkeiten für Arbeitskräfte aus ländlichen Gebieten geschaffen wurden, um Einkommen außerhalb der Landwirtschaft zu generieren.

In Folge der Intensivierung der landwirtschaftlichen Produktion stieg die Schadstoffbelastung in Böden und Grundwasser stark an. Neben den ökologischen Aspekten einer nachhaltigen Produktionsweise bilden vor allem ökonomische und soziale Nachhaltigkeitskriterien den Forschungshintergrund für die vorliegende Arbeit. Gerade mit Blick auf zunehmende soziale Spannungen und

Ungleichgewichte zwischen dem ländlichen und urbanen China und des immer noch relativ hohen ländlichen Bevölkerungsanteils ist es wichtig, die Hintergründe der Entwicklung des (materiellen) Wohlstandes in den ländlichen Landesteilen seit Beginn des wirtschaftlichen Öffnungs- und Transformationsprozesses zu verstehen. Als eine Provinz mit hoher Bevölkerungsdichte und der unmittelbaren Nähe zu den städtischen Ballungsräumen Beijing und Tianjin ist Hebei ein geeignetes Untersuchungsgebiet, um Entscheidungen ländlicher Haushalte bezüglich der Partizipation im nicht landwirtschaftlichen Arbeitsmarkt zu analysieren.

Es ist wichtig, die in Hebei existierenden landwirtschaftlichen Betriebsformen in Vollzeit- und Teilzeitbetriebe zu unterscheiden, um den Zusammenhang zwischen Betriebsform und Entscheidungsprozessen auf Haushaltsebene zu verstehen, und um Veränderungen in der Faktorallokation und Effizienzverbesserungen in Hebeis Landwirtschaft analysieren zu können. Institutionelle Veränderungen innerhalb des Agrarsektors, z.B. in Bezug auf die Verteilung von Land und Wasser, haben nicht nur einen starken Einfluss auf die landwirtschaftliche Produktion sondern auch auf den Wohlstand der Landbevölkerung. Für diese Arbeit steht ausländischen Forschern erstmals ein repräsentativer Paneldatensatz für die Jahre 1986 bis 2006 des Research Center for Rural Economy (RCRE) zur Verfügung, welcher zur Analyse der Armutsentwicklung in Hebei verwendet wurde. Darüber hinaus wurden diese Daten genutzt, um Armut in chronische und transitorische Armut zu zerlegen, außerdem um Einkommen nach Quellen zu zerlegen, bei gleichzeitiger Wertung des Beitrags jeder Quelle zur Einkommensungleichheit. Damit erhöht sich auch das Verständis für die Arbeitsallokationsentscheidungen landwirtschaftlicher Haushalte. Ebenfalls basierend auf diesem Datensatz erfolgte die Untersuchung der Beständigkeit agrarischer Betriebsstrukturen. Die Beschränkungen der Analysen auf den Zeitraum 1986 bis 2002 ist notwendig, da die Inhalte der Umfragen für 2003 bis 2006 nicht vergleichbar sind mit den von 1986 bis 2002 erhobenen Informationen. Deshalb wurde der längere Zeitraum mit einer höheren Anzahl an Beobachtungen als Grundlage für die quantitativen Analysen gewählt. In der Zeit von 1990 bis 1993 wurden umfangreiche Reformen durchgeführt, welche eine stärkere Öffnung des ländlichen Arbeitsmarktes zum Ziel hatten. Die Ergebnisse früherer Arbeiten zeigen jedoch, dass die Implementierung institutioneller Veränderungen in China sehr lange dauern kann, so dass Analysen von längeren Zeiträumen notwendig sind, um Einflüsse dieser Veränderungen auf Haushaltsentscheidungen zu identifizieren. Die verwendeten Untersuchungsmethoden stellen ein geeignetes Instrumentarium für die Einkommens-, Armuts- und Farmstrukturanalyse aktuellerer Datensätze dar.

Landwirtschaftliche Institutionen und Produktionsstrukturen verändern sich schrittweise. Dabei werden die Veränderungen sowohl durch externe Faktoren beeinflusst, als auch durch Faktoren aus dem Agrarsektor selbst. Durch die Vernetzung der verschiedenen Sektoren wirken sich die veränderten institutionellen Rahmenbedingungen in nicht-landwirtschaftlichen Bereichen auch auf Institutionen aus, welche die Entscheidungsprozesse in der Landwirtschaft beeinflussen, wie zum Beispiel Veränderungen im Bereich der individuellen Arbeitsanreize und der Arbeitszeitallokation.

Die vorliegende Arbeit informiert politische Entscheidungsträger über den rückläufigen Anteil der landwirtschaftlichen Produktion am (materiellen) Wohlstand der ländlichen Bevölkerung. Unter Anwendung der Methoden „Variationskoeffizient"- und „Shorrocks"-Zerlegung wird das Haushaltseinkommen nach Einkommensquellen zerlegt. Der Anteil des landwirtschaftlichen Einkommens am gesamten Haushaltseinkommen ging von 47% im Jahre 1986 auf 24% in 2002 zurück. Es zeigte sich, dass nicht-landwirtschaftliches Lohneinkommen besonders stark zur Ungleichverteilung von Einkommen innerhalb eines Dorfes beiträgt. Schlussfolgernd aus dem rückläufigen Anteil des Agrareinkommens ergibt sich für aktuelle Programme zur Angleichung von ländlichen und städtischen Lebensverhältnissen, dass eine Steigerung des landwirtschaftlichen Einkommens allein zum Erreichen des von den Entscheidungsträgern gewünschten Angleichungsziels nicht geeignet ist.

Hinsichtlich der Armutsentwicklung in der Hebei Provinz wurde die Hypothese formuliert, dass das absolute Armutsniveau im Zeitraum von 1986 bis 2002 gesunken ist. Verschiedene Armutsindizes wurden nach Foster, Greer und Thorbecke (1984) für die untersuchten ländlichen Regionen der Hebei Provinz berechnet. Diese Indizes zeigen, dass im Untersuchungszeitraum ein Rückgang der absoluten Armut zu verzeichnen ist. Um die Armutsentwicklung detailliert zu untersuchen, erfolgte eine Zerlegung von Armutselastizitäten anhand von ortsspezifischen und individuellen Charakteristiken der untersuchten Haushalte. Es ist das erste Mal, dass Daten für die Hebei Provinz für diese Zerlegung zur Anwendung kamen. Da für andere Provinzen in China vergleichbare Datensätze Analysegegenstand waren, stellen die Ergebnisse dieser Arbeit eine Erweiterung der Wissensbasis über die Veränderungsprozesse in China seit 1978 dar und ermöglichen einen Vergleich der Entwicklungen zwischen Provinzen mit einem ähnlich hohen Anteil landwirtschaftlicher Produktion. Es wurden zwei Ansätze zur Armutsmessung miteinander verglichen. Der erste misst Armut basierend auf dem durchschnittlichen Wohlstand der Bevölkerung. Der zweite Ansatz dagegen untersucht die Anzahl an Situationen in denen der Haushalt sich in einem Zustand des Mangels befindet. Die Vorstellung und Diskussion beider Ansätze ist wichtig, da sie sehr unterschiedliche Ergebnisse in Bezug auf die Unterscheidung zwischen chronischer und transitorischer Armut liefern können. Die Unterscheidung beider Armutskomponenten ist für sozialpolitische Entscheidungen sehr relevant. Chronische Armut lässt sich eher durch Investitionen in Humankapital reudzieren, wogegen Maßnahmen zur Stabilisierung von Einkommensströmen eher geeignet sind, transitorische Armut zu reduzieren. Es kann aus der Zerlegung der Armutselastizität festgehalten werden, dass die Faktoren Bildung, Fachwissen im Rahmen spezifischer Berufsausbildung und weniger regulative Eingriffe in den Arbeitsmarkt bessere Ansätze zur nachhaltigen Verbesserung des Wohlstandes in den ländlichen Regionen in Hebei darstellen als Transfers oder andere Zahlungen, die nicht im Zusammenhang mit erbrachter Arbeitsleistung getätigt werden.

Mit Hilfe von „fixed-effects“ Regressionsmodellen wurde die Hypothese getestet, dass die Arbeitsangebots- und Arbeitsnachfrageentscheidungen der untersuchten Haushalte nicht getrennt voneinander getroffen werden können. Eine Separabilität dieser Entscheidungen kann sowohl für die gesamte Stichprobe als auch für Teilstichproben der Vollzeit- und Teilzeitlandwirtschaftsbetriebe verworfen werden. Als Schlussfolgerung ergibt sich, dass die Haushaltsarbeitszeit, die für die Mehrzahl der ländlichen Haushalte in Hebei den wichtigsten verfügbaren Produktionsfaktor darstellt, nicht effizient verteilt werden kann; der Markt für ländliche Arbeitskraft ist (nicht unerwartet) unvollkommen. Die Vermutung liegt nahe, dass die Migrationsbeschränkung der ländlichen Bevölkerung, eine bedeutende Arbeitsmarktunvollkommenheit darstellt. Diese Schlussfolgerung lässt sich aber im Rahmen dieser Arbeit nicht weiter quantitativ überprüfen, da keine genauen Charakteristika von Arbeitsmigranten in den zugänglichen Erhebungen erfasst wurden. Die Ergebnisse anderer Untersuchungen sowie qualitative Befragungen bestätigen jedoch diesen Zusammenhang.

Im Anschluss an eine Diskussion der Entwicklung von individuellen und Haushalts-arbeitsangebots- und Allokationsmodellen kam ein statisches Agrarhaushaltsmodell zur Anwendung, um die Bestimmungsfaktoren der Haushaltsarbeitsangebotsentscheidungen zu identifizieren. Es zeigt sich, dass Haushalte mit mehr Familienmitgliedern, relativ mehr Arbeit in der eigenen landwirtschaftlichen Produktion einsetzen als kleinere Haushalte. Das kann ein Hinweis auf Einschränkungen der Möglichkeiten zum Angebot von Arbeit außerhalb des landwirtschaftlichen Sektors sein und sollte in zukünftigen quantitativen und qualitativen Untersuchungen genauer untersucht werden.

Für die Analyse von Veränderungen der landwirtschaftlichen Betriebsstrukturen in Hebei kam ein Hazard-Modell zur Anwendung, um die Hypothese zu überprüfen, dass die Wahrscheinlichkeit für einen Wechsel zwischen Teilzeit- und Vollzeitbetrieb, abnimmt, je länger ein jeweiliger Zustand bereits andauert. Obwohl Wechsel zwischen den Betriebsformen beobachtet wurden, zeigt sich, dass ein einmal vom Haushalt eingenommener Zustand, Vollzeit- oder Teilzeitbetrieb, mit geringer Wahrscheinlichkeit wieder verlassen wird. Aus dieser Stabilität der gewählten Betriebsform über die Zeit lässt sich ableiten, Vollzeitbetriebe so zu unterstützen, dass sie sich stärker spezialisieren und insbesondere die Produktivität der haushaltseigenen Arbeitskräfte steigern können. Aktuelle Programme zur Verbesserung der Lebensverhältnisse im ländlichen China folgen kaum dieser Erkenntnis. Es wird vielmehr versucht, über die Subventionierung von Maschinen und anderen Einsatzfaktoren die Produktionskosten zu senken bzw. zu stabilisieren, sowie durch direkte Transfers das Einkommen der Landbevölkerung zu erhöhen. Langfristig würden aber gerade Haushalte, die einen Teil oder die Gesamtheit ihrer verfügbaren Arbeitszeit für nichtlandwirtschaftliche Erwerbstätigkeit einsetzen eher von der Schaffung von Ausbildungsmöglichkeiten außerhalb des landwirtschaftlichen Sektors profitieren.

Im Rahmen dieser Arbeit wurden verschiedene Ansätze und Methoden kombiniert, um die Informationen aus dem verfügbaren Datensatz bestmöglich zur Beantwortung der gestellten Forschungsfragen zu nutzen. Dabei könnte in der Kombination aus parametrischen und nicht-parametrischen Ansätzen eine Chance bestehen, in zukünftigen Untersuchungen Paneldatensätze eingehender zu analysieren, und die Bedeutung individueller Charakteristika einzelner Haushaltsmitglieder auf Arbeitsallokations-entscheidungen zu analysieren. Die aktuellsten Jahrgänge der Befragungen (2007 bis 2009) waren nicht verfügbar. Diese Restriktion war durch eigene quantitative Datenerhebung nicht zu beseitigen, da ausländischen Forschern die Erhebung repräsentativer Daten in den gleichen Dörfern in Hebei, in denen das RCRE Daten erfasst, untersagt ist. Es erscheint für die Analyse von Arbeitsallokations- und Betriebsformentscheidungen viel versprechend, in zukünftigen Untersuchungen die aktuellsten RCRE Erhebungen für die Jahre 2003 bis 2009 zu verwenden, da in diesen Datensätzen mehr Informationen über alle im Haushalt lebenden Individuen, z.B. in Bezug auf Alter, Bildung und Arbeitszeit, enthalten sind. Weiterhin ist zu empfehlen, die Auswirkungen von institutionellen Veränderungen, wie die Abschaffung aller landwirt-schaftlichen Steuern im Jahre 2006, auf die ländliche Entwicklung und strukturelle Veränderungen im Agrarsektor anhand der aktuellen Daten für Hebei aber auch für andere chinesische Provinzen zu untersuchen.

Summary

The Hebei province, as one part of the North China Plain, is an important area of grain production within the People's Republic of China. Over the three decades since the start of the reforms in 1978 rural institutions changed tremendously. The responsibility for agricultural production was reassigned from the collectives to individual households and land use rights were assigned according to the household size. Combined with a strong population growth this led to a rather small average size of farms in Hebei compared to world averages but also compared to other Chinese regions. Migration of the rural population and especially the rural labor force was and is still regulated and restricted by the household registration system. This and other imperfections in (rural) labor markets led to a surplus of agricultural labor. But due to the development of the Chinese economy since the beginning of the 1980s the importance of the industry and service sector increased and more opportunities were created for rural laborers to earn income outside agriculture.

Agricultural production systems change stepwise and the changes are fueled by drivers that are both external and internal to the agricultural sector. The intra-sectoral changes, e.g. in land and water institutions not only affect agricultural production but also the well-being of the rural population. Therefore, it is important to understand the characteristics of different farm types and how they affect households' decision making and well-being. It is the first time that an extensive panel data set covering the period from 1986 to 2006 was used to assess the development of poverty in rural Hebei, to decompose poverty, to decompose income and income inequality, and to explain labor allocation decisions of agricultural households and farm type persistence. The interplay with the other sectors, whose institutions changed tremendously as well during the last decades in China, also contributes to changes in rural institutions such as incentive systems and labor allocation behavior.

Present research has emphasized that it is important to assess the development of inequality among the rural population in China, to analyze poverty trends and to decompose poverty in its components, and to assess the interaction between geographical diversity, poverty trends and farm households' labor allocation decisions. To the best knowledge of the author it is the first time that this assessment is done for Hebei province based on a comprehensive longitudinal data set. In addition this work provides an understanding of the determinants of Chinese rural households' labor allocation decisions which helps in the assessment of applied and intended policy measures that focus on rural development.

This study provides valuable information to policy makers about the declining importance of agricultural production for well-being of the rural population. Income was decomposed by sources applying the coefficient of variation method and the Shorrocks decomposition method. The share of agricultural income in total household income declined in the rural areas of Hebei from 47% in 1986 to 24% in 2002. In addition the non-farm wage income contributes strongly to income inequality within villages. The increase in the importance of income that is earned outside the own village is shown by the fact that migratory wage income increased on average by 8% per year, and by this is the income source with the fourth highest growth rate. The per year growth rates of income from fruit production (14%), income from transportation (12%) and income from other family businesses (10%) are higher but fewer households receive income from those sources than from migratory wage income. It is also worth to mention that the share of households earning migratory income is constant and is 36% in 1986 and 2002.

Foster-Greer-Thorbecke-type poverty indicators have been calculated for rural Hebei to assess the hypothesis that absolute poverty declined in Hebei between 1986 and 2002. In general, poverty declined over the assessed period. Poverty elasticities are decomposed according to different location specific and individual characteristics of the assessed households. This was done by using one approach that links poverty to an average in welfare in comparison to an approach that links poverty to ill-fare statuses experienced by households. The amount of land holdings of farmers became less relevant for the explanation of poverty differences between rural households in countries that experienced agrarian change. The results of the decomposition of poverty elasticities indicated that education, the provision of training to the rural population and less restrictions in labor markets are much better measures to increase the chance of long-lasting (sustainable) improvements in rural well-being than transfers or other non-earned income measures. Regarding the results of the decomposition of poverty into transitory and chronic poverty both methods differ strongly. With the approach of Jalan and Ravallion (1998) all of the estimated poverty was explained as transient whereas with the approach of Duclos et al. (2008) two thirds of poverty could be explained as chronic poverty.

Fixed effect regression models have been applied to test the hypothesis that labor demand and supply decisions of rural households are not separable. For the full sample but also for population sub-samples separability was rejected. So it can be concluded that labor time, as one important production factor, was not allocated in the most efficient way.

A static agricultural household model was used here to identify the determinants of farm households' labor supply after reviewing the development of individual and household level models to assess labor supply and allocation decisions. Interestingly, households with more family members used relatively more family labor in agricultural production. This might be an indication for restricted possibilities to provide family labor off the farm. In comparison to common labor supply models this kind of probability model to assess the labor market participation of agricultural households allows to assess the determinants of agricultural households' demand for non-family labor.

A hazard model was applied to reflect dynamics in the farm structure in Hebei. It was found that the chosen states (either full- or part-time farming) were relatively stable over time, beside the fact, that state changes did occur. The longer a household remained in one of the two labor market states the lower was the probability of a change to the alternative state. As a consequence of this duration dependence it can be recommended to provide full-time farm households with support to increase the degree of specialization in agricultural production so that they improve their production efficiency. It would be beneficial for those households allocating some or all labor to non-farming activities if labor migration was less restricted and if more possibilities for job specific trainings outside the agricultural sector were provided. Increased possibilities for the leasing of land would offer the chance to better utilize the agricultural land that is not longer farmed by migrating laborers by increasing the farm size of the full-time farm households.

In this study different methodologies have been discussed and combined to best utilize the information contained in the data set. The approach of combining parametric and non-parametric methods should be the basis for future in-depth assessments of panel data sets covering rural areas in China.

The Research Center for the Rural Economy (RCRE) started the collection of socio-economic and production data on rural households in China in 1986. So, with the comprehensive data set at hand it is possible to assess institutional changes in the agricultural sector and changes in well-being in the rural areas that are closely related to the beginning of the transition period in the end of the 1970s and the beginning 1980s.

Several data quality and variable content problems, e.g. regarding the unique identification of observations, could be solved by carefully cross-checking the data for every year and observation and by restricting the analysis only to those years (1986 to 2002 for the income and poverty analyses and 1995 to 2002 for the other assessments) where variable information is compatible from year to year. Remaining limitations of the work at hand are the application of static approaches, the use of partial models and the restriction of the analysis to the household level. For furthers studies it seems promising to use the most recent panel data for rural Hebei which also include more individual level information than the data set used here to assess the characteristics of individual labor allocation decisions of rural laborers. Also recent shifts in fiscal institutions like the abolishment of agricultural taxes since 2006 might be interesting to be analyzed with respect to their impacts on rural development and intra-sectoral changes in Hebei and other rural provinces in China.

1 Introduction

1.1 Background

Gai ge kai fang which means "change the system, [and] open the door" (Dollar, 2007, p.4) [author's addition] is the reform program of China's economic system. Following this goal China opened its economy and got stronger involved in world wide economic exchange. Parallel to these globally oriented reforms the internal policy agenda shifted the attention from a promotion of secondary industries and urban areas to the rural areas, which had received less attention in terms of the development of welfare and infrastructure during the 1960s and 1970s. What happened since the mid 1980s in rural areas of China? Aspects of this question will be answered with the help of a case study on the development of rural areas and respective institutions in times of societal transition and structural changes in agriculture in the Hebei province.

Structural and institutional changes in the agricultural sector are a common pattern found during the development of economic systems from subsistence agriculture to a more diversified economic system (Kirschke et al., 2007). During the structural transformation of an economy the share of the agricultural sector declines and it is expected that the sector provides capital (including land and labor) to other sectors, which allows expanding the activities of the secondary and tertiary sector (Johnston and Mellor, 1961).

Recent research revealed that land renting institutions are differing quite strongly among different regions in the North China Plain and that land rental markets are not completely developed and by this cannot fully fulfill their economic function of allocating land to its most productive uses (Piotrowski, 2009). With respect to credit institutions not only are households found to be constrained in formal credit markets but also substitutability between formal and informal credits appears to be limited in rural China (Jia, 2008).

The term institution in general refers to all measures that are related to organizational processes in all sectors of an economy, to the modes of use rights and resource allocation, social and political norms, but also to other societal and system related mechanisms that could have an impact on individual behavior (Krug, 1990) and the enforcement mechanism behind those measures (North, 1994). In theory, this means that formal and informal institutions are an omnipresent framework that is – purposively or unintentionally – implemented by humans and that determines all human interaction (North, 1990). In the present study more specific institutions such as local measures of land allocation and land renting, implicit or explicit restrictions to migration as well as the role of land for social security (see e.g. Li et al., 2007) and the production of food for subsistence are assessed. As indicated by North (1990), an important role of institutions is to reduce uncertainty and by this the provision of a stable framework that helps individuals or societal agents to organize their interactions. If the efficiency concept of North (1990) is applied then a situation can be called efficient if it leads to economic growth under a set of constraints. Even if institutions should be designed to reduce those constraints, such as transactions costs, it well never be possible to eliminate all constraints. There will be always some constraints like institutions which are constraints in themselves, alongside with economic constraints like technology, budget and time constraints. Or as North (1990) also states, since there is always some degree of uncertainty, e.g. about future development regarding prices or labor demand, it is just not possible to reduce transaction costs to zero and by this to reach the theoretically possible maximization of objectives that might be profits or investments in human capital. When positive transaction costs are included in theoretical models to assess economic transition then the inter-temporal resource allocation is influenced by the role of the state (Buchenrieder, 2001). In such a situation of non-zero transaction costs, the institutions designed by policy to assign property rights do not necessarily follow the argument of Coase (1960). He states that the initial assignment of property rights (e.g. when privatizing former state companies) does not matter in the case of zero transaction costs and freely transferable property rights, since the transactions between market agents will always lead to a distribution of rights that increases the value of production.

Nonetheless, institutions are, beside their stabilizing character, themselves subject to changes during periods of transition (Buchenrieder, 2001). Especially because large societies are facing complex adjustment processes North (1990) favors the adaptive efficiency approach. According to him, adaptive efficiency is linked to the assessment of the kind of regulating structures that have an effect on the pathway of the development of economies over time. As one consequence of adaptive efficiency North (1990) argues for decentralized processes of decision-making which he judges as being appropriate to enable societies to maximize their attempts to find alternative ways of solving problems. In Hebei it can be observed that the organization of formal institutions differs from county to county or even from village to village (Böber, 2008 and 2009). Following the argumentation about decentralized decision making, this could be considered as being efficient to set up institutions that support local economic development by providing growth despite existing constraints. Adger (2000) discusses the necessity of institutions to be resilient and adaptable. To a large extent the resilience of institutions depends on their exclusivity and on the degree of trust that the society has in them. That is important to be kept in mind when evaluating farmers' attitudes towards the formal institutions to which they are liable to. Social resilience is defined by Adger (2000) "...as the ability of communities to withstand external shocks to their social infrastructure." (p. 361). Farmers in Hebei are subject to natural shocks that affect the output of production directly such as floods or droughts but they are also faced with policy or administratively induced shocks such as unscheduled redistributions of land rights.

It is not always possible to identify direct effects of an institutional change. Especially for the micro-economic analyses, based on a data set that is limited to the household level, quite often changes in price systems or policies can hardly be included directly but need to be approximated instead. Also changes in non-market institutions such as attitudes or habits that occur rather slowly (Kuiper, 2005) are difficult to cover with the models and available data. However, it is worthy to be aware of potential impacts of institutional changes because they might serve as a key for the interpretation of results that will be presented and discussed later in this document.

Regarding the goals of Chinese policy self sufficiency in food production is one major aim (Fang and Beghin, 2000; Solot, 2006). To achieve this, agricultural production systems are needed that allow for the effective use of scarce natural resources1 and for more participation of the rural population in production decisions and adequate incentives for individual farmers to increase production (Lin, 1997). In the end of the 1970s some production teams started a system where land, other resources and output quotas have been contracted to individual farm households, the household responsibility system (Sachs and Woo, 1997). Since the nation wide introduction of the HRS in 1981, agricultural production in China experienced massive changes in productivity (Davis, 2002; Sanders, 2000) and the rural areas developed rapidly. But Fan (2007) argues that the productivity of labor is still the lowest in agricultural production compared to the industry and the service sector.

Another policy aim is to reduce the rural labor surplus to overcome the problems of rural poverty and low income of farm households (Tuan et al., 2000). Lohmar (1999) mentions that there is an ongoing debate to how far the institutional changes in the rural labor market are considered as being successful. One group of scholars argues that there is a higher increase in opportunities for rural laborers to supply labor off the farm since the end of the 1970s in China than in countries with comparable rural (labor) markets. But Lohmar (1999) also

---

[1] China is feeding around 1/5 of the world's population but only having access to around 8% of the worldwide available arable land (own calculation based on data for 2008 available at FAOSTAT, FAO, 2010).

lists the arguments of other scientists who consider the relatively large share of human labor in the mix of agricultural production inputs, in comparison to other countries with a similar level of economic development, and the high and increasing inequality between agricultural and non-agricultural household income as facts that indicate imperfections in the labor market. Zhen and Zoebisch (2006, p. 62) emphasize, that the gap in income equality between (rural) households should not be "too great".

The transition of rural China and the agricultural sector was not free of costs. Chinese policy makers are challenged by keeping a balance between industrialization (also of rural areas), urbanization, and self-sufficiency in food production (Zhang et al., 2004). Beside the increase in absolute well-being of the rural population in comparison with the period before the transition from a fully state planned economy the distribution of welfare became more unequal. Not only are the costal areas outperforming the inner provinces of China in terms of income and infrastructure development but especially the gap between the rural and urban population has been widening since the start of the (agricultural) reforms in the end of the 1970's. By the household registration or *hukou* system individuals are categorized in two classes of citizenship, rural and urban. Rural residents are excluded from a wide range of benefits provided to the urban population such as public transport, urban schooling or urban health care and they are not allowed to take up every kind of work in urban areas. Just jobs that are considered as dangerous or dirty and offer low payments are accessible for rural laborers in cities without constraints (Chan and Buckingham, 2008). Rural-urban migration was and is hindered by the household registration system and by this also fueled the emergence of a wide gap in income and welfare between urban and rural areas (Dollar, 2007). But well-functioning labor markets are considered to be a pre-condition for facilitating the successful modernization of the Chinese economy (de Brauw et al., 2002).

Also in Hebei province the rural economy and society and the related institutions underwent structural changes. As can be seen from *Figure 1* the share of the rural labor force working in agricultural production declined relative to the other sectors. But also the absolute number of rural labor employed in agricultural production decreased in Hebei. The information for 1978 is provided to have an overview about the composition of the rural labor force at the start of the reform period. For the years 1992-1994 no data are available for Hebei.

Hebei as one major area of grain production is of great importance to achieve high and constant levels of food production. According to Hu (1997), apart from rice, wheat, maize, sorghum, millet and other miscellaneous grains, in China grains also include potatoes, sweet potatoes, soybeans and beans (Hu,

1997).2 The quota was applied to all of these so-called grain crops. As such Hebei is the agricultural backbone of the urban areas of Beijing and Tianjin. Due to a high population density Hebei itself is faced with pressures on the rural society stemming from land fragmentation and surplus of agricultural labor (Bhattacharyya and Parker, 1999).

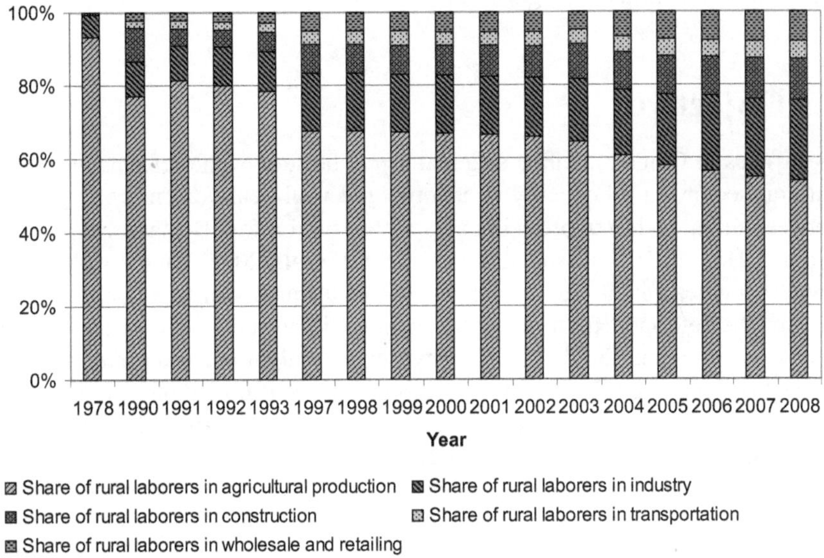

Source: Basic statistics for agriculture ACMR (2010).

Figure 1: Share of rural laborers employed by sector, Hebei 1978-2008

Moreover, input levels for mineral fertilizer in Hebei province are high and environmentally unsustainable (Zhao et al., 2006). The current migration policy does not allow rural residents to permanently exit agriculture and rural areas. Motives to establish or to stabilize part-time farming like e.g. positive external effects of German small holder farms on the landscape or in Norway and other developed countries to prevent farmers to migrate from the rural areas do not seem to be the first priority on the policy agenda in China.

The research for this thesis was conducted in the framework of Subproject 3.3: "Property Rights and Access to Credit, Inputs and Agricultural Knowledge:

2 According to Hu (1997) special conversion rates help translating quantities of tuber crops into an equivalent of 1 kg of grain.

Implications for Technical Efficiency, Sectoral Change, and Rural Income Inequality", which is part of the International Research Training Group (IRTG): "Modeling Material Flows and Production Systems for Sustainable Resource Use in Intensified Crop Production in the North China Plain", supported by the German Research Foundation (DFG) and the Ministry of Education (MoE) of the People's Republic of China. In Appendix A, a structural outline of the whole research project is given (*Figure 12*).

1.2 Objectives

Farm sizes in China remained stagnant since the start of the reforms in the agricultural sector, and inequality in income and well-being did not only increase between urban and rural areas but also within rural areas (Benjamin et al., 2007; Lin and Ho, 2003; Wan and Zhou, 2005, Yu et al., 2007). But Rozelle (1994) reviews studies which found falling levels of inequality in rural China after the start of the reforms. Rural non-farm income3 is not only seen as an important contribution to household food security but also might act as an inhibitor of urbanization, because migration is of less importance if households are able to diversify income at their rural location of residence. In addition non-farm income is also one measure to prevent natural resource degradation that could occur from overexploitation because of non-sustainable agricultural production systems when people depend solely on agricultural income (Reardon et al., 1998). A rising share of farms in China is managed by older people (Pang et al., 2004), and many rural laborers work only part time on the farms (Carter et al., 1999).

This increase in off-farm activities affects inequality among the rural population whereby different income sources contribute differently to overall income inequality of rural households (de Janvry et al., 2005). But it is also found that those households that continue farming as full-time farmers and by this specialize in agricultural production have characteristics that make them more productive than those households that leave the sector partly or fully (de Janvry et al., 2005).

Social welfare is a topic of rising interest in socio-economic research in China and different approaches are discussed from different perspectives with respect to either the function of rural social security nets, the development of the rural economy and infrastructure and the role played by family and relationship

---

3 Rural non-farm income is defined by Reardon et al. (1998) as all income earned by wage paid activities in agricultural production, industries and services. Farm wages and migratory income are excluded by this definition.

structures (Hebel, 2004). The transition from a state planned to a market economy can be considered as an economic shock that affects the well-being of population subgroups differently (Araar and Duclos, 2006). During the 1970s and 1980s income inequality decreased but welfare inequality increased. Social policy measures with respect to the provision of education and health care and the maintenance of income favored urban over rural areas (Davis, 1989). Also Fan (2007) emphasizes the growing disparity between urban and rural regions. In 2002 the urban per capita income in Northeast and East China was around three times higher than the rural per capita income.

As recent research has emphasized it is important to assess the development of inequality among the rural population in China (Benjamin and Brandt, 1999; Benjamin et al., 2005), poverty (Benjamin et al., 2007; Duclos et al., 2008), the interaction between geographical diversity, poverty trends (Chen and Ravallion, 2004) and farm households' labor allocation decisions (Wang, 2007; Glauben et al., 2008). To the best knowledge of the author it is the first time that this assessment is done for Hebei province based on a comprehensive longitudinal data set. In addition this work provides an understanding of the determinants of Chinese rural households' labor allocation decisions which helps in the assessment of applied and intended policy measures that focus on rural development.

Poor people in rural China are not only affected by inequality in income but also they are less well equipped with the provision of education and health care (Zhu and Jiang, 1995). Also Dollar (2007) shows, there has been increasing inequality regarding education and health care provision in China. Because the data set, as described later, only contains household level data and no regional or census information, the focus of the present assessment of inequality will be on income and on expenditure based poverty measures. Yu et al. (2007) review several studies on inequality in rural China and figure out that the studies differ with respect to the chosen inequality indicators and/or the time span assessed. But in general inequality is found to be more related to regional differences (costal vs. western provinces or urban vs. rural areas) than to differences among households in a specific location.

Benjamin et al. (2005) find in their Shorrocks decomposition of rural households' incomes from nine Chinese provinces that self employment income from non-agricultural occupations and the relatively slow growth of agricultural income after 1995 led to an increase in income inequality in rural areas.

The assessment of the sustainability of agricultural production systems in the North China Plain is one of the overall aims of the IRTG project. Sustainability is often defined as a concept made up of "three pillars", where attention is equally paid to the economic, environmental and social dimensions of decision-making (Pope et al., 2004), which are also referred to as the normative dimensions of sustainability (Zhen and Routray, 2003). A sustainable agricultural production system is also based on the time and space-specific dimension of sustainability (Zhen and Routray, 2003). While the net farm income or the crop productivity are examples for economic indicators of sustainability, inequality in poverty and in income are social indicators (Zhen and Routray, 2003). The latter ones are used in this study for the assessment of the social dimension of agricultural sustainability in rural Hebei. They reflect both; the spatial aspect of sustainability, here with respect to different households in one region (province), but also the time dimension of this concept, with inequality indicators containing information about short-term but also about long-term aspects of sustainable development.

The first objective of this study is to assess determinants that influence income generation and the well-being of rural households in Hebei. Research questions related to this aim are:

- How did income and poverty develop over time?
- What changes occurred in the composition of income?
- Which role does the fragmentation of the agricultural sector (small farm size and low degree of specialization) play with respect to household's well-being?
- How do different on- and off-farm income sources affect income inequality?
- Which determinants are relevant for household's labor market participation?

The agricultural sector in the research area is still dominated by high-input, low-output (per farm and arable land area) part-time smallholder agriculture (Piotrowski, 2009). Following the argumentation of increasing economies of scale, larger, more commercially oriented full-time, farms should be more efficient. On the other side part-time farming in combination with off-farm wage labor activities is seen as a strategy to diversify income based on different perceptions of risk by part-time and full-time farmers (Lien et al., 2006). Wan and Cheng (2001) and Chen et al. (2003) found in their studies on Chinese farms negative economies of scale.

Research in other countries showed that farm exit rates are strongly influenced by family, farm and regional characteristics (e.g. for Germany see Glauben et al., 2006; for Israel see Kimhi, 2000; and Ahituv and Kimhi, 2006). In China there are no studies accessible in English which investigate questions related to the succession of family farms and the changes in farm size structure. The formal reason is that land is not allowed to be passed on to a member of the household if the holder of the land use right dies. But instead the land use right goes back to the village pool of responsibility land and will then be reallocated.

In addition most of the households in rural China are considered agricultural households (Zhu, 1991; and Glauben et al., 2008). By this they represent a production unit that is referred to in this work as farm. Also there is no general decision mechanism about the succession of a farm like in other countries because the household holds only use rights of the agricultural land that was distributed by the village usually based on per capita measures. The village, in other words the state, collectively owns the land (Gale et al., 2005). Differences in the amount of land per household are related to differences in the demographic composition of the farm family but are at the same time also based on administrative land allocation schemes. This is different to the finding of Tschajanow that differences in land holdings can be explained by differences in the reproduction patterns of peasant families (Bernstein and Byres, 2001).

Generally, agricultural income is just one of the various income sources of farm households in developing countries (Schwarze and Zeller, 2005). Due to structural changes in the Chinese economy and the development of the secondary and tertiary sector, a lot of possibilities evolved for the rural population to supply labor also to other activities than to family based agricultural production. So it is worth to analyze the evolution of labor supply decisions of farm households in rural Hebei. The provision of off-farm labor can reduce the surplus of rural labor (Feng and Heerink, 2008) that otherwise cannot be fully employed in agricultural production. The development of job opportunities outside the agricultural sector already reduced the labor surplus in rural areas of China to some extent (de Janvry et al., 2005). Despite the fast growth in China's non-agricultural sectors the reallocation of labor out of agricultural production was rather low during the past decades of transition due to restrictions in labor mobility (WDR, 2008). The assessment of individual, location and institutional factors that have an impact on households' decisions to participate in the agricultural and non-agricultural labor market could help to understand this low rate of labor reallocation.

A large share of farm households in Hebei derives income from non-agricultural sources. The question then is, why they continue farming as part-time farmers and do not specialize into being either full-time farm households or by giving up agricultural production and being households of employed workers or running an own business? Often it is argued by scientists that discuss the assignment of land use rights in China, that rural households keep their land use rights as a means of social security even if they would not really need to farm the land anymore since the household income is earned outside the agricultural sector or is send home as remittances by migrant workers (e.g. Zhao and Wen, 1999). But Phimister and Roberts (2006) show, that part-time farm household are less efficient in their use of inputs, if one discusses efficiency as the "surplus" after deducting input costs from the output (Sen, 1962). Those part-time farm household apply relatively more chemical fertilizer than larger commercially oriented farms. One explanation could be that part-time farm households have lower capital costs for investments in farm production, since they use cash from income earning activities outside the agricultural sector. As another explanation those part-time households might have lower labor costs, at least for those household members (e.g. teenagers or elderly) that don't have sufficient skills which would allow them to participate in off-farm occupations. The results of Barning (2007), Jia (2008) and Piotrowski (2009) seem to indicate, that economies of scale, scope and risk are not fully exploited in the intensive agricultural production systems of Hebei. But other authors provide evidence that farms in China not necessarily have to be large to be considered as being efficient (Wan and Cheng, 2001; Chen et al., 2003). In the section that focuses on the separation of household labor supply and demand (chapter 1.3) an explanation of Sen (1962) is discussed that indicates the potential pitfalls if one uses market based wage rates to include the costs of family labor into the assessment of farm efficiency.

The distinction between part- and full-time households has important implications not only for the income generation of the assessed households but also for the levels of chemical inputs applied, and by this also for the assessment of the environmental pillar of the sustainability of the agricultural production systems in Hebei. An assessment of the impact of intensive input use in agricultural production and farmers' awareness about the relationships between agricultural production and the degradation of environmental resources for Hebei province is provided in Böber and Zeller (2009). So, the second objective of this thesis is to analyze the determinants of change in the number and types of farm households over time. Related questions to this part of the work are:

- Which farm types exist in Hebei province with respect to the distinction between part-time and full-time farming?
- What determines the size of the farm?
- How does the sectoral diversification of labor time influence farm types and structure?

In the next part of this work hypotheses which relate to the two research objectives are presented.

1.3 Hypotheses

Based on the review of theoretical literature and of empirical studies the following hypotheses are formulated and assessed in the empirical part of this work.

Poverty

Chen and Ravallion (2004) state, that between different geographic regions China's WTO accession had diverse effects on poverty development. They simulate the gains and losses associated with the WTO accession for rural and urban areas in three Chinese Provinces. Even if the WTO accession is found to have only a slight positive impact on poverty, Chen and Ravallion (2004) indicate that rural households mainly involved in agricultural production might loose most from integrating China into world trade. This is especially true for assessments that focus at the short-run effects of the WTO accession, since rural wages are expected to fall while the prices for consumption goods are expected to increase. The well-being of farm households in China can be affected by different price and income effects. If wholesale prices for agricultural products drop, the income of farm households is reduced, but farm households might also cash in on a drop of consumer prices and higher wages for off-farm labor (Chen and Ravallion, 2004). However, the study by Chen and Ravallion (2004) did not take into account possible specialization of Chinese farms into high-value, labor-intensive crops. In contrast, Hertel et al. (2004) assess possible welfare effects of the WTO accession in the long-run and argue that also poor and specialized agricultural households might gain from increasing labor mobility between the different economic sectors.

The structural changes in rural China contributed largely to the alleviation of poverty (Swinnen and Rozelle, 2006). The growth of the agricultural GDP is considered to be mainly responsible for China's success in poverty reduction because it is estimated that it contributed around 3.5 times more to poverty alleviation than the growth of industry and services (WDR, 2008). This is mainly because China comes from being a country dominated by rural population, which also makes up the largest share of the total poor population. But it is shown in previous studies that absolute poverty in China did not decrease in every year. Especially in the years 1987 to 1990, where some reforms have been stopped or reversed, poverty increased (Dollar, 2007). Since the beginning of the reforms in the 1970s the reduction of absolute poverty was the main aim of policy makers (Hussain, 2004).

In addition to the distinction between absolute and relative poverty, poverty can also be decomposed into a transient component, which indicates the intertemporal variability in peoples' consumption, welfare or ill-fare status, and into the component that represents the proportion of poverty that persist over time; chronic poverty (Jalan and Ravallion, 1998). The distinction between these poverty components is of relevance for applying respective policy measure for poverty alleviation. As Jalan and Ravallion (1998) explain, chronic poverty might be reduced by investments in human capital or physical assets whereas a reduction of transient poverty could be reached for instance by stabilizing income-streams of rural households. An example for such a stabilization are cropping insurances that partly cover losses incurred due to bad harvests.

It is hypothesized that absolute poverty in rural Hebei declined during the period 1986 to 2002, even if there might have been years in which absolute poverty increased and that the larger share of absolute poverty in 2002 can be classified as chronic poverty. This hypothesis will be assessed in chapter 6.1. In addition, location and household related characteristics (e.g. the educational level attained by the household head) are used in this part of the work to assess determinants of poverty elasticity and inequality in the poverty elasticity among different population groups. The elasticity of poverty with respect to growth is used as one tool to measure to how far economic growth reduces poverty (Son and Kakwani, 2004).

Separation of household labor demand and supply

The assumptions regarding existing and functioning markets are critical to the formulation of an agricultural household model (Benjamin, 1992). Benjamin (1992) focuses in his discussion of agricultural household decisions on the separation between labor demand and supply. Tschajanow (1923) finds evidence that large households employ relatively more labor per given amount of land than households which have less members and hence a lower endowment with family labor. This is seen as an indicator of labor market constraints that hinder the household to supply labor outside the own family farm. Sen (1962) discusses the appropriateness of applying wage rates to value the amount of family labor input when assessing the productivity of small scale farms. He describes the inverse relationship between farm size and human labor used as input in agricultural production. While the amount of employed labor is decreasing the smaller the farm size gets, the amount of family labor used as production input is increasing, to an extend that in total more human labor is employed per unit of land. In addition, Sen (1962) describes that in many cases small farms are found to achieve a higher output per given area of land. This would seem intuitive, if one assumes farming at the small scale as being more productive. Sen (1962) does not see the size of the farm as the determining factor of the efficiency of the agricultural production but he argues that the production system itself is more relevant for the explanation of farm productivity. If most of the human labor input in small-scale farms consists of non-wage family labor and one uses a market wage to value this labor in terms of production costs, it is often found that the production costs are higher than the (monetary value of the) output of small farms. The conclusion of Sen (1962) is that one has to be careful with using a market wage rate as an indicator for the production costs of family labor, since this wage rate does not necessarily represent the marginal social opportunity costs of labor, especially in situations where no alternative uses for family labor outside the own agricultural production exist.

Benjamin (1992) considers the separation property as ideal to recognize that farmers can be characterized as being workers and capitalists at the same time. He assumes that the optimum (profit maximizing) allocation of farm labor does not depend on household preferences or the amount of land farmed, but only on the available production technology and on the wage rate for labor. Every combination of family and hired labor is possible if separation holds. As indicated by Benjamin (1992), in the context of separability of consumption and production decisions of farm households the supply of household labor is considered in the household utility maximization problem as a consumption decision, based on e.g. consumption preferences of household members and the demographic composition of the household(s' labor force). And the demand for labor is considered as production decision that involves the decision about the desired level of production, the choice between different activities and the input use decision (de Janvry and Sadoulet, 2003). In general, microeconomic household models reflect the trade-off between time and consumption of goods, where leisure is one, by a time constraint. This constraint states that time can be converted into goods if less of it is used for enjoying leisure but more time is devoted to work (see e.g. Becker, 1965).

If separability holds for an agricultural household model, then the amount of family labor that is employed in own agricultural production of the household should not be determined by the amount of laborers or the composition of the household's labor force, e.g. whether there are male or female laborers available in the household (Benjamin, 1992). Or as Arcand and d'Hombres (2006) explain, if separability holds than only plot characteristics, the applied production technology and prices are the determinants of the marginal productivity of all farm inputs. Therefore in chapter 7.1.1 structural variables will be explained that are suited for the assessment of separability between households' labor demand and supply decisions.

In the case of separability of rural households' decision about labor demand and labor supply, the household would act as profit maximizer and would allocate production factors separately from its own factor endowment (Kuiper, 2005) as well as consumption and leisure preferences (de Janvry and Sadoulet, 2003). Thus, the household would choose an allocation of family labor time that maximizes the households' overall utility (Hanf, 1996). In its' decisions about allocation of family labor time, the household would consider the marginal utilities of all possible uses of family labor time.

A well functioning labor market could help in determining the marginal utility of household labor supplied to off-farm occupations and in identifying the marginal costs if non-family labor has to be employed at the family farm (Hanf, 1996). Despite the existence of labor markets still difficulties could arise for the household if it wants to make long term labor allocation decisions: there is instability in off-farm labor demand and uncertainty about the future development of off-farm income for unskilled and skilled laborers (Coutu, 1957).

Coutu (1957) argues in his assessment of part-time farm decisions in the U.S. in the 1950s that some part-time farm households seem to value leisure higher than the marginal product of family labor time allocated to agriculture. He considers the limited knowledge of part-time farm households about agricultural production possibilities as the reason for this finding. The shadow wage of family labor could be distorted downwards due to the social security function of family labor (young laborers taking care of retired household members) in intergenerational contexts (Rosenzweig and Wolpin, 1985). In the context of the present study, labor surplus in rural areas in Hebei could lead to distortions in the valuation of leisure and farm labor time.

As Benjamin (1992) argues, assumptions about separability are made quite often but models that test for specific reasons of the existence of non-separability, e.g. constraints in rural farm and non-farm labor markets are not often applied.

Bowlus and Sicular (2003) explicitly assess separability in the context of farm household labor allocation decisions based on panel-data for the years 1990 to 1993 for Shandong province. They reject separability between households' labor demand and supply and conclude that even more than one decade after the reforms of the agricultural sector started, the labor market is strongly constrained and does not allow for an efficient allocation of rural labor.

Based on the theoretical discussions of Benjamin (1992) and the results of Carter and Yao (2002), Bowlus and Sicular (2003) and Kuiper (2005), it is hypothesized that labor demand and supply decisions of farm households in Hebei are non-separable.

It is necessary to test this hypothesis because non-separability would not allow solving agricultural household models recursively. The labor demand would depend on the composition of household labor and the labor supply would be dependend on the household endowment with the fixed production factors land and capital (Yotopoulus and Lau, 1974). If non-separability is found, then profits cannot be maximized independently of the utility function during utility maximization (Benjamin, 1992). Lopez (1984) also assesses the interdependence of profit and utility maximization of agricultural households and emphasizes that the agricultural household models have to account for the differences in cases of interdependence or non-interdependence of utility and profit maximization. In addition, the recursivity between agricultural households' labor demand and supply decisions is one major aspect where the respective agricultural household models differ from the assumptions and considerations that led to the development of household models that are applied to assess the labor allocation of workers' households in developed or industrialized countries. In chapter 4.2.2 the model to test for the hypothesis of non-separability is presented and in chapter 7.1 the hypothesis will be assessed.

Labor market participation

Education is a main explanatory variable with respect to individuals' and households' labor market participation decisions. It increases the productivity of farm and off-farm labor and leads to reductions in transaction costs (Glauben et al., 2008). Ahituv and Kimhi (2006) consider human capital as being more productive in off-farm employment. Higher levels of education achieved are associated with higher earnings (de Janvry and Sadoulet, 2001). Tuan et al. (2000) indicate in their study on Chinese census data that skills necessary for non-farm activities are mainly developed at the secondary or high school level. A decrease in the probability to participate in agricultural production with increasing education is also found by Babatunde and Qaim (2009) for farm households in Nigeria. They argue that households which have access to sectors with higher wages than in agriculture follow a pattern of demand-pull diversification of labor supply.

It is hypothesized that better education of the household head and specific training provided to individual household members have a positive effect on the participation of the household in the non-farm labor market.

Whether this hypothesis holds is assessed in chapter 7.2.

Farm structure persistence

The literature about labor allocation decisions of individual farmers or farm households discusses two main aspects with respect to labor market states. Some authors provide evidence for structural state or inter temporal dependence of labor supply decisions (Weiss, 1997; see also the discussion in Brosig et al., 2009). True structural state dependence is found if the previous state, in which the observation unit (here household) was, changes the constraints and parameters the household faces in the recent state or if the attitudes of household members are changed by the previous state the household belonged to (Corsi and Findeis, 2000). If there is structural state dependence then policies that affect farmers' labor market participation decisions at one point in time would have an impact on the outcome of future decisions of farmers to participate in the labor market (Ahituv and Kimhi, 2001). Other authors argue that it is also important to discuss impacts of the amount of time that a person remained in a specific labor market state on the probability that he or she might leave the state at a specific point in time (Chan and Stevens, 2001; Knight and Yueh, 2004).

Following Brosig et al. (2009) it is of interest to assess the choice of farm households of either exclusively engaging in own farm production or of supplying labor off-farm as well. By this an insight in the persistence of part- and full-time farms in rural Hebei is gained.

It is hypothesized that the time that a household operated as either part- or full-time farm household decreases the probability that the household will change the state.

For this hypothesis the assessment is presented in chapter 7.3.

1.4 Outline of the thesis

Chapter 2 shortly introduces the Hebei province and the socio-economic and environmental conditions framing the development of agricultural production and the involvement of the rural population in agricultural and non-agricultural labor supply. This also builds the basis for understanding why the size of a farm in Hebei is rather small compared to other Chinese provinces. In addition the decision of farm households about the types of crops to be planted, and by this the decision between staples or cash crops, depends on soil, climate and other location related characteristics.

In part 3 of this work time periods that are important for understanding and discussing the recent institutional framework in rural China and Hebei are reviewed. The transformation of the Chinese economy from a planned to a market oriented one went different than in other former planned economies. Some reasons for this different development can be found in China's past institutional system.

In chapter 4 theoretical agricultural household models are discussed that provide the basis for empirically analyzing household behavior regarding the allocation of family labor and for the assessment of the determinants of part-time and full-time farm persistence.

The data set used for the empirical analysis is described in chapter 5. Results for the analyses of poverty and income are presented and discussed in chapter 6. The respective variable sets used and results from the different parametric analyses of the separability test of households' labor demand and supply decisions, households' labor time allocation and the persistence of farm structures are presented and discussed in part 7 of this work. Chapter 8 provides conclusions and suggestions for policy and further research.

2 Hebei province

In this part the Hebei province is described regarding the conditions that are decisive for the dominating role of agricultural production and with respect to socio-economic developments in rural areas of Hebei and regional institutional patterns.

2.1 Location, population and natural conditions

The Hebei province is located in the North-East of China. Together with the provinces Henan and Shandong and to some part Beijing, Tianjin, Anhui and Jiangsu province most of the area of Hebei belongs to the North China Plain (*huabei pingyuan*) (NCP)4. It has a size of 187,700 km² (NBS, 2008) with fertile alluvial soils found in those counties that belong to the NCP (Rumbaur, 2008). The sediment soils are mainly chromic or calcaric cambisols (Rumbaur, 2008). The yellow river and its tributaries flooded the plain areas over centuries. The population of Hebei reached almost 70 million people in 2008 (ACMR, 2010) which results in a population density of around 372 people per km².

The average temperature ranges between -20 to -14 degrees Celsius in January and 20 to 27 degrees Celsius in July (CBW, 2010). The average annual rainfall for Hebei varies between 400 mm and 800 mm (CBW, 2010) but it is very seasonal with low or no precipitation in winter and some periods of heavy rainfalls in spring and July and August. There is high variation between years with droughts experienced in some years and floods occurring in other years (Rumbaur, 2008).

Due to these environmental conditions the NCP is considered to be the major area of grain production of China. Hebei as well has intensive agriculture with mainly grain production in the plains. The Western and North-Western regions of Hebei province do not belong to the fertile plain areas and are mainly mountainous with altitudes up to above 1,000 meters above sea level. In this region less grain and therefore more horticulture production can be found. Typical crops cultivated are for example apples and chestnuts.

---

[4] See the respective maps for China and Hebei in appendix A.

2.2 The rural areas of Hebei province

Still around 60% of the population in Hebei province are classified as rural (NBS, 2008). In 2008 an area of 6.3 million ha was under cultivation (ACMR, 2010) which represents 5.2% of the total area of arable land in China (NBS, 2008).[5] The total area cultivated declined since the 1950s (*Table 1*). Most of the farm land is irrigated and cultivated within the traditional double cropping system that is practiced in most of the plain parts of Hebei.

Table 1: Population, rural labor force, agricultural land, and irrigation area in the Hebei province (various years compared)

			Area in 1000 ha						
					Sown Area				
Year	Population	Rural Laborers	Culti- vated	Total sown	Grain	Vege- tables	Cotton	Peanut	Irrig able
	(1000 persons)								
1949	30,860	11,688	7,266	7,750	7,243	n.a.	n.a.	n.a.	n.a.
1978	50,570	17,260	6,675	9,370	7,944	n.a.	n.a.	n.a.	3,556
1990	61,590	23,605	6,556	8,787	6,828	n.a.	n.a.	n.a.	3,618
2000	66,740	27,701	6,883	9,024	6,919	n.a.	n.a.	n.a.	4,346
2003	67,694	27,480	6,883	8,639	5,944	1,069	581	490	4,404
2007	69,430	28,465	6,315	8,653	6,168	1,180	680	392	4,579
2008	69,888	28,948	6,317	8,713	6,158	n.a.	n.a.	n.a.	4,453

Note: n.a.: not available.
Source: ACMR (2010) and NBS (various years).

The classical crop rotation includes winter wheat and summer maize or cotton double cropping, for which irrigation is necessary especially for winter wheat because it requires up to 3 times more water during its cropping period than is available from rainfalls during this time (Zhen and Routray, 2002). The precipitation is rather high on average but there is a quite uneven distribution with most of the rainfalls occurring in summer. Some portion of the decrease in

[5] As Lin (2009) states one has to be cautious with Chinese official statistics especially regarding the amounts of arable land available. There was a tendency of underreporting of cultivated land area by official administration at various levels. This tendency was uncovered by the first national land census that was undertaken between 1984 and 1996.

the sown area of grain crops is due to increases in the sown areas for e.g. vegetables, cotton and peanuts. Also the expanding production of cotton is based on intensive underground water irrigation.

Besides its importance for whole China in the production of grain, Hebei is also the province with most of orchard area (in 2007 around 1 million hectares). Orchard areas are dominating in the western and northern parts of Hebei.

The demand for infrastructure leads to land conversion for new settlement areas or roads and railway systems. As can be seen from *Table 2* below, the trend in the change of land use or the reclassification of land from crop production area to other purposes such as garden land (mainly vegetable production) or for state infrastructure projects continued. Together with the still growing population this results in a very small available per capita area of arable land (0.084 ha/person in 2008) in comparison to the world average of 0.236 ha (Lin and Ho, 2003) or even the average for China of 0.092 ha (own calculation based on ACMR, 2010).

Table 2: Changes in cultivated land in the Hebei province, 2000-2008

	2000	2005	2007	2008
Cultivated area at the beginning of the year (1000 ha)	6,868.80	6,441.51	6,315.34	6,329.79
Increase in cultivated area in this year (1000 ha)	2.00	8.10	53.90	15.81
Barren brought under cultivation	0.50	4.39	5.44	10.14
Garden converted to farmland	n.a.	0.91	44.58	1.84
Decrease in cultivated area in this year (1000 ha)	14.80	53.37	54.72	13.65
State capital construction	5.90	7.02	6.84	5.96
Farmland converted to gardens	n.a.	44.70	0.51	2.69
Farmland converted to pasture	n.a.	0.73	44.97	3.06
Cultivated area at the end of the year (1000 ha)	6,857.10	6,396.25	6,314.53	6,331.89
Per capita cultivated area (ha/person)	0.097	0.087	0.085	0.084

Note: n.a.: not available.
Source: Hebei Statistical Yearbook 2009 available at ACMR (2010).

This low amount of arable land per captia leads to small scale production and the average farm size is small. In terms of output, grains (mainly wheat and maize) are still the main agricultural production occupation for farm households in Hebei province. A large proportion of the agricultural production in the assessed region is subsistence agriculture, with e.g. large shares of the output for grain or eggs used for household consumption.

Over the period from 1986 to 2002 the total amount of arable land per household declined in the study region as did the amount of land per capita, although to a lesser extent showing the relative egalitarian per capita distribution of land (*Figure 2*).

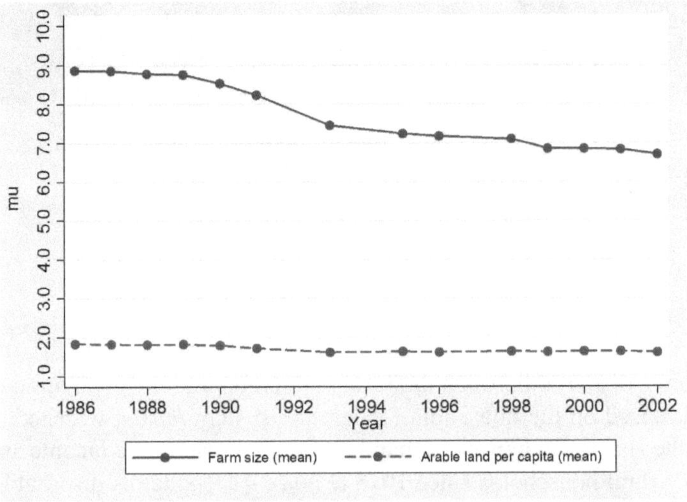

Source: Own computations based on RCRE data for Hebei, 1986-2002.

Figure 2: Arable land per household and per capita by year

The land is farmed by a high number of small agricultural households. This led to a high fragmentation of the land. In most areas the plot size is small and the households operate on plots that are scattered around the farm yard or house in the village.

Despite the policy aim of grain self sufficieny, the high amount of available rural labor and the scarcity of arable land per capita are a comparative advantage for the production of labor intensive crops; fruits and vegetables (Sandrey and Edinger, 2009). In reverse, China does not have favorable conditions for the production of land intensive crops as cereals or oilseeds.

The assessed villages differ in the per capita amount of land provided to the household (*Figure 3*). This is mainly due to different amounts of arable land available for distribution among villagers.

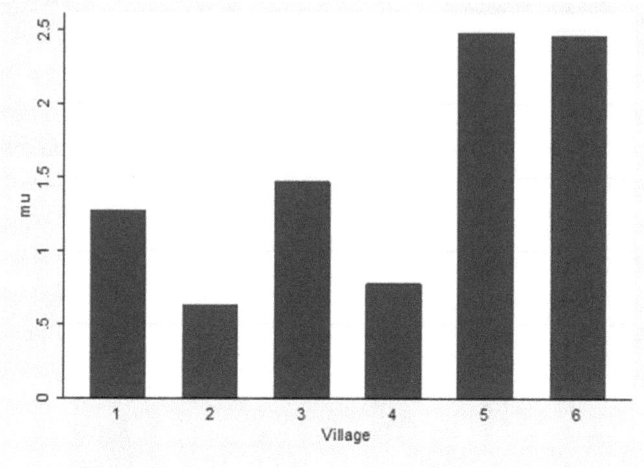

Source: Own computations based on RCRE data for Hebei, 1986-2002.

Figure 3: Arable land per capita by village

Also the disparity between the rural population and the population classified as urban, based on the household registration system *hukou*, widened as can be seen by the rising gap between urban household's disposable income and the net income of rural households since 1978 (*Figure 4*). The terms disposable and net income refer to the distinctions made in the Chinese statistical yearbook between urban and rural income available for the coverage of living costs. However, the costs of living are lower in the rural areas, as also shown in *Figure 4*.

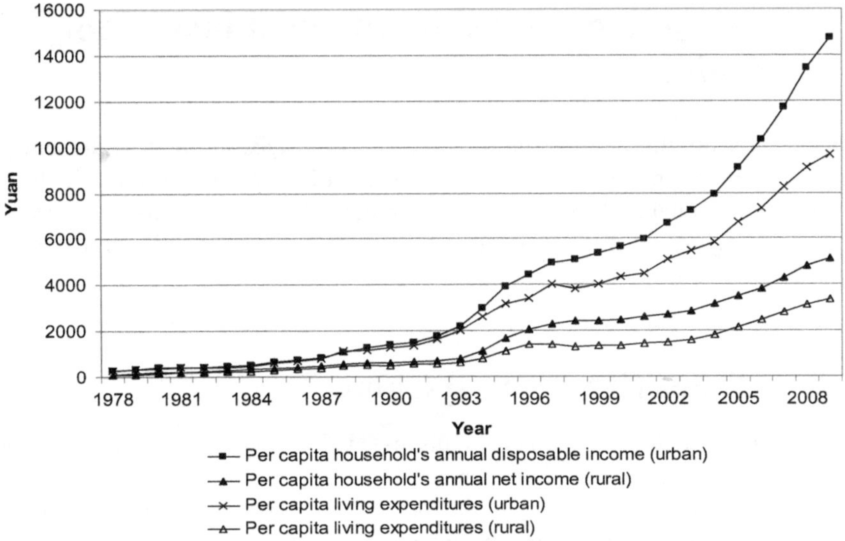

Source: Basic statistics for people's livelihood, Hebei province, ACMR (2010).

Figure 4: The urban rural gap in income and living expenditures

2.3 Summary

Most of the population in Hebei province is classified as rural. The agricultural production system is still dominated by small scale farms. Grain crops dominate in terms of cultivated area, especially in winter wheat summer maize double cropping system, but shifts to cash crops such as cotton and vegetables can be observed. Since the start of the reforms the disparities in income and living expenditures increased. But also the villages within Hebei differ in terms of development and well-being. The reasons for those differences are partly related to differences in the population density and partly to the institutional developments that occurred since 1978, which will be discussed in the next chapter.

3 Development and state of rural institutions in China

This chapter provides an overview of the various stages in the development of rural institutions in China in general and some of which are also specified for Hebei. It is devoted to the historical development of institutions that supports the understanding of the micro-economic assessments in Chapter 7. As a starting point the term transition is explained.

3.1 Transition in rural China

Transition can either be defined or discussed focusing on sectoral transition (Spiertz and Oenema, 2004; Swinnen and Rozelle, 2006) or as an overall transition of the economy and society in the light of normative and positive economic theory. Also agrarian change can be analyzed from different perspectives (Rigg, 2006). One aspect is the deagrarianization which is driven by structural changes within the assessed economy. But also the assessment of poverty trends is included in studies on agrarian change as well as the analysis of changes in the culture and livelihoods of the rural population (Rigg, 2006), which can be seen as more societal changes then as structural changes.

Here the sectoral and the overall transitional view will be combined because from the early 1980s onwards the rural areas in China experienced at the same time a restructuring of production processes within the agricultural sector and an opening and system change occurring for the whole society and economy. Skinner et al. (2001) explicitly argue that the development in rural China has to be assessed with respect to the interaction between agriculture and the secondary sector but also in the context of changing environmental conditions (e.g. increases in environmental costs due to land use changes) and the impacts on local decision makers that arose from the orientation of the Chinese political economy towards markets.

McMillan and Naughton (1992) state that with the transition of a planned economy the whole set of fiscal, monetary, legal system, ownership and price institutions must be changed. Also Swinnen and Rozelle (2006) emphasize that the transition of a communist or socialist economy involves necessary changes in property rights regimes, an adaptation of incentive systems to improve labor and capital productivity and the creation of exchange institutions or markets that are more efficient than the ones under central planning of exchange. The most important effects of well functioning exchange institutions are that they facilitate transactions between different economic agents and by this promote specialization and trade. Those institutions involve a price mechanism by which information about the degree of scarcity of specific factors is provided to consumers and producers (Swinnen and Rozelle, 2006).

The transition of former socialist or communist societies with centrally planned economic systems is discussed in the economic theory mainly from two different perspectives (McMillan and Naugthon, 1992). The first way of transition discussed in theory and also observable with respect to some East-European societies is the "big bang"-approach. Theorists favoring this approach argue that private property rights and a market oriented system of allocation and distribution should replace the former system as soon as possible (Tsang, 1996). The school of thought promoting the second approach, "gradualism", argues that a fast transformation of all spheres of society and the economic system at the same time is not appropriate especially for large and relative homogenous centrally planned communist societies (Gregory and Stuart, 2001). Because a fast and complete transition of a whole state system is accompanied by many stakeholders that loose influence, power or their economic basis a stepwise change of the structures provides a feasible way to prevent resistance from those interest groups. So the compensations necessary for people to agree to changes are lower if the gradualist approach is followed (Dewatripont and Roland, 1992). As Schüller (2002) explains the homo oeconomicus would favor the "big bang" to achieve efficiency in allocation and production and competition based actions and decisions as soon as possible. But if one thinks of the socio-economic actor as homo sociologicus (Schüller, 2002) this would not be the prime interest because the benefits of a fast transition could be outweighed by the risk that the transition becomes a failure due to high pecuniary and non-pecuniary transition costs. China was in a comfortable position as the institutional reforms in the agricultural sector started in the end of the 1970s. The society had recovered from the chaotic years of the Cultural Revolution and the economic system was relatively stable (Bajpai and Jian, 1996). As a consequence there was no need to transform the rural institutions too fast, as it might have been the case in East-European countries, where societies had to cope with a sudden break down of the economic and political structures at the same time.

Following Spiertz and Oenema (2004) transition in agriculture is seen as a process of sectoral change in response to internal or external drivers that results in a change of the incentives for the sectoral actors. The term transition itself implies that this process is anti-systemic (Ness and Raichur, 1989) by changing know institutions. Some examples for drivers of change are: population growth, market and price changes, policy changes, adoption of new technology, changes in the level of education of the rural population, and climatic changes or flooding (Spiertz and Oenema, 2004). The actors respond by adapting their (production) decisions to the perceived changes.

Figure 5 provides a graphical illustration of these processes. Transition as a process entails the movement from state determination of productive endowment and income values to market determination of those values (Benjamin et al., 2005). The change from a socialist to a market-oriented economy goes along with changes in factor prices. For example, returns to education or special skills are expected to be higher (Benjamin et al., 2005) than under the commune system that hardly rewarded differences in labor productivity or human capital.

Following Happe (2004) 'structure' is used here as a term that refers to an entity which consists of several components that are inter-related to each other. With respect to the agricultural sector those components are the farm firm or household itself and the available production factors land, labor and capital (Happe, 2004). The OECD (1995) defines structural changes in agriculture as the movement or exchange of production factors within the sector (e.g. among farm households), and between the agricultural, the industrial and the service sector of an economy.

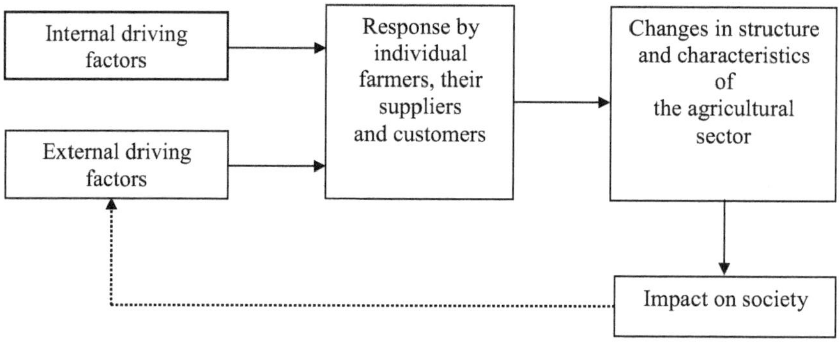

Source: Adapted from Spiertz and Oenema (2004).

Figure 5: Drivers of change in agricultural production structures

As suggested by the feedback loop it is not always possible to clearly distinguish between the cause and effect of externally induced changes due to the simultaneity of change in the sector but also society wide. Based on the interactions of rural actors, especially agricultural households, with other sectors and administrative levels of the state societal and policy changes during the opening process of China also influenced the structure of the agricultural sector. Farm households are the core production decision unit in the agricultural sector of Hebei. Their decisions about the provision of off-farm labor had an impact on the development of non-agricultural industries. Institutional changes regarding land use rights, the abolishment of the commune system, and the stronger focus on agricultural subsidies influenced on the other side the decision processes of the farm households. In general, the agricultural sector is of great importance for the development of an economy at its early stages (von Urff, 1982) because it provides food and non-food commodities and labor force that could be used in other sectors (Swinnen and Rozelle, 2006).

With respect to the development of the agricultural sector in Hebei one can identify some inhibitors of change:

(1) The de facto breakdown of the formerly centrally organized extension service. This resulted in a gap in knowledge transfer about up to date farming methods and pest control that could only partly be replaced by private actors, such as sellers of agricultural inputs.
(2) Urbanization in combination with the reclassification of rural agricultural land into urban development or infrastructure land.
(3) Population growth that further contributed to land fragmentation and by this facilitated the trend of decreasing farm size.
(4) At the same time also the share of elderly people, who are less productive due to their age and health status, increased.
(5) Politically induced changes in the price and distribution system that are observed in general in whole China.

This list does not claim to be complete. What is clear is that the assessment of the changes in rural institutions has to involve the discussion of societal and political factors influencing the transition. Therefore time related variables are included in the microeconomic assessment later in this work that might unveil impacts of policy or macroeconomic changes on rural households' decisions.

3.2 Rural China prior the period of communism

Over a long period of time (from the first dynasties until the appearance of the People's Republic) land was privately owned in China. Almost 50% of the cultivated land before the socialist revolution was owned by landlords. The landlords rented land to peasant households so that a system of independent but fragmented agricultural production and decision units, private farms, existed in rural China (Lin, 1997).

Land was the most important component in a system that Zhao and Wen (1999) describe as a "combination of intergenerational and inter-temporal transfer of wealth, with emphasis on intergenerational transfers" (p. 3). Land protected its owners in two ways from old age poverty. First, land was traditionally inherited to the sons of the family after the death of the father. Being aware of the heritage to receive the young generation behaved well with respect to their parents and provided their income to the intergenerational household (intergenerational transfer). In the case of a loss or non-existence of children aged land owners could, as a second way to ensure old age security, sell the land or rent it out (inter-temporal transfer) and by this make a living either from the revenues generated by the land sale or from the land rent flows (Zhao and Wen, 1999).

Before the foundation of the People's Republic of China in 1949 income inequality was relatively high in China (Rozelle, 1994). Roll (1980) calculates a Gini coefficient for income of 0.443 for overall rural China in the 1930s. Brandt and Sands (1990) estimated Gini coefficients with respect to income for three villages in northeastern Hebei in the 1930s of 0.346, 0.349 and 0.391 respectively and 0.46 for the province as a whole. In the 1930s rural households in China derived a significant share of their income from sideline agricultural income such as weaving and spinning (Roll, 1980). Income earned by those sideline activities and a higher share of household laborers being involved in non-agricultural activities contributed positively to income inequality reduction. The marginal contribution of these variables to inequality reduction was lower than the negative impacts on income equality stemming from the amount of owned farm land or the amount of hired agricultural laborers (Roll, 1980). The land reform contributed to a decrease in local income inequality but did not address reasons and did not change inter-regional inequality (Roll, 1980). In addition, the rural population received a dividend from the abolition of land rents (at the expense of the former landlords) and changes in the tax system (Roll, 1980).

Before the revolution in 1949 most agricultural taxes were related to the amount of land owned or farmed and tax collection was in the responsibility of provincial governments. The tax system was regressive; the higher the amount of taxed items the lower the tax rate. In 1951/52 a progressive tax system based on per capita crop income was introduced which helped in reducing inequality in overall household incomes (Roll, 1980).

3.3 Collectivization

This section reviews the main features of the period of a collectively organized agricultural production system in China to build the basis for discussing institutional changes that occurred during the reform of the sector (see chapter 3.4).

Hartford (1985) provides an overview of seven principles that have been the basic characteristics of the collectivized agricultural production system in rural China from the beginning of the collectivization in the 1950s up to the structural reforms of the agricultural production from 1978 onwards:

(1) Every kind of (quantitative) allocation of material inputs and distribution of monetary funds between all levels of production units was *planned centrally*. Production units at lower hierarchical levels had to deliver predetermined amounts of output to higher hierarchies.
(2) All means needed for agricultural production have been *owned collectively*.
(3) The production was oriented at *large scale*. The production teams had to fulfill pre-determined production plans and worked on relatively large and unified fields.
(4) Based on a system of work points every member of the production team received its income according to a *unified distribution* system based on the net income of the production team.
(5) Ideally every commune provided all services to its members so that they were integrated in a system that provided consumption goods and social services but also organized the political life among the commune members.
(6) All people that were not able to take care for their well-being themselves got provided all necessary goods and services to satisfy basic living, health and education needs under a system of welfare guarantees.
(7) The rural population was assigned to specific production and exchange units (cells). It was aimed to keep those units as self-reliant as possible. Individuals required the permission of the unit before changing the location of residence.

Looking at these principles describing how the agricultural production was organized and was intended to be working, it is obvious that the system was lacking mechanisms that allowed for incentives for both, individual workers but also local decision makers to improve production and to use scarce resources as efficiently as possible. Lin (1988) explains that close supervision in agricultural production goes along with high supervision costs and therefore reduces the incentives to work as part of an agricultural production team. In addition, rural labor productivity was very low due to relative low amounts of arable land per capita (de Janvry et al., 2005).

From the point of view of politics, the agricultural sector was not of first priority. It was considered to support the development of other industries and to provide support for urban development (Gale et al., 2005) and industrialization (Karplus and Deng, 2008). This was reflected in the socialist price system which set high prices for industrial products and low prices for agricultural outputs and via this mode of price setting lowered the real income of farmers (de Janvry et al., 2005).

But the socialist ideology was oriented to diminish inequality especially among the rural population (Rozelle, 1994). As Roll (1980) shows in his seminal assessment of income inequality development in China in the early1930s and 1950s, rural Gini coefficients, with respect to income, declined from the 1930s to the 1950s. Putterman (1990) indicates that in the 1960s and 1970s there was hardly a change in intra-rural income inequality.

Because most social and health care services were also provided by the collective they were by this likely to contribute to equalization in well-being among the rural population. Therefore, Benjamin et al. (2005) argue that household's well-being was less sensitive to household's productivity during communism than it might have been from the start of the transition of rural China until now.

3.4 Policy changes during the transition and the development of market institutions

Over the last two to three decades the completely centrally planned and organized economic system has been replaced by an institutional framework in which a Party-state decides about the parameters that condition market forces (Lin, 2009). This process started between 1976 and 1978 as Chinese policy makers formulated higher levels of efficiency in production and (resource) allocation as important topics in economic policy (Krug, 1990).

1978 is often referred to as the starting point of opening reforms or structural change in rural China (Lin, 1988; Swinnen and Rozelle, 2006) due to the fact that in this year institutional changes, like the provision of incentives to individual households to increase production and some relaxations in the quota system started in Anhui province and later resulted in the HRS, that was gradually implemented in the other regions of China and formally accepted in 1981 (see an overview in Jia and Fock, 2007).

Due to the focus of the present work, the institutional frameworks regarding the use of land and the generation of income by rural households will be reviewed in this part. Beside national laws and provincial regulations the local institutional setup varies strongly. This is a major challenge especially for foreign researchers. Therefore the institutional framework is outlined based on how it should be according to national regulations, but if possible references are made to actual patterns and differences between different locations in Hebei based on own qualitative information.

One has to have in mind, that policies that have been formulated to explicitly address a specific, e.g. macroeconomic, topic implicitly also affect the development and distribution of welfare and income (Roll, 1980). For rural China examples for such implicit impacts could be adjustments in the foreign exchange rate system that occurred often in the 1980s and 1990s (Wang, 2004). Also China's WTO accession influenced its terms of trade and changed relative prices between agricultural and industrial products. Carter and Zhu (2009) find evidence that the opening of China to world trade had a positive impact on those relative prices and therefore agricultural producers could be expected to economically profit from relative to industrial products higher rewards for their outputs.[6] But also the decentralization of fiscal revenue raising and public spending (Zhang and Zou, 1998) can have an impact on rural (economic) development, for example with respect to public spending for health care and education. Between 1986 and 1995, public spending for education decreased from a share of 63.4% in Chinese overall public spending to a share of 45.6% (Zhang and Fan, 2004).[7]

Even if it is argued that decentralization in general is enhancing the efficiency in revenue collection and spending, Zhang and Zou (1998) find for the period 1987 to 1993 a negative relation between fiscal decentralization and economic growth on provincial level. This might be due to the general political turbulenc-

6 As can be seen from Mundell's (1961) discussion about optimal currency areas, flexible exchange rates based on national currencies work well for countries with high internal but low international factor mobility. Wang (2004) considers a Mundell-Fleming model as being applicable for the assessment of China's real exchange rate between 1980 and 2002. He considers the opening of China's trade, the elimination of price controls, the increased orientation towards markets and other institutional changes during the reform process as leading to a higher relevance of applying macroeconomic models developed to assess open economies (see Krugman and Obstfeld, 2004, for a theoretical discussion of related macroeconomic models).

7 According to Zhang and Fan (2004) public spending in China comprises expenditures for research and development, for education, and for the construction and maintenances of irrigation schemes, roads, electric power plants and grids and communication facilities.

es during this time. Zhang and Zou (1998) argue that a central level fiscal system can better support investments in public goods that have nation-wide positive externalities in societies that are at early stages of economic development.

In China land, as the core input factor for agricultural production, serves two main goals of policy makers. It is the basis for the country's food subsistence and fulfills traditionally a social security function (Zhao and Wen, 1999). According to Lin (2009) land is perceived society wide as so important for food production and provision of at least some part of old age security, especially to the rural population, that this perception even outweighs positions such as the need of exclusive property rights, the principle of utility maximization and the request for fully functioning (land) markets.

The first sentence of Article 2 of the Chinese Land Administration Law (in force since 1 of January 1999) states, that:

> "The People's Republic of China practices socialist public ownership of land, namely, ownership by the whole people and collective ownership by the working people." (National Development Reform Commission, 2010)

As a consequence of this, the agricultural land in rural areas belongs to the rural collective as mentioned in the 2nd sentence of Article 8 of the Land Administration Law.

> "Land in rural and suburban areas shall be owned by peasant collectives, except for those portions which belong to the State as provided for by law; house sites and private plots of cropland and hilly land shall also be owned by peasant collectives." (National Development Reform Commission, 2010)

Or as Chin (2005) points out, the farmers' collective *nongmin jiti* holds the ownership of the land but it is not clearly defined who the farmers' collective is. According to the first two sentences of Article 14 of this law, there is the possibility to issue user rights for agricultural land. Land contracts should be concluded for a period of 30 years. But quite often land is found to be reallocated before the end of the official allocation period for example because of changes in the village population (Lohmar et al., 2001).

Article 3 of the Rural Land Contract Law of the People's Republic of China (RLCL) explains that a contract system should be applied for entitling user rights of land in rural areas (MoA, 2010). But also in this law no clear definition of the composition of the collective economic organizations in the countryside is provided. This leads to difficulties in applying the law in practice. Who should decide how to allocate the land and to whom? According to Skinner et al. (2001) the responsibility for land use decisions lays mainly in the hands of province, county and town(-ship) decision makers. Chin (2005) states that at the basic administrative level, the village, de facto the village leaders control the distribution of the land. This is partly confirmed by results of own surveys (Böber, 2008 and 2009) where farmers stated that there have been reallocations in villages beside official reallocations and without the need to reallocate land use rights due to correct for changes in the composition of the population in the villages. Such "out of turn" reallocations at village level, accepted or even arranged by town or province administration, quite often occur to change the legal status of land from "agricultural land" into "non-agricultural land" that is allowed to be used for e.g. infrastructure construction (Lin, 2009). Lin (2009) hints towards another conflict that arises with respect to land use rights, their allocation and the conversion of land between different purposes. Due to the hierarchical relationships in the Chinese political system there is hardly a possibility for rural (farmers') collectives to claim their rights. So the state or urban administration can convert rural to urban land without the need to involve rural stakeholders in the decision process. The ordo-liberal principle of freedom of decision about private property (see Eucken, 2004) does not hold for the current conditions in the Chinese economy. Farmers, besides their re-granted responsibilities for agricultural production, still do not possess land titles or are not allowed to rent-out or rent-in land in some regions. But the transition from "a planned economy under the law of exchange value" to a "socialist market economy with Chinese characteristics" (Sachs and Woo, 1997) provided the rural population with more direct decision power over their agricultural production, off-farm labor allocation and by this ultimately also over their income and overall well-being.

Decentralization also took place with respect to the monitoring of environmental resources resulting in sometimes overlapping and not well structured responsibilities and funding sources (Rozelle et al., 1997). The degradation of natural resources directly affects human health but also increases human insecurity due to the uncertainness of the links between pollution and the future development of the living base (UNDP, 2008).

The introduction of the household responsibility system shifted the decision about household's labor allocation from the collective to individual households. At the same time, the emergence of township and village enterprises offered employment opportunities especially in industrial production (Qian, 2000). So households that where endowed with more labor than needed for agricultural production practically got a chance to supply this surplus labor to off-farm jobs. Fan (1990) cites Lin (1987) who finds that the introduction of the household responsibility system as one major institutional change in rural China was responsible for 60% of the growth of agricultural production in China between 1980 and 1984, and for around 51 percent of the poverty reduction during the same time (Fan et al., 2004). Even with improved possibilities for rural households to decide about labor allocation rural labor markets as such did not function perfectly in the 1990s (Benjamin and Brandt, 1997).

Since the opening policy started in China's rural areas in 1978 the institutions and regulations for the agricultural markets and the price system were changed several times. Heerink et al. (2007) list at least three main periods or stages in the development of market structures in the rural areas. They see the first period lasting from the end of the 1970s till 1984. This period is characterized by the responsibility of the farm households to produce state mandated fixed amounts of agricultural products and by a state buying-up system with state fixed prices. From Šik (1968) one learns that such a centrally planned and controlled system seeking for equality gives more or less no incentive for individual engagement and productivity improvement. But Sen (1966) argues that Chinese leaders have been aware of lacking incentives and encouraged local political leaders to increase outputs by offering non-monetary incentives. He shows in his assessment of labor allocation in cooperative systems that even a system of centralized labor allocation decisions can lead to a Pareto optimal allocation of labor and a maximization of social welfare. Putterman and DiGiorgio (1985) discuss several combinations of centralized and community level decision making and voting procedures about individually or collectively organized agricultural production. They find that democratic local choices about the degree of collectivity might be more efficient than centralized decisions and could increase social welfare of the local communities. If local communities are provided with the choice between individual household farming or agricultural production organized in a collective their decisions would be mainly influenced by the following motives: level of community control over land allocation, the equality in access to land and to how far the institutional parameters of the allocation decisions are defined in a democratic manner (Putterman and DiGorgio, 1985). Transactions costs, which are in general the costs of finding a contract partner, setting up a contract and enforcing agreements (North, 1990), are higher in a collective decision system (Berggren and Karlson, 2003) but this is not discussed by Putterman and DiGorgio (1985).

Heerink et al. (2007) state, that the Chinese government readjusted the price system to encourage developments in the rural areas by rising prices for output. So it can be argued that the political decision makers were partly aware of the discouraging nature of plans, the negative impact of distorted rural-urban price systems and the low labor productivity (in rural areas) in a centrally planned economy. The policies applied in the second period between 1985 and 1993 seem to confirm this argument. According to Heerink et al. (2007) a dual price system was installed. This system focused on state mandated fixed prices for a state planned fixed quota that had to be delivered of every agricultural product to the state on the one side. On the other side farmers were allowed to sell above quota amounts for market prices. To raise the agricultural production the prices for products in the contract farming system were quite often increased. Qian (2003) also mentions the dual-track concept regarding prices that allowed farmers to sell (grain) production above the quota requirements to market prices.

Heerink et al. (2007) see 1994 as starting point of the third period. In the end of 1994 the former procurement system was again put in force for grain (Buschena et al., 2005). The motivation behind this re-installment was the promotion of grain production instead of producing cash crops as rapeseed or cotton. The reason for this behavior was to produce enough grain to reach self-sufficiency in grain supply in China (Chen, 2006). Because of this, state intervention into market processes remained persistent especially for grain.

With opening the market for food and also for housing in urban areas the policy makers lowered the barriers for the rural population to migrate to cities even beside the fact that they continued the *hukou* system (de Janvry et al, 2005).

At the beginning of the reforms possibilities for provincial and local governments to tax and collect fees for investment have been linked to locally generated revenues. At the same time the ability of the central government to redistribute funds between provinces was limited by putting a cap on the taxation of state owned industrial companies (Rozelle, 1994). Some local leaders responded to those changes by increasing the taxation of local industries to subsidize agricultural production (Rozelle, 1994). But in reality the tax burden on the agricultural population was not relieved. In 2002 the tax-for-fee reform started with the aim to sum up all local fees rural residents were confronted with in a single agricultural tax (Kennedy, 2007). But still this agricultural tax was a burden for the rural population. In addition the tax revenues to local administrations were lower than the revenues from the fees collected before. Empirical studies indicate that the lower revenues might have resulted in a less efficient provision of services, especially due to deficiencies in local transfer systems, and this might have negatively affected rural areas especially in the poorest regions (Kennedy, 2007).

To finally counterweigh discrimination against agricultural production by heavily taxing farm outputs directly or rural labor indirectly, e.g. by forcing households to provide it as an input to infrastructure construction, China started the abolishment of all central state and local agricultural taxes and fees in 2004 (Gale et al., 2005). By 2006 the agricultural tax was abolished (Yu and Jensen, 2009). In addition subsidy programs have been initialized to provide income support to rural households. Currently different measures of direct and indirect income support for farmers are applied at province and county levels (Gale et al., 2005). Some examples are fertilizer subsidies that lower purchase prices, area related subsidies if households plant grain crops but also direct support if farm households invest in mechanization (13 billion Yuan in 2009 for agricultural machinery purchases; peopledaily, 2010). It is planned to reform this fragmented subsidy system so that farmers are only supported ones per year to stabilize subsidy flows (Chang and Zhang, 2010). With all these policy measures the Chinese government aims to solve the 'San-Nong' problem, which consists in the relatively declining income from farming in comparison to non-farm income and by this the widening of the gap between rural and urban income (Yu and Jensen, 2009). However, the average amount of subsidies received by every farm household was rather low (Gale et al., 2005). As Huang et al. (2011) state, in 2002 the central government provided subsidies to agriculture that where equal to only 0.007 per cent of the agricultural output. So it was questionable if these measures significantly increase agricultural and total income. Also the goal of stabilizing and securing grain production hardly seemed to be achievable with average payments of 10 Yuan per mu if grain crops are planted (Gale et al., 2005). The policies to support farmers changed radically since 2002. In 2008, 95 billion Yuan have been provided as subsidies for the agricultural sector (Huang et al., 2011). Around 82 per cent of this amount were made up by grain subsidies (*liangshi butie*) and input subsidies (*nongzi zonghe butie*). Huang et al. (2011) conclude that the subsidies do not lead to any distortions in farmers' decisions regarding the amount of area of land sown with grain or in the decisions about the use of fertilizer. So, subsidies can rather be seen as income transfers to rural households than as influencing the grain production area and consequently the grain output. But such a type of income transfer (unearned income) might have distorting effects on the labor time allocation decisions of the households regarding different agricultural or non-agricultural occupations, as will be assessed in part 7 of this work.

The second most important (non-labor) production factor for agriculture, besides land, is water. Because production in Hebei province heavily depends on irrigation and almost 80% of irrigation water originate from groundwater (Zhang et al., 2008), the distribution and management of water is crucial for agricultural producers and the society as a whole. The importance of a reasonable management of the production of water is increased in face of declining groundwater resources all over North China. Water provision and distribution is regionally organized in several ways. In the period of de-collectivization private ownership of tube wells significantly increased (Zhang et al., 2008). Major characteristics especially of the markets for groundwater in North China are that they are informal, localized, unregulated and impersonal (Zhang et al., 2008). Water is provided to farmers sometimes from the village, sometimes from a farmers' association but also from private entrepreneurs. Usually, the latter ones are local residents that privately invested in digging wells and building tube infrastructure (Böber, 2009). So even though de jure water is the property of the people (Zhang et al., 2008) de facto water management institutions are not transparently organized and lack efficiency (Varis and Vakkilainen, 2001) and it is quite likely to observe that no one in the different administrative bodies that are involved in ground water management seems to assume him- or herself being responsible for the implementation of existing laws and rules (Zhen and Zoebisch, 2006). In addition Zhen and Zoebisch (2006) explain that there are no monitoring and reporting methods included in the existing regulations for ground water management. Although the price of water seems to be reflecting the actual costs for ground water pumping (Zhang et al., 2008), price distortions might arise in the water market as soon as state interventions bias the prices for energy.

3.5 Farm households in China and Hebei

3.5.1 General overview

In China more than 200 million farms exist (Swinnen and Rozelle, 2006). However, one has to bear in mind that the concept of a farm in China differs from the concepts of farms in Europe, the U.S. but also in other parts of Asia. For example McConnell and Dillon (1997) distinguish six basic farm types for Asia (excluding China):

Type 1: Rather small family farms with subsistence agriculture
Type 2: Farms that are still small family farms but partially commercialized
Type 3: Small family farms that are independent and specialized
Type 4: Small and dependent family farms (where the farm family does not possess the de facto power to make decisions)
Type 5: Large family farms that are commercialized and specialized
Type 6: Commercial farms, which are managed by hired personnel and mainly focusing on mono-cropping systems

During the transition, most of agricultural land was transferred via the use right system to farm households, so that the majority of arable land in China still is cultivated by family farms on a small scale (Swinnen, 2009).

At present the actual size of an average Chinese (family) farm is rather small in comparison to the size of production units during commune time. There are also new developments regarding the participation of agricultural households in businesses other than agricultural production. In 2008, around 14.8 million households in Hebei are classified as rural household, which equates to around 70% of all households in Hebei (Hebei Statistical Yearbook 2009 available at ACMR, 2010).

Sandrey and Edinger (2009) summarize, that it is not easy to define what is meant by a small farm or a small-holder farm household in China. Elements of the former communal system can still be found in the institutional setting in rural China. So, Sandrey and Edinger (2009) refrain from the concept of clearly defined individual farm households but assume that it is more appropriate to use the concept of farming cooperatives to describe the linkages between rural households. In the present study, the farm households are considered to be individual decision units, even if they sometimes depend on community level cooperation like regarding the exchange harvesting machinery.

As Zhu (1991) explains, the term 'peasant household' is usually applied to differentiate between rural households and households of workers and state employees. De facto, almost every rural household can be considered as a unit of agricultural production or farm household. This is mainly due to the fact that at least in the villages assessed here, almost 96% of households possessed use rights for agricultural land and devoted at least some hours of work to the allocated plots. In addition the household head is usually classified as 'rural' according to the *hukou* system. Also Chen et al. (2004) state, that Chinese households are classified as rural as long as they engage to some extent in agricultural production no matter if they devote household labor to non-agricultural occupations.

Wang (2007) provides a slightly changed definition of Nakajima's (1986) definition of the farm household that is applied here. Instead of behaving strictly profit-maximizing the rural farm household is defined as "semi-commercialized" rural production unit that uses a mix of purchased input factors and input factors available from the household's endowment, especially family labor and land (Wang, 2007). The output of the farm household's agricultural production is partly consumed by the household itself and partly sold. The distinction between own consumed and marketed outputs is relevant especially for the discussion of income and poverty trends.

3.5.2 Part- and full-time farm households

The assessment of differences between full-time and part-time farm households is one of the major aims of this study. Poverty indices are calculated separately for the sub samples containing full- and part-time farm households respectively in chapter 6. In chapter 7.1 separability is tested for part- and full-time farm households and in chapter 7.3 an ex-post analysis of intra-sectoral change with respect to trends in farming population and farm size is applied. Therefore it is necessary to distinguish different types of rural households with respect to part-time and full-time farming activities.

Different concepts can be used to define part-time and full-time farming. One group is based on the sources of income and the other on the allocation of working time to on-farm and off-farm activities. According to Ahearn and Lee (1991) there are advantages of both concepts. The income-based concepts are useful in cases of yearly collected data without panel data character and have the advantage that they display which proportion of the household income is derived from farm and off-farm work. Income-based concepts offer a good possibility to analyze the diversification abilities and strategies of rural households. In contrast to these income-concepts the time-based concepts define part-time farming in a different way. Time-based concepts allow detecting the activities to which the household in total or the individual household member devote their available working time. The disadvantage of this concept is the difficulty to draw conclusions on the contribution of a given activity to the livelihood and the well-being of the household based on the amount of hours spent on that activity. This is particularly difficult because of a high variation in the required amount of working time for different types of farm products (Ahearn and Lee, 1991). As Fuller (1991) states there is the potential for an operator bias if only the time allocation or income sources of the main operator (often the household head) are considered. An operator's labor could be substituted by family members so that the operator can work part-time off the farm and the farm as such could still be counted as full-time farm. Following Croll (1994) the household in China is seen as an economic, social and political unit that determines production and consumption and utilizes family labor, land, capital and other resources. Furthermore she describes the most typical form of a Chinese household as one consisting of 4-6 members belonging to two to three generations (Croll, 1981). Although family per economic definition of input factors may not be regarded as an "input factor" it could well be argued that the ties and specialization inside the family and the social functions of a family provide a necessary basis especially for the functioning of a rural economy. Chinese farmers that devote some part of their labor time outside the own agricultural production are officially considered to be part-time workers rather than being classified as part-time farmers as in other countries (Zhu, 1991). So, according to Zhu (1991) the terms 'peasant household' and 'farmers' families' are used interchangeably in China when referring to a rural household that is involved in farming.

The interest to look at part-time farming activities arises from the fact that part-time farming can be seen as one part of many problems discussed in relation to agriculture (Hildreth, 1991). Zhou et al. (2001) state, that part-time farming is likely to evolve in societies or economic systems where land is a scarce resource and distributed equally and the transfer of land or land use rights is restricted. Some of the problems listed by Hildreth (1991) are of importance for discussing part-time farming in China. One of these problems is the distribution of income within the agricultural sector but also between agriculture and the other sectors. As can be seen in Chapter 6.2.1 there is rising importance and an increase in the share of income components derived from non-farming activity in the income composition of rural households in Hebei. Other aspects discussed are the impacts of part-time farming on land use patterns (Hildreth, 1991), land-use intensity (Suh, 1985) and the intensity of fertilizer and pesticide use among part-time farm households (Phimister and Roberts, 2006).

Rawski (1972) mentions, that the holding of multiple jobs was a strategy of peasants in ancient China to achieve a higher standard of living by complementing agricultural production with craft work and retail activities. Croll (1994) sees the development of part-time farming as a phenomenon that was new for rural areas in China as it became obvious in the 1980s. It arose with rising numbers of Chinese farmers working full-time as wage earners outside the farm. In parallel to the argumentation of Chaplin et al. (2003) it could be assumed that households' diversification of production activities in present China is a process of decreasing dependence on agricultural activities and that the strategy to diversify farming activity can contribute to rural development. De Janvry et al. (2005) find positive spillover effects from non-farm activities to the agricultural production. So part-time farming is seen as a way for rural households to compensate for failures in credit or insurance markets that would increase the risk to well-being of the household if agricultural income is fluctuating strongly due to fluctuations in production as well as due to in- and output price fluctuations.

In the classification of part-time and full-time farm households of Brosig et al. (2009) every household that allocates all family labor to on-farm production is considered as full-time farm household. Households that allocate some or all of the family labor to off-farm occupations and still farm any amount of land are classified as part-time farm households. This definition of part- and full-time farm households is applied in chapter 7.3 for the assessment of the persistence of those farm types over the period 1986 to 2002. The choice of this definition allows consistently adapting the model of Brosig et al. (2009) to the recent study. For the income and poverty assessments (chapter 6) farm households are defined as being part- or full-time farm households based on the information provided in the data set about the self classification of farm households as to which activity they devote their labor time.

Both definitions above refer to the distribution of labor time to distinguish between part- and full-time farm households. As already discussed (and further elaborated in chapter 6) a large proportion of farming was and still is subsistence agriculture. If agricultural products are not marketed but consumed by the household itself an income based classification of farmers would likely understate the share of farm income in total income if a large share of the products is not sold in markets but consumed by the household. So, more households might be classified as part-time farm households than in the case where a labor time based classification is chosen.

In chapter 7.2 households are grouped in four different labor market participation regimes that are defined by using the information about the allocation of family labor time combined with the information if non-family labor is employed by the household.

3.6 Alternatives to small scale farming?

This part shortly addresses the question, if there is the possibility to adopt an institutional structure for rural Hebei province that allows the creation of larger and less scattered farms. The small size of the farm "enterprise" can especially be a problem for agricultural households when they want to market their production since their market power is rather low compared to the market power of middlemen or wholesalers.

In North and North-East China (e.g. Heilongjiang province and Inner Mongolia Autonomous Region) farm sizes are larger than in Hebei because the population density is lower so that family based farms cultivate more land. Besides family farms, the state operates large farms which can exploit economies of scale regarding their production and have market power also with respect to the processing and marketing of their products. The World Development Report (WDR) for 2008 presents an example of a marketing cooperative for water melons. This kind of farmer cooperative is seen as a measure to enable small farm households to get linked to the supply chain.

As long as land use rights are distributed based on population size to guarantee equality among the rural population in a specific location and a large share of population remains classified as rural, it is obvious that farm size will remain small in Hebei. Voluntary and market induced (as opposite to mandatory state/policy forced agglomerations) farmer associations with appropriate mechanism to control individual members' behavior could be a feasible way to overcome the disadvantages of small farm entities especially with respect to their low market power compared to agricultural input suppliers or wholesalers. Because no representative data about such institutions are available in the examined data set those possibilities of overcoming potential inefficiencies of family farms in Hebei due to scale inefficiencies will not be further discussed in this work.

In terms of production efficiency farms in Hebei do not have to be explicitly larger as long as rural institutions allow for the application of improved technologies or the efficient use of labor. As Schultz (1964) argues, changes in farm size, either farms getting larger or smaller, may be a consequence of a modernization process in agriculture but are not a pre-condition for modernization. Small farms can be efficient if they are provided with sufficient knowledge about farming technologies and practices and if the household laborers are adequately educated. So it is rather a question of factor proportionality instead of asking for the "right" size of a farm (Schultz, 1964).

3.7 Summary

This chapter provides the background information about the development and recent state of rural institutions in Hebei province and reviews different approaches to define part- and full-time farming.

After centuries of private land ownership and market based agricultural production systems the aim of policy during the communist period was to reorganize the rural institutions to distribute land more equally and by this also to achieve a lower inequality in income and well-being among the rural population. The organization of farms into collectives and the introduction of non-market price systems lowered the incentives for individual agricultural workers but also for the collective production units to produce sufficient amounts of agricultural outputs (especially grain) as efficiently as possible. Based on the household registration system around 70% of all households in Hebei are currently classified as rural. A farm household is defined in this study as an agricultural production decision unit that may follow the motive of profit-maximization (among others) and acts as a semi-commercial unit that is self-sufficient to some extent. Farm households are classified into part- and full-time farms based on the allocation of household family labor time to farming or to off-farm activities instead of distinguishing farm types based on the shares of income derived from agricultural production and off-farm activities. Different classifications of farm households will be applied in the following chapters.

Exchange institutions that function well should contribute to an efficient allocation of production factors and should also contribute to prices and income values that are determined by the market rather than the state. The transition of an agricultural production system is a stepwise process that is fueled by internal and external drivers and results in the change of incentives of decision units in the agricultural sector. During the stepwise transition of institutions in rural China more rights and responsibilities were assigned to the agricultural households. Many of these households were not limited anymore in their possibilities to earn income and to allocate their family labor to only agricultural production. Instead, the share of part-time farm households rose. Already in ancient China a mixed system of agricultural production and the provision of family labor off the farm was considered as improving the household's well-being.

Another finding of this chapter is that the current system of rural institutions differs strongly within Hebei. In addition to national and provincial laws and rules, village and community level differences with respect to agricultural production systems are observed. Those differences are included in the empirical assessments in chapters 6 and 7 by the use of village dummy variables. Further information to reflect differences in institutions are not available.

4 Theory and methodology

4.1 Development economics and measures of poverty and well-being

Governmental and administrative decisions affect income inequality. For rural China the long lasting system of taxes, subsidies and grain quotas influenced factor prices (Benjamin and Brandt, 1999). The structural and administrative reforms undertaken in the last decades in China are considered to change households' factor endowments, especially regarding land and labor due to regular and irregular reallocations and the development of rural non-agrarian industries. Allowing the development of market institutions has an impact on the distribution of land and affects its social security function (Benjamin and Brandt, 1997). As it is also stated by Benjamin et al. (2005), it is difficult to separate between effects from the transition of rural China and growth or development effects in empirical (income) inequality assessments. Wages for instance can change due to better accessibility of local and migratory labor markets and improved incentive mechanisms in agricultural production but also due to overall economic development.

In welfare economics, the common values of a given society can be represented by a social welfare function (SWF). A social welfare function depends "on the personal conditions of all individuals" (Harsanyi, 1955, p. 315) and expresses the subjective preferences of all members of the society (Harsanyi, 1955). Consequently, social welfare functions are more than just the sum of individual utilities (Harsanyi, 1955). Usually well-behaved welfare functions rank more unequal distributions of welfare lower than more equal distributions even if the mean value of the respective welfare indicator (based on either income or consumption) is the same (Benjamin et al., 2005). Different economic variables can be used as indicators to express welfare of a society (Mueller, 2003). Therefore a SWF can be formulated for example with respect to utility levels, income or poverty. Usually, utility concepts include factors that can be expressed in monetary terms such as income or the value of housing but also non-pecuniary social measures for well-being as trust, reciprocity or fairness.

Following Schumpeter (1909), not only the sum of individual welfare is necessary to be known for utility and welfare assessments but also the distribution of welfare among individuals matters. In theory, inequality within a population or between regions can be assessed with respect to different factors like land and other production factor endowments (e.g. machines), health status, education, infrastructure development or consumption. For example Deutsch and Silber (2004) state, after a review of inequality studies, that inequality in income is usually higher than inequality in consumption. They explain this with the smoothing of consumption[8].

Kakwani (1980) distinguishes two different schools of thought regarding the assessment of income distribution and income inequality. He names the first of these schools the "theoretical statistical school" (Kakwani, 1980, p. 2). Authors classified as belonging to this school apply stochastic models. These models examine income distribution only partially since they do not provide information about the economics of the distribution (Kakwani, 1980). In contrast the second so called socio-economic school of thought tries to assess the distribution of income or welfare based on economic and institutional factors, e.g. age, education or geographical location, and the distribution of wealth. Within this school Kakwani (1980) identifies three groups of authors. The first group follows the human capital approach that focuses on the maximization of income over the lifetime of an individual (e.g. Becker, 1965). This approach builds on the relationship between the differences among individuals' human capital and the power of these individuals to earn income. The differences between individuals have then implications regarding the distribution of income within the whole analyzed population (Polachek, 1981). The human capital approach focuses mainly on the supply side of the labor market and by this concentrates on different levels of skills and education of laborers (Kakwani, 1980). It is not possible to fully assess the reasons underlying the distribution of occupations, which might be one cornerstone in the explanation of income inequality, by using the basic human capital approach, since no differentiation is made between different kinds of human capital (Polachek, 1981). The second group of authors form the "education planning school" which argues that the demand for different kinds of labor originates from production functions (Kakwani, 1980). Tinbergen (1975) is one of the protagonists of the "supply and demand school" as he assesses the distribution of income based on both sides of the market; the demand and supply of different types of labor (Kakwani, 1980).

No matter which school of thought builds the fundament for an inequality assessment, Araar and Duclos (2007a) emphasize that the type of inequality and

8 Measures that help households to smooth their consumption such as the sale of household assets, family and village level networks or functioning rural credit markets and the importance of consumption smoothing in terms of rural welfare are assessed for example by Rosenzweig and Stark (1989) and Zeller et al. (1997).

the kind of poverty, absolute or relative, have to be clearly specified when discussing linkages between poverty, inequality and growth.

Besides the fact that welfare also includes social components like the provision of education and health services (Bigsten and Levin, 2000), the assessment of economic welfare in this work focuses on two dimensions; on the distribution of income or consumption and on the assessment of poverty. Like in many other developing countries, in China the portion of economic welfare of rural households that stems from agricultural production is not only determined by the amount of income that they receive from selling their agricultural outputs but also by the expenditures for purchasing consumption goods provided by the industrial sector (Carter and Zhu, 2009). So for the assessment of welfare one also would have to have a look on the impacts that changes in relative prices between the different sectors of the Chinese economy had on the sample households during the period 1986 to 2002 that is analyzed in this study.

Chen and Ravallion (1996) state that for rural areas in China consumption based measures represent economic well-being better than income based methods because there is a high fluctuation in income from farming. Another important point when thinking of consumption and expenditures of rural households is the proportion of own produced and consumed goods. Especially agricultural households in developing countries (Bardhan and Udry, 1999) or in countries in transition, such as China, act at the same time as consumers and producers of consumption goods. As Chen and Ravallion (1996) emphasize it is especially important to include self-retained grain into poverty analyses. In addition, measures should be selected to allow for a good targeting of the poor in rural areas (Fan, 2007). For a better targeting of the poor, the distinction between chronic and transient poverty can be one aspect. As Li et al. (2007) indicate most poverty alleviation programs in rural China have failed in really targeting the poor at household level. Their results show that the wealthy population groups benefited more from the programs than the poor. The central poverty alleviation program, which was launched in 1986 and covered 592 counties that were classified as poor on the national scale, was designed to raise the level of general income especially of poor households in the designated poor regions. One criticism against this program is that it does not necessarily benefit poor households in counties that are not designated to be poor counties (Li et al., 2007).

Li et al. (2007) emphasize that it is not only necessary to assess the overall trend in poverty reduction but also the poverty dynamics and to distinguish between chronic and transient poverty to answer the question if this program is appropriate and the most effective policy to reduce poverty. Panel data are the right source for dynamic poverty assessments since they contain information about income consumption levels of households over time as well as location related information that might change over time. In their study Li et al. (2007) could even include the poverty funds received at county level and direct support to households in the form of subsidized loans as explanatory variables for transient and chronic poverty. This makes their results highly valuable since it can be examined if the provided funds have the capacity to reduce poverty directly at the level of poor households or if only better off households benefit from the welfare enhancing effect of the funds.

4.1.1 Decomposition of income inequality

Around two thirds of rural households in China are involved in both agricultural and non-agricultural occupations (WDR, 2008). The focus of the present study is not on a comparative analysis in economic well-being at provincial level but on the analysis of inequality in households' income. Income is chosen here, because land as another measure to assess inequality among households is by law equally distributed within a location on a per capita basis. Fluctuations in the main source of income can have a considerable effect on total household income (WDR, 2008). Based on Roll's (1980) definition, inequality in income is considered in this study as the inclination of incomes among rural households in Hebei that receive income from various agricultural and non-agricultural sources.

The decomposition of the Gini coefficient by income sources reveals that policies promoting investments into agriculture helped in reducing income inequality in rural China, whereas support to rural non-farm industries had the opposite effect of increasing inequality among the rural population (Rozelle, 1994). Azam and Shariff (2009) also decompose the Gini index and find that the contribution of agricultural income to overall income inequality declined in rural India between 1993 and 2005, a period where the importance of non-agricultural sectors in generating income for the rural population increased similarly to the case of rural China.

Income inequality measures that allow breaking down total income inequality into a "weighted sum of inequality contributions of various income components" (Estudillo, 1997, p. 73) are considered as being source-decomposable (Estudillo, 1997). As will be described in the next paragraphs two of such source-decomposable measures are applied in this study.

De Janvry and Sadoulet (2001) decompose income by sources using the coefficient of variation method to assess how specific income sources affect inequality among farm households. For the case of Mexican farm households they show, that not every source of non-farm income leads to an increase in inequality. They find that income from non-agricultural household business reduces total income inequality. Following de Janvry and Sadoulet (2001) total income inequality can be decomposed by:

$$\sum_i w_i r_i \frac{CV_i}{CV} = 1, \tag{1}$$

where CV = coefficient of variation of total income,

CV_i = coefficient of variation from source i,

$w_i = \frac{\mu_i}{\mu}$ = weight of income source i,

μ_i = mean of income form source i,

μ = mean of total income and,

$r_i = corr(y_i, y)$ = correlation between income y_i from source i and the total income y.

If a source has a relative concentration coefficient $r_i\, CV_i/CV$ lower than one it contributes to a decrease in inequality and all income sources with a concentration coefficient larger than one contribute to an increase in inequality (de Janvry and Sadoulet, 2001).

Benjamin et al. (2005) use the stochastic method of Shorrocks (1983) for decomposing income by sources into various income components to illuminate the importance of income structure as an explanatory factor for a rise of inequality over population groups and regions in their data set of nine Chinese provinces. The coefficient of variation is just one possible index for income inequality. The Shorrocks decomposition of income inequality by source can be applied to three different inequality indices (Kimhi, 2007). Those indices are the Gini index, Theil's T index and the squared coefficient of variation inequality index.

The aim of decomposing income as suggested by Shorrocks (1983) is to identify the proportion of inequality in total income that can be related to one specific income component. The Shorrocks decomposition is a purely descriptive tool and offers hardly causal explanations for the reasons of income inequality but it still offers some insights in the contribution of income sources to overall income inequality between households.

Following Benjamin et al. (2005) the index of inequality $I(y)$ for total income y can be expressed as:

$$I(y) = \sum_{k=1}^{K} S_k I(y_k), \qquad (2)$$

where the index of inequality from income source k is $I(y_k)$.

The above described methods are both applied in chapter 6 to decompose the per capita household income inequality. Both methods are compared to assess if controlling for potential errors in the measurement of income (see 4.1.2) yields different results regarding the importance of the contribution of one specific income source to overall income inequality than the coefficient of variation method.

Kimhi (2007) argues that the decomposition applying the Theil's T rule of decomposing income inequality does not necessarily yield intuitive results. Especially the quantitative interpretation of the results after the application of this rule could be misleading. This is the case if the sign of an estimated contribution of a specific income source to total income is negative but the contribution to a change in inequality of the same income source is positive when its variance is increased by one standard deviation. Therefore only the inequality decomposition rule based on the squared coefficient of variation is applied in the Shorrocks decomposition in this study.

Other theoretical concepts to review income inequality are the Lorenz curve or the respective Gini coefficient of concentration. Lorenz curves offer a non-parametric tool to assess the robustness of methods used to analyze inequality (Deaton, 1997). The Lorenz curve graphically represents the distribution of wealth, income or assets among the analyzed population. If there would be prefect equality e.g. in income among a population then 10% of the population (x-axis in graphical illustrations) would earn a share of 10% of the income (y-axis in graphical illustrations). The Gini coefficient is equal to twice the area in between the line of perfect equality, p and the particular Lorenz curve $L(p)$ for a population (Arrar and Duclos, 2007a) or equal to one minus twice the area under the Lorenz curve. The larger the area between a specific Lorenz curve and the 45-degree line of equality the larger is the Gini coefficient or the more unequal is the distribution e.g. of income. So the Gini is a relative measure of inequality because it only depends on the shares of the respective variable of interest, here income (Kleiber, 2005).

Following Araar and Duclos (2007a) the Lorenz curve can be defined as

$$L(p) = \mu^{-1} \int_0^p Q(p) dp, \quad (3)$$

where $Q(p)$ is the income below which a proportion p of the population is found, and $\mu = \int Q(p) dp$ is the average income of the population. According to this the Gini coefficient for income inequality is calculated as

$$I = 2\int_0^1 (p - L(p)) dp. \quad (4)$$

One disadvantage of the widely used Gini index as unit-free inequality indicator is that it is always possible to identify utility functions that reverse the ranking of two income distributions, which have the same Gini index, in the case of intersecting Lorenz curves (Atkinson, 1970). So, is not possible to find an additive social welfare function which ranks distributions by their Gini coefficients for income distributions with the same mean income (Newbery, 1970; Chipman, 1985 cited in Rozelle, 1994). But as Kakwani (1980) discusses, the condition of additive welfare functions is a rather strict condition. He refers to Dasgupta et al. (1973) who show that there are no strictly quasi-concave welfare functions that would result in the same ranking of income distributions as the ranking provided by the Gini index. And Kakwani (1980) also confirms the results of Dasgupta et al. (1973) and Rothshild and Stiglitz (1973) who find that it is allowed to rank any class of income distributions by the Gini index if the Lorenz curves of those income distributions do not intersect. Dasgupta et al. (1973) show that Atkinson's result regarding the reversal of the ranking, in case of intersecting Lorenz curves, holds even if the assumption of additive separability of social welfare functions is not fulfilled.

As Atkinson (1970) argues, the Gini coefficient is sensitive to transfers because it weighs transfers in the middle of a (income) distribution highest. This might be conflicting with social values or norms that would prefer transfers provided to individuals at the lower end of the (income) distribution. This disadvantage is most relevant if different measures of inequality or different transfer schemes to reduce inequality would be compared at one point in time. For comparing income distributions over time this negative property of the Gini coefficient is considered less severe because the focus is not on assessing the social acceptance of transfer schemes but on the changes of income distribution in the society over time. For time comparisons the Gini coefficient even has the advantage that it is not affected by inflation or changes in purchasing power (Bandourian et al., 2002). Therefore, the Gini coefficient or in reversal the concept of the Lorenz Curve is used later in this work to illustrate differences between the income distribution in rural Hebei between 1986 and 2002.

Benjamin et al. (2005) suggest the use of generalized Lorenz curves (second-order stochastic) for inequality comparisons. In general a distribution is second order stochastically dominated by another distribution if, and only if, $\int \alpha(x) dF_1(x) \geq \int \alpha(x) dF_2(x)$ holds "for all monotone nondecreasing and concave functions" (Deaton, 1997, p. 163).

Generalized Lorenz curves allow for a ranking of the distribution when one is not only interested in inequality but also in social welfare (Deaton, 1997).

Other measures for the assessment of income inequality are the Theil and MLD (mean logarithmic deviation) index (Yu et al., 2007) which are belonging to the class of generalized entropy single parameter indices (Shorrocks, 1984). The Theil index can be interpreted as a "direct measure of the discrepancy between the distribution of income and the distribution of individuals between mutually exclusive and completely exhaustive ... groups" (Conceição et al., 2001, p. 492). Both of these indices are decomposable by groups e.g. for assessing regional inequality. The MLD has the advantage that its total index value is a combination of "the sum of the between-groups MLD and the population weighted average of within-groups MLD" (Motonishi, 2003, p.5). Using data from 6 provinces, including Hebei, and assessing township and village inequality Yu et al. (2007) find that changes in income inequality are not large if the focus is on the community level.

Regression based approaches for the decomposition of income inequality offer the possibility to identify and quantify the reasons and explanatory components of income inequality (Wan, 2002). Liu and Sicular (2008) find in their three-step decomposition analysis based on the China Household Income Project survey data, that education influences inequality in non-agricultural income stronger than it influences inequality in agricultural income.

4.1.2 Estimation of income inequality

For the estimation of inequality in per capita household income stemming from different sources following the Shorrocks decomposition it is possible to include regional variables to control for location effects. In the decomposition of per capita household income inequality by income source using the coefficient of variation the effect that the location of the household has on income inequality is not considered. Because village dummies are the only regional variables that cover differences in household's per capita income inequality it is interesting to assess to how far the regression based Shorrocks decomposition yields similar results compared to the decomposition using the coefficient of variation.

As described in section 6.2.2 it is aimed to estimate the proportion of inequality S_k that is related to inequality in k. The respective estimator is given by:

$$\hat{S}_k = \frac{Cov(y_{ik}, y_i)}{Var(y_i)}. \quad (5)$$

$\hat{S}_k$ can be estimated using the regression model provided by Benjamin at al. (2005):

$$y_{ik} = \beta_{0k} + \beta_{1k} y_i + u_{ik}, \quad (6)$$

where $\beta_{1k} = \hat{S}_k$.

So, actually the correlation of a particular source of income y_{ik} with overall income y_i of the household is estimated. Or as Jenkins (1995a) states, one derives with a "point estimate of the slope coefficient from a regression of total income on [the respective income] source" (p. 39, [author's addition]).

The estimator $\hat{S}_k$ is based on a decomposition rule that underlies two restrictions regarding the weights of two income sources if the sum of them is equal to the total income (Shorrocks, 1982 and Kimhi, 2007). The first of these restrictions is that the contribution to overall inequality of an income source that is equally distributed is zero. And the second restriction is that the inequality contribution of two income components, as a result of dividing total income, is equal if the factor distributions of those income components are variations of each other. This requirement that the factor contributions from two income sources sum up to the total inequality can even be replaced by the weaker assumption that the sum of the contribution of any two factors can be derived from the individual inequality contributions of these factors (Shorrocks, 1982). The decomposition rule is independent of the inequality index chosen. Shorrocks (1982) also indicates that feedback effects between income sources are not taken into account by the factor decomposition rules discussed by him because every income component is separately assessed. This simplifies the analysis since no behavioral relationships between income components have to be assessed.

Benjamin et al. (2005) suggest applying two-step least squares estimation to prevent impacts from possible measurement errors regarding specific income sources. If income from one source is overestimated it would lead to an overstatement of the correlation of this income source with total income. As a valid instrument Benjamin et al. (2005) use household consumption, because it is assumed that it is not affected by the same measurement error as income component y_{ik}. For example Lubell (1947) demonstrates that households have a tendency to understate their income and this understatement is found to be more important for low income households. By applying ordinary least squares (OLS) and two step least squares (2SLS) estimates on the decomposed incomes for 1987 and 1999 Benjamin et al. (2005) show that farm income declined and by this became less important as a factor contributing to the equalization of incomes. Also income from non-agriculture family activities, which is as such contributing to inequality, became relatively more important in farm households income composition (Benjamin et al., 2005). Because the non-agricultural labor market is not able to provide sufficient possibilities to earn income, especially for the poorest households, the equality destabilizing effect of the declines in agricultural income cannot be fully covered.

4.1.3 Poverty development and differences in poverty inequality for different population subgroups

Friedman (1971) formulated his hypothesis about permanent income and argued that the best explanation of consumption decisions is offered by a real measure of wealth of an individual, the physical and non-physical ability of the individual to earn income over a longer period, and not by the real disposable current (specific point in time) income of this individual. As a consequence, indicators of welfare or well-being that are based on consumption (expenditures) of individuals or households are considered to be a better indicators for the assessment of well-being over longer periods than pure income based indicators (Muyanga, 2008) that might be sufficient to explain differences among a population at a specific point in time.

Different approaches for measuring welfare and poverty are discussed in Haughton and Khandker (2009). Bigsten and Levin (2000) distinguish between income-consumption related measures for poverty on the one hand and output related measures for poverty like school enrolment rates or life expectancy on the other hand. An argument for income or consumption based measures is that income can be used to satisfy other needs. One disadvantage of social poverty indicators is that they are sensitive to distributional effects. Such indicators could signal an improvement where only improvements that benefit the better off are responsible for the observed change in the indicator value (Bigsten and Levin, 2000).

Duclos (2002) discusses welfarist and non-welfarist approaches for the assessment of well-being in poverty analyses. Beside the distinction between income and expenditure or consumption based methods to measure poverty there is also the question which income sources or purposes of expenditures to include. The basic needs approach, as a non-welfarist approach, focuses on physical inputs that individuals require to accomplish functionings (Dulcos, 2002). Functionings as such are multidimensional and could be for example the enjoyment that is caused by the consumption of a specific commodity or by the fact of being healthy. Basic needs could then be interpreted as being able to generally access functions instead of actually experiencing a specific outcome. Duclos (2002) offers the example that living close to a health care provider can be considered as a basic need that is fulfilled but this does not necessarily imply that the individual is in a healthy condition at a specific point in time. Because consumption also includes the value of own-produced goods it is not equal to expenditures (Duclos, 2002). Income and consumption based welfare measures can be compared to derive a better understanding of poverty (Li et al., 2007). The respective poverty indices or estimated poverty levels will be different since the income approaches also include the saving and borrowing activities of the households into the assessment. Also the factors that have an impact on the poverty level as such are very likely to differ between income and consumption based poverty measures. And these different impacts also matter in the design of poverty alleviation programs.

Zhang and Fan (2004) develop an approach based on the method of the Shorrocks decomposition to assess the impact of public spending on differences in economic inequality among 25 provinces in China. This kind of inequality assessment also allows to reveal the importance of different sources of public spending on the well-being of different population subgroups, such as the poor and the non-poor. The authors find that poor population subgroups in western provinces suffer from a bias in public investments that favored the coastal provinces. While Zhang and Fan (2004) developed a provincial comparison, the present study contributes to the academic discussion by assessing the differences in poverty trends between households in the same village as well as between households in different villages.

In the "cost of basic needs approach" that will be applied here, non-food consumption is included (Haughton and Khandker, 2009). Haughton and Khandker (2009) offer explanations why it is reasonable to include the cost for housing and service in the cost of basic needs method to define poverty lines. A poverty line as such represents the minimum level of income or consumption that an individual would need to cover his/her basic needs. Since the valuation of what is considered being a necessary minimum varies across time but also across societies, it is necessary to define poverty lines that reflect the state of societal development and respect the norms and values (informal institutions) of the society (Bigsten and Levin, 2000). The calculation of the absolute (food and non food consumption) poverty line used in this work will be described in chapter 6.1.

One common criticism against indices that just represent the number of people below the threshold level of the poverty line is that these indices do not explore the situation of poor people in more detail, like the extent to which poor people suffer from poverty (Kakwani, 1980; Sen, 1986). As Kurosaki (2003) states, it is important to include the welfare costs caused by the variability in consumption of people who are always below the poverty line into poverty assessments.

Foster, Greer and Thorbecke (FGT) (1984) developed a class of poverty indices that are additively decomposable. Due to the decomposability the impact that a change in subgroup poverty has on total poverty can be assessed quantitatively but also qualitatively (Foster et al., 1984). Those poverty gap indices represent measures of the distance between the actual income of a poor household and the (absolute or relative) poverty line (Foster et al., 1984). Following Duclos, Araar and Giles (2008) FGT poverty indices can be written for the observation of a population of n individuals over t time periods as

$$P_{\alpha}(g) \equiv (nt)^{-1} \sum_{i=1}^{n} \sum_{j=1}^{t} g_{ij}^{\alpha} \qquad (7)$$

where α can be interpreted as a parameter that displays the sensitivity of the poverty indices to the distribution of poverty among individuals and variability of individual poverty or poverty gaps respective over time. Setting α equal to 0 would result in the headcount poverty rate. $\alpha = 1$ gives the average poverty gap. $\alpha > 1$ yields in distribution sensitive poverty indices or measures of "poverty aversion" (Duclos et al., 2008).

Duclos et al. (2008) present approaches for separating poverty into the components of chronic and transient poverty and discuss differences in the results of different approaches. This is a dynamic decomposition of poverty (Araar and Duclos, 2006) and a useful tool to assess how vulnerable households are to instability in well-being over time (Muyanga, 2008). Transient poverty is herein understood as the poverty that is related to intertemporal variability in consumption (Jalan and Ravallion, 1998) or risk (Duclos et al., 2008). The distinction between chronic and transient poverty is important for the evaluation of poverty targeting programs (Reyes, 2003). Chronic poverty is a permanent inability of individuals or households to leave poverty due to e.g. illness or age whereas fluctuations in agricultural outputs and related prices (e.g. as a consequence of bad harvest) might cause transient poverty (Muyanga, 2008). Jalan and Ravallion (1998) conclude that if transient poverty is really a severe component of Chinese rural poverty, than policy programs to target poor in specific areas based on current consumption data might not be successful. To reduce transient poverty, an insurance mechanism against the high risk related to agricultural income fluctuations might be a better means.

Duclos et al. (2008) compare the measurement of chronic and transient poverty based on the welfare approach of Jalan and Ravallion (1998), further called JR approach, with the concept of "equally-distributed equivalent" (EDE) poverty gap $\Gamma_\alpha(g)$which is based on understanding "poverty as an aggregate of "illfare" in society" (Duclos et al., 2008, p. 4). The concept of the equally-distributed equivalent level of income was introduced by Atkinson (1970) who shows that this level of income can be interpreted in analogy to the certainty equivalent, which is used in the theory of making decisions under uncertainty, and "is equal to the proportional risk premium as defined by Pratt…" (Atkinson, 1970, p. 251). If one uses (7) and sets $\alpha > 0$then it follows that:

$$\Gamma_\alpha(g) \equiv P_\alpha(g)^{\frac{1}{\beta}}, \tag{8}$$

where $\Gamma_1(g)$is the average poverty gap (Duclos et al., 2008).

The difference between the normalized poverty gap$\Gamma_\alpha(g)$and $\Gamma_1(g)$ for a given α is an appropriate measure for the costs that are associated with the "inequality in the distribution of normalized poverty gaps among the whole population" (Duclos et al., 2008, p. 5). These costs of inequality $C_\alpha(g)$are provided in money metric terms on a per capita basis and reflect the costs of an increase in the average poverty gap that a Social Decision Maker (SDM) would be willing to bear if it is aimed to remove all inequality in the poverty gap distribution and it is always non-negative (Duclos, et al. 2008; Muyanga, 2008).

Total poverty is derived in a theorem by Duclos et al. (2008) as the sum of the cost of transient poverty ($\Gamma_\alpha^T(g)$), the average poverty gap in the underlying population ($\Gamma_1(g)$), and the cost of inequality in individual EDE poverty gaps ($C_\alpha(\gamma_\alpha)$).

Jalan and Ravallion (1998) consider a household level intertemporal measure of poverty as a stream of a household's consumption over time. $P = P(y_{i1}, y_{i2}, \ldots, y_{iD})$, where P is the poverty measure of household i over D dates. So they define chronic poverty C_i as

$$C_i = P(\bar{y}_i, \bar{y}_i, \ldots, \bar{y}_i), \tag{9}$$

and transient poverty T_i as

$$T_i = P(y_{i1}, y_{i2}, \ldots y_{iD,}) - P(\bar{y}_i, \bar{y}_i, \ldots, \bar{y}_i). \tag{10}$$

Following this decomposition, C_i is the poverty component that does not vary over time and T_i reveals the remaining part of overall poverty that displays the variation of poverty around the time mean $(\bar{y}_i)$. Jalan and Ravallion (2000) list two conditions that have to be fulfilled to consider a household as experiencing transient poverty. At least in one date during the analyzed period the household must be poor. And as second condition the standard of living of this household within this period has to vary over time. Similarly, defined by Reyes (2003, p. 1), people are transient poor if they "move in and out of poverty" during the period analyzed.

Following the notation of Duclos et al. (2008) equation (3) can also be written as

$$P_{\alpha}^{T}(y) \equiv P_{\alpha}(g) - P_{\alpha}^{*}(y), \tag{11}$$

with $P_{\alpha}(g)$ as total poverty and $P_{\alpha}^{*}(y)$ as estimate of chronic poverty.

The EDE poverty gap approach also sees total poverty as the sum of transient and chronic poverty. But it does link the chronic poverty to an average of ill-fare in comparison to the approach of Jalan and Ravallion (1998) that links C_i to an average of welfare. As other differences between both methods Duclos et al. (2008) mention the link of chronic poverty to out-of-poverty spells. Because the JR approach averages welfare over time it could be concluded that someone is not poor over the whole time if his/her income during some periods far exceeds the income of the other periods. The EDE approach takes into account the ill-fare statuses experienced by the household i over t periods. Also the JR indices cannot be interpreted in a cardinal way if α differs from 0 or 1. This leads to difficulties in combining FGT type indicators with metric indicators based on monetary terms as in cost-benefit analysis or efficiency analysis. As a last disadvantage Duclos et al. (2008) mention that an increasing value of α would result in decreasing values of the FGT indices and by this a decrease of the measured level of both components of poverty would be reported.

Duclos et al. (2008) use estimators that correct for biases that derive from the small number of time periods available because otherwise the estimated poverty levels would be systematically different from the true unobserved level of each individual's poverty. So they provide a second-order analytical bias corrected estimator for an individual's true chronic poverty

$$\hat{\tilde{P}}_{\alpha,j}^{*} = \left(1 - \hat{\bar{y}}_i\right)_{+}^{\alpha} + \frac{\alpha(1-\alpha)}{2t}\left(1 - \hat{\bar{y}}_i\right)_{+}^{\alpha-2} \operatorname{var}\left(y_{ij}\right), \tag{12}$$

for the JR approach and a similar corrected estimator for the measurement of transient poverty:

$$\hat{\hat{\gamma}}_{\alpha,i}=\gamma_{\alpha}\left(g_i\right)+0.5\alpha^{-2}\left(\alpha-1\right)\bar{\gamma}_{\alpha,i}^{\left(1-2\alpha\right)}t^{-1}\mathrm{var}\left(g_{ij}^{\alpha}\right), \qquad (13)$$

where $\bar{\gamma}_{\alpha,i}$ is the true EDE poverty gap of individual *i* (Duclos et al., 2008).

In addition Duclos et al. (2008) apply the method of bootstrap bias correction. They show that both methods are able to reduce the biases of the uncorrected estimators for chronic and transient poverty by around 50%. Even with panel data the number of observations per individual over time is in most cases limited. In the panel examined here, a maximum of 14 observations for income figures or the respective poverty levels are available if the household remains in the sample over the whole period from 1986-2002. Therefore, it is a big advantage of the bias corrections by Duclos et al. (2008) that they allow for better estimations in the sense of approximating estimated and true poverty levels even if the number of time periods is limited. So those corrections provide an alternative to increasing the panel by additional spells. The JR and EDE measure of poverty gaps will be applied to the RCRE data set available using the Distributive Analysis Stata Package[9].

Several studies assess the contribution of growth to poverty reduction by using the concept of the growth elasticity of poverty which is an estimate of the percentage change in poverty if per capita income changes by 1 percent (Son and Kakwani, 2004). If a country's economy grows as in China, average living conditions improve every year. As a consequence the growth elasticity decreases but the inequality elasticity increases. Therefore, it is important to calculate the long-term poverty elasticity if one wants to calculate the economic growth necessary to reduce absolute poverty (Son and Kakwani, 2004). The assessment of poverty and inequality elasticities is useful to evaluate policy programs as seen by Son (2006), who analyses the possibilities of fiscal policies to generate pro-poor growth for the case of Thailand.

As presented in the next two paragraphs, there is some debate, to which extent inequality among groups of people affects development and reduction of poverty and which explanations for poverty evolution or inequality reduction can be provided by focusing on changes in group disparities (Araar and Duclos, 2007a). Those differences in extent can be assessed with a static decomposition of inequality (Araar and Duclos, 2006).

---

9 A free version of the Stata DASP 1.4 package is available under: http://dasp.ecn.ulaval.ca/. The support and comments of Abdelkrim Araar and Jean-Yves Duclos are gratefully acknowledged by the author.

The calculation of poverty inequality elasticities with respect to different population groups could help in an impact analysis of how socio-economic policies and economic shocks affect individuals differently at the same point in time (Araar and Duclos, 2007a). This is important for the assessment of how far different groups of the rural population in Hebei province (e.g. differentiated by the educational level attained by the household head) are affected by measures to reduce chronic poverty. Especially the FGT poverty indices are decomposable and allow allocating overall poverty among population subgroups which as such could be defined based on location or labor market participation characteristics (Shorrocks, 1999). With the data set described in section 5.2 it is possible to assess the impact that changes in the distance between each value of an income component k and the overall mean or average income $\mu(k)$ of this component have on poverty and inequality (Araar and Duclos, 2007a).

Araar and Duclos (2007a) present two sources of distributive changes that are associated with changes in poverty inequality. The first source is a change in inequality that stems from changes in specific socio-economic groups. Whereas the second source for changes in poverty inequality is the inequality of specific income components. With Shorrocks' income decomposition a tool is already introduced to reveal changes in inequality from different income sources. But inequality can also be assessed for differences in average poverty across subgroups or due to inequality among the respective subgroup of the population (Shorrocks, 1999; Duclos, 2002). The methodologies to evaluate growth effects on poverty inequality developed by Araar and Duclos (2007a) differ from the ones used by Shorrocks (1999) who derives with a procedure that allows for an exact additive decomposition of a statistical inequality indicator into the contribution of every factor contributing to inequality in a specific setting.

The methods developed by Araar and Duclos (2007a) will be used to consider the differences in households poverty equality that can be related to the location of a household in a specific village or to the labor time that the household devotes to farming activity. The assessment of differences between farm groups or types is one major aim of the recent study. Therefore those methods of Araar and Duclos (2007a) are chosen to analyze if poverty inequality is for example different between part-time and full-time farm households.

Following the approaches of Araar and Duclos (2007a) for the bipolarization of inequality the elasticity of total poverty related to within-group inequality is given as:

$$\varepsilon_{\sigma}(z;\alpha;\rho)=\left.\frac{\partial P(z;\alpha;\sigma(g))/\partial\sigma(g)}{\partial I(\rho;\alpha(g))/\partial\sigma(g)}\frac{I(\rho;\sigma(g))}{P(z;\alpha;\sigma(g))}\right|_{\sigma=1} \quad (14)$$

where: $\sigma(g)$ = group -g- specific factor of bipolarization,
$I(\rho;\sigma(g))$ = overall single parameter Gini (S-Gini) after the bipolarization factor,
$P(z;\alpha;\sigma(g))$ = total FGT poverty,
z = poverty line,
α = parameter of "poverty aversion".

Within-group bipolarization refers to the change in inequality that spreads the income below which one finds a proportion p of the population away from the mean income $\mu(g)$ of those people that belong to the respective group g. Whereas between-group bipolarization refers to the dispersion of population groups from each other whereby the within-group inequality is not affected (Araar and Duclos, 2007a). S-Gini indices have the same properties as the usual Gini index. So it follows that incomes which are non-positive are easily accommodated, "and inequality can be decomposed by income type if the rank-order of incomes does not vary by source of income" (Donaldson and Weymark, 1980, p. 74). The advantage of S-Gini indices is that they are more flexible regarding the distribution of the equivalent income (Donaldson and Weymark, 1980).

The elasticity of total poverty related to between-group inequality is:

$$\varepsilon_\gamma(z;\alpha;\rho)=\left.\frac{\partial P(z;\alpha;\gamma)/\partial\gamma}{\partial I(\rho;\gamma)/\partial\gamma}\frac{I(\rho;\gamma)}{P(z;\alpha;\gamma)}\right|_{\gamma=1} \qquad (15)$$

where: $\gamma(g)$ = between group specific factor of bipolarization,
$I(\rho,\gamma)$ = between group inequality,
$P(z;\alpha;\gamma)$ = total FGT poverty with respect to between group bipolarization,
z = poverty line,
α = parameter of "poverty aversion".

Both elasticities are calculated using the -db efgtg- procedure as given in Stata DASP 1.4 (Araar and Duclos, 2007b). The overall marginal impact on inequality (MII) is given by $\partial I(\rho)/\partial()$, whereas $\partial P(z;\alpha)/\partial()$ is the overall marginal impact on poverty (MIP) and $\varepsilon_0(z;\alpha;\rho)$ is the elasticity of poverty with respect to overall inequality (ELS).

The groups of interest for the estimation of the poverty elasticities above are defined by using different villages for spatial grouping, educational level of household head as socio-demographic criterion for grouping or income from different sources (e.g. part-time versus full-time farmers) as an economic criterion for the group formation. In difference to the study of Araar and Duclos

(2007a) for the analysis in chapter 6.1 per capita consumption expenditures will be used instead of household per capita income.

4.2 Labor allocation

Due to restrictions in the possibilities for rural laborers to migrate to urban areas and to take up urban work and other deviations from a well functioning labor market the overall economic allocation of labor was distorted in China even after the start of the reforms. Knight and Song (2005) present an illustration of a model of labor allocation between the urban and rural sector in China, where they show the extent of prevented urban unemployment and the difference between rural employment under competitive vs. restricted labor market conditions.10 To provide a better understanding of the constraints in the macroeconomic allocation of labor in China during the period assessed in the study at hand the theoretical considerations of Knight and Song (2005) are presented in *Figure 6*.

Following Knight and Song (2005) it is assumed that the amount of labor available for the whole economy is fixed and equal to the distance between 0 and $0'$. The share of rural labor is measured from 0 onwards to the right, e.g. as the distance between 0 and L_1. As a simplification the rural sector is seen here as only to consist of agricultural production and hence MPL_a represents the curve for the marginal product of rural peasant labor or the rural labor supply price to the urban sector. The certain urban wage is the wage from which onwards rural-urban migration takes place. The amount of labor allocated to the urban sector (again simplified as just consisting of one urban labor occupation possibility) is measured to the left of $0'$. The wage rate and the marginal product of labor are indicated on the y axis.

If the Chinese labor market were competitive, then MPL_a would represent the supply curve of rural labor, MPL_u the urban employers' labor demand curve and the market would be cleared at the competitive wage of w_c. At this wage the amount of $0L_2$ labor would be allocated to rural occupations and $0'L_2$ would be the amount of labor employed in the urban sector. However, the wages are assumed not to be competitive but instead the urban wages w_u is set higher than w_c. Assuming a competitive labor market this would result in an amount of urban labor equal to $0'L_5$. As Yang and Zhou (1999) indicate especially for state

10 The additional explanations and clarifications provided by John Knight are highly appreciated. I also thank Lina Song for forwarding my questions to John Knight.

enterprises (in urban areas) it was quite common, also in the 1980 and 1990s, to set wages higher than would be appropriate based on labor productivity.

In the two sectoral model presented by Harris and Todaro (1970) the rural supply price is equal to the expected wage, which would be the wage in the urban sectors times the probability that it will be obtained. If this probability is equal to the ratio of urban employment to urban labor force, then labor is shifted from rural to urban occupations until the supply price of rural labor is equal to the expected wage. If the geometric construct xx', which shows how much urban unemployment there will be at a given urban wage, intersects MPL_u at point b then L_1L_5 is the amount of open unemployed urban labor. At the intersection point of xx' and MPL_a, risk-neutral rural laborers receive the (rural) certain-wage-equivalent of the uncertain urban wage w_u.

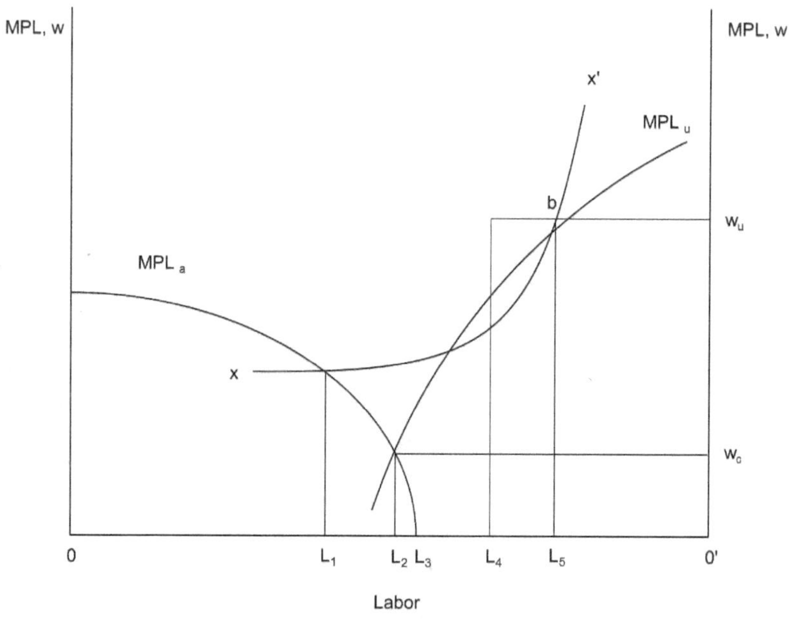

Source: Adapted from Knight and Song (2005).

Figure 6: Labor allocation between the urban and rural sector in China

Therefore they are indifferent between staying in rural areas and migrating to the urban labor market. The most important assumption of the model developed by Harris and Todaro (1970) is that the prospective rural migrant laborers migrate "as long as the *expected* urban real income at the margin exceeds real agricultural product" (p. 127) and by this are considered as being "maximizers of *expected* utility" (p. 127) [highlighting in italics in original, note by the author]. In China, policies intend to prevent open urban unemployment. Therefore surplus urban jobs are created to the extent of L_4L_5 and migration of rural labor to urban jobs is hindered. So the distance $0L_4$ is equal to the amount of labor employed in the rural sector and $0'L_4$ is the amount of labor employed in the urban sector. This 'non-market' separation of the labor force results in a hidden rural unemployment beyond L_3, where the marginal product of agricultural labor is equal to zero.

In difference to this sectoral assessment of labor allocation the present study is focusing on the determinants of households' labor allocation decisions. Microeconomic models for the assessment of individual or household decisions are applied in several fields of economics such as labor economics, health or educational economics. In the following paragraphs the origins and characteristics of such models are reviewed and discussed.

Becker (1965) introduces the concept of full income which is the maximum money income that is achievable by a household if the household provides all time and other family endowments to income earning activities without taking consumption into consideration. This income concept follows the human capital approach and provides a resource constraint that combines all consumption goods and available household time. Because money income can be considered as a conversion of time into goods this combination of resource constraints into a single one is possible. The household is seen as a "small factory" (Becker, 1965, p. 496) that combines resources, human labor and capital to produce commodities. According to Abbott and Ashenfelter (1976), for such a household wages are not just important as they indicate achievable income but the wage rate is perceived as a price that influences the households' decision about labor time allocation that is not marketed.

Because a household consist of two or more members, following the concept of methodological individualism would require analyzing household decisions based on the assessment of individual utility functions (Chiappori, 1988).

As Hodgson (2007) mentions in his explanation of the origins and interpretation of 'methodological individualism', one has to be careful in using this term because it is applied in different contexts with different meanings. Schumpeter (1909) uses this concept in his sense of pure economic theory; social values and utilities can only be assessed if one starts with the analysis of the wants and wealth of individuals. Watkins (1952) explains the principle of methodological individualism as one that "states that social processes should be explained by being deduced from principles governing the behavior of participating individuals and from analyses of their situations," (p. 186). So he believes that, "if social phenomena are generated by individuals they can only be explained individually" (Watkins, 1952, p. 186). Later in his work Watkins (1952) argues that 'methodological individualism' holds for economic systems where individuals are guided by egoistic economic motives. The strongest criticism that Hodgson (2007) formulates is, that 'methodological individualism' is mostly used in the last five decades not only to explain individuals and their behavior but also relations among them and by this social or societal structures, whereas he considers 'individualism' as an inappropriate term for such institutional assessments. Therefore this term will not be used in this work. But it is kept in mind, that for a better understanding of the functioning of a household based and largely self-sufficient economy it would be the best option to assess the time allocation of each household member (Ilahi, 2000), but this is not possible because the necessary information is aggregated at the household level.

Blundell and MaCurdy (1999) present an overview of different labor supply models, starting from the standard static model of individual labor supply following the full income concept. In this model an individual worker maximizes his/her utility over consumption and the decision about allocating the total time budget to labor or leisure time, under consideration of the wage rate and all unearned income, including asset income (the budget constraint). Since education, experiences but also past periods of sickness influence working decisions it is suggested to apply dynamic or life cycle labor supply models (Blundell and MaCurdy, 1999). Labor supply models also differ by either including or excluding uncertainty of individuals or households e.g. about the future distributions of wages and wealth or their own way of life (Blundell and MaCurdy, 1999). Following the seminal distinction of risk and uncertainty in Knight (1921) uncertainty can be seen as a term for a state in which the decision maker can not assign any probability to the future events (changes) whereas the term risk refers to situations where the decision maker can mathematically assign probabilities to future events. Knight (1921, I.I.29) distinguishes between "Risk as a know chance and true Uncertainty" or as he (Knight 1921, III.VIII.2) explains later in his work for risk "the outcome in a group of instances is known […], while in the case of uncertainty this is not true".

In the neoclassical model of the family it is assumed that a set of preferences that is common to all household members is the reason behind the decision of individual household members to pool their labor resources and to set individual labor market participations aside (Schultz, 1990; Alderman et al., 1995). From this neoclassical point of view household decisions about demand and supply of labor are considered to satisfy the criterion of maximizing one single utility function of the household. But a pooling of labor resources on the household level would require that one family member is able to monitor all family members and to sanction them if they don't follow the implicit rules and conditions of the household pooling agreement (Alderman et al., 1995). For developed economies with a higher degree of specialization among the household labor force and more opportunities of labor supply outside the own family this supervision is hardly possible. But for less differentiated rural economies it could be assumed, that e.g. the household head would be able to monitor the household labor time allocation. To prevent the labor and preference pooling problem it is reasonable to incorporate individual specific time constraints and reservation wages into family labor supply models.

For the standard unitary model of family labor supply (with two individuals in working-age), as described by Blundell and MaCurdy (1999), it is assumed that the family maximizes its joint utility over total family consumption and, in difference to the individual model of labor supply, two separate decisions about leisure time, one for each of the two potential workers are made. Two family labor supply regimes are distinguishable. In the first regime both workers supply labor, whereas in the second regime only one of the workers supplies labor time to the market, and the other one allocates all available time to leisure. Further it is assumed that the marginal value of non-labor income is the same for all working and decision making household members. This income pooling restriction is considered as unreasonable, because it would imply that all sources of unearned income would affect family labor supply decisions in the same way, and therefore it is relaxed in collective or joint decision models of family labor supply (Blundell and MaCurdy, 1999). One of the main advantages of the unitary model is that it allows for explicit recovering of preferences from observed household behavior which helps in assessing the effects of policy changes on households' comportment. For a better account of differences in individual preferences11, and by this labor supply decisions, of household members it is sufficient if information about individual labor supply is available which is then used to differentiate between (two) sub-utility functions (Blundell and MaCurdy, 1999).

The estimation of individual labor supply curves for the husband and wife is included in the maximization of a joint utility function with after-tax income and the respective leisure of the spouses as explanatory variables, as presented by Wales and Woodland (1976). If wage rates are assumed to differ strongly across individuals, then work efforts of the husband and wife are also determined by

11 In most contexts and data sets information about consumption of other goods than leisure is only available as household level aggregate and individual consumption is not observable, even though individuals have different preferences (Blundell and MaCurdy, 1999).

the wage received (or the wage rate receiveable) by the respective partner (Wales and Woodland, 1974).

Goldin (1994) describes the U-shaped labor market participation function for married women during the development of an economy. At the early stage of an economy, which is dominated by agricultural production and characterized by low incomes, the labor participation of women is high. But most of this labor is employed as unpaid labor in own family business and especially as family farm labor. Due to the income effect related with the development of new markets and labor occupations, e.g. in industry and services, the participation rate of women declines. As Goldin (1994) states, in agriculture the demand for women as laborers decreases due to new production technology or in non-farm household businesses with the household production being not competitive anymore with the prices of industrially produced goods. In later stages of the economic development the share of female laborers increases due to an increase in the education level of women and the new opportunities to work outside the agricultural sector, which is mainly caused by more financial resources available to also educate women and by a decline in the 'social stigma', which states that women should not work but take care of the household and family (Goldin, 1994).

Rozelle et al. (2002) apply discrimination analysis approaches but also econometric tests to assess the significance of differences between wage rates for men and women in rural China and to explain differences in wage inequality regarding the degree of competitiveness of the rural labor market. Based on cross section data for 8 provinces and the years 1988 and 1995 they find that the wage differential increased between different industries (e.g. construction or light industry) but they did not find evidence for a rise of the wage gap related to discrimination between men and women within one industry. But in both years wages for women, after controlling for e.g. education and location effects have been significantly lower than the wages for men. Rozelle et al. (2002) explain this with the Confucian ideology that is deep rooted in rural areas and which propagates the subordination of women and their destiny to serve their husband and family; an argument following the line of thought of Goldin's (1994) 'social stigma', as described above.

Information about different wage rates for differently qualified persons or for men and women are not included in the labor allocation decision models later in this work, because this information is not available in the data set.

Chiappori (1988) presents a collective model to explain the behavior of a two-member household, which is guided by the principle of Pareto Efficiency rather than focusing on the maximization of a single household utility function where both members supply labor. A situation is called Pareto Efficient if at least one member of the household has improved his/her situation (and thus reaches a higher utility level) and the other household member(s) is (are) at least as well-off as before. Pareto Efficiency is a qualitative concept because the assessment of the situation depends on the judgment of the economic agents or actors itself (Stephan and Ahlheim, 1996). The judgment about situational changes that change the well-being of individuals is subjective. Chiappori (1988) shows that the results of the assessment of the sharing of resources within the household and households' labor supply decisions depend on the assumption whether the individual household members are seen as being egoists (only interested in maximizing their own well-being) or as being altruists (taking the well-being of other household members into account). As Blundell and MaCurdy (1999) state, it is possible that the allocation of household labor time deviates from the optimal allocation under the unitary (utility maximizing) model even when the allocation as such is Pareto Efficient and the household members are altruists. Collective household labor supply models have the big advantage that they reflect differences in the bargaining position of household members (Blundell and MaCurdy, 1999).

Since the time allocation rule in the model of separable utility functions depends on individual wages, it is difficult to include household production in collective labor supply models (Blundell and MaCurdy, 1999). In the case of home production non-marketed time does not only consist of leisure but instead it is used in a productive way. Non-market labor can be either substituted by market labor time, or is hardly to be substituted, e.g. time spent for taking care of dependents. But as demonstrated by Apps and Rees (1997) household production can be included in the collective labor supply models if some preconditions, such as linear homogeneity in household production and a non-sensitive reaction of demand for pure leisure to changes in the price of the good produced by the household, are fulfilled.

If labor markets are competitive then the neoclassical (unitary) model of family labor supply is assumed to be better suited for the explanation of households' labor market supply decisions in developing than in developed countries (Rosenzweig, 1980). This is because labor in developing countries is considered to be more homogenous, wage paid jobs are assumed to be less different regarding non-monetary benefits, and taxation and saving considerations are more likely to be able to be ignored in the analytical framework, and there might be more flexibility in labor time provision (Rosenzweig, 1980). Those 'developing country criteria' are assumed by the author to also hold for the less developed agrarian study region during the analyzed period. In addition men were, and might still be, the dominant decision makers in Chinese households and for such a patriarchal situation a unitary model with just a single utility function and a single decision maker seems to be appropriate for assessing households' labor supply (Chau et al., 2007). But even in the developed country context household models of labor supply are of importance since the effects of several welfare policies or tax programs need to be assessed based on a profound understanding of the process of intra-household labor market participation decisions (Blundell and MaCurdy, 1999).

Yotopoulos and Lau (1974) apply general equilibrium models to assess decision processes in the agricultural sector in developing economies. They formulate a microeconomic model for the assessment of farm households' behavior, in which they directly specify and estimate labor supply functions for agricultural households. Their specification of the labor supply function includes the number of laborers in the household, the total number of household members, the wage rate, the monetary profits from agricultural production, the output prices and fixed obligations less the income from assets. They do not focus so much on the differentiation between the reasons for labor supply off the farm because the supply decisions of the household will not depend on this distinction, as long as the marginal rate of compensation (marginal wage rate) is the same for agricultural or non-agricultural labor supplied off the farm. Yotopoulos and Lau (1974) extend the microeconomic model to include macroeconomic variables that also determine the labor supply decisions of farm households. To derive the macroeconomic relations underlying the decisions of the assessed households, they multiply the estimated labor demand and supply functions by the total number of analyzed households. But this would represent exact approximizations of the overall labor supply and demand only under the assumptions that all the observation units are identical, especially regarding their utility function or their initial factor endowment. While the microeconomic model of Yotopoulos and Lau (1974) rests on the assumption of perfect markets, the assessment of macroeconomic equilibria can be done for different situations, including an institutional environment where one or more of the markets of the rural sector are regulated by the government. Examples for such governmental interference in markets are fertilizer subsidies or migration restrictions imposed to rural laborers.

The household supply of labor depends on the returns to labor and those returns itself depend on the production decisions of the farm households (Sicular and Zhao, 2004). So, in general, microeconomic models to estimate farm households' off-farm labor supply contain variables regarding households' demographic characteristics and the amount and type of human capital available in the households (see e.g. Fafchamps and Quisumbing, 1999) and concentrate only on factors determining the supply of family labor off the farm (Wang, 2007). In the labor supply model specifications, additional variables are used that provide information about transaction costs and local wage rates (Lohmar, 1999). But the inclusion of shadow wages is of great importance if labor supply is intended to be estimated under conditions as in rural China, where not much of the agricultural labor is hired but self-employed family labor (Sicular and Zhao, 2004). Such an inclusion of shadow wage estimates as explanatory variable for household labor supply allows assessing if households' labor supply is more responsive to the agricultural shadow wage or to the market wage rate (Sicular and Zhao, 2004). Information about wage rates is not available and also transaction costs cannot be quantified for the available observations. It is also not possible to derive with estimates for shadow wages from the estimation of production functions, as done by Sicular and Zhao (2004), because important information for the estimation of production functions like local prices for agricultural and non-agricultural outputs of household production is not available. Therefore, an alternative approach is chosen to estimate the determinants of farm households' labor allocation decisions.

The labor market participation model applied in the study at hand allows estimating the probability that a household chooses to be in one state of labor demand and supply compared to a reference state (autarky). Within this framework of assessing household labor allocation, the household is modeled regarding two aspects. Firstly, the household decides about the amounts of labor time to be used as input in family farm production and about the amount of leisure to be consumed, and secondly the household decides about the amount of labor that is "marketed", according to the labor market regime the household participates in (Glauben et al., 2008; Key et al. 2000). No labor supply equations are estimated in this study due to the constraints in wage and labor hour's data. It is one advantage of the chosen labor allocation probability models that they do not only reflect the supply side but also assess labor market participation regimes which are characterized by agricultural households demanding labor from the market (Wang, 2007). All results that are derived in chapter 7.2.3 are based on these quantitative models.

Individual incentives and their impact on all social interactions, where interactions at markets are a part of it, matter if the allocation of resources is discussed in economics (Manski, 2000). Non-marketed interactions among individuals are not reflected in the neoclassical framework of the general competitive equilibrium (Manski, 2000). Therefore Becker (1965) and other authors extend the assessment of labor allocation decisions from the discussion of the decision about wage labor to a wider one that also incorporates family and household decisions that e.g. reflect the sharing of responsibilities for child care. So, labor supply decisions are modeled as non-cooperative games of individuals that have differing objectives, preferences, interests or incentives (Manski, 2000). Manski (2000) considers it as critical to focus on the assessment of the outcome of decision processes; as is done, when quantitative data are used for estimations. According to him, a lot of information about individuals' decision making is lost by looking only at the end results instead of analyzing the process of decision making itself. For the present work this loss of information represents a limitation in the sense that only quantitative data are used to assess the probability that households "choose" between different specific labor allocation regimes but no qualitative triangulation is possible. Past working experience, attitudes towards different kinds of work or individual perceptions are some criteria that might influence individual labor allocation decisions. Sometimes the observed behavior of individuals differs from the economically or socially ideal behavior (Scrimshaw, 1990). Information about individuals and their behavior is usually considered as being qualitative innatures and hence hidden in a quantitative analysis. In fixed effects regressions these variables are assumed to be time-invariant; random effects models allow, if applicable, the identification of some of these effects, but both types of models still require a quantitative data base. Quantitative modeling in economics or other social sciences usually seeks to achieve results that are replicable and that can be discussed in more depth as soon as larger amounts of observations become available. But especially for specific case studies about human interactions and decision making, the property of replicability is not easily fulfilled just by conducting the same study with an increased number of individuals (Piore, 2004). Despite the criticism on economic approaches to assess households' behavior expressed by sociologists, in this work households are considered as being a decision unit that chooses among different alternatives to achieve an specific outcome (highest utility level) based on a set of preferences and that face certain constraints.

Some studies include questions about potential institutional restrictions imposed to individuals' or households' labor supply decisions. Wales and Woodland (1976) could make use of a panel data set that included a question to the household head in which he/she was asked if he/she had the possibility to work more or to work less in his/her present occupation than he/she did. If the household head could not work more or less hours then he/ she was asked in a follow up question if he/she wanted to contribute more labor hours to his/ her main occupation. Such a type of questions could not be applied in the study at hand.

As another alternative to pure quantitative economic studies one could think about qualitative assessments to gain insights into individuals' (and by this also into households') decisions about the allocation of family labor. Qualitative methods, such as formal or informal interviews or focus group discussions can be used to triangulate the results of quantitative analyses. Especially open questions like: "How do you decide about the distribution of your household's labor time?" or "Why do you work off the farm?" could provide additional information about farmers' labor allocation behavior.

During field studies in 2008 and 2009 the team of students and interviewers did not hold permission for qualitative assessments in RCRE villages in rural Hebei (Böber, 2008 and 2009). But during interviews (in villages that are not identical to the RCRE villages) some farmers made qualitative statements regarding their personal motives for labor supply off the farm and for the migration of rural laborers to urban areas which are not contained in the available quantitative data but also influence their labor supply decisions. Since this information have not been collected randomly, due to administrative restrictions, and could hardly be validated and assessed in terms of reliability, official representatives have always been in the same room as the interviewee, they have not been used in the work at hand. Therefore the assessment of households' labor allocation decisions is restricted to quantitative analyses.

4.3 Agricultural household models

According to Singh et al. (1986) the full income approach was useful in developing agricultural household models that integrate demand and supply decisions of the household. Tschajanow (1923) and Nakajima (1986) develop and discuss different agricultural household models of which some also allow to account for missing markets or market imperfections. Heterogeneity between family and hired labor could be one imperfection at the agricultural labor market. Deolalikar and Vijverberg (1987) discuss several reasons that might explain limited substitutability between family and hired labor. The first reason could be that both types of labor differ in their effect on farm output since the composition of the labor differs. There might be a higher share of female, child and unskilled labor among family labor than among hired labor, due to limited access of those labor groups to the off-farm labor market. Another reason would be that hired labor is sometimes employed in activities that require a higher degree of specialization of the laborer, e.g. plowing with tractors, so that the productivity of the hired laborers is higher and by this it is not a perfect substitute to family labor. Also seasonality could be an argument for a higher marginal productivity of hired labor since this labor is quite often only employed in busy seasons where the output per unit labor is higher than during the slack season. A fourth reason would be that the shadow price of family labor is low if there are no off-farm employment possibilities and therefore farmers who want to maximize their profits lower the marginal product of family labor compared to the one of hired labor. Also family and hired laborers differ in their incentives, because family members have an ownership interest that could lead to higher labor productivity in comparison to hired laborers whose main interest is the generation of income (Deolalikar and Vijverberg, 1987).

Other labor market imperfections are for example transaction or search costs for hired labor (de Janvry and Sadoulet, 2003). Market failure as such is specific to the farm household not to the traded commodity because one can argue, with a more general definition of market failure, that markets even if they exist are not used by the household if the gains from providing goods to the market, including family labor, are below the transaction costs of doing so (de Janvry et al., 1991).

The household is the decision unit under consideration in this study because the interest is on assessing decisions about the allocation of the total amount of family labor.

In countries with a high share of the population living in rural areas and working in agriculture which is mostly done on the family (owned) farm, the use of agricultural household models is important for policy analysis because three dimensions of policy decisions can be assessed (Singh et al., 1986). First, the direct well-being effects of policy measures on farm household can be analyzed which is important if policies are aimed to increase the well-being of large parts of the rural population in monetary or non-monetary terms. The second field of examination are spillover effects from the agricultural sector to the other sectors of the economy, e.g. from the promotion of investments in agricultural production. Those effects can be assessed if one understands the behavior and reactions of the agricultural households to these policies. Third, from a more macroeconomic point of view, agricultural household models can be used to analyze the reaction of the agricultural sector to price policies.

4.3.1 The concept of utility maximization of agricultural households

Despite the arguments against the pooling of individual labor allocation decisions as outlined in chapter 4.2, for the study at hand decisions about labor demand and supply will be assessed at the household level. The first reason is the already mentioned argument that labor allocation decisions of households in developing countries (and mainly agricultural economies) seem to fulfill some of the neoclassical assumptions of the model of family labor (see chapter 4.2). Because the agricultural sector was dominating in terms of laborers employed but also in its contribution to GDP during the assessed period from 1986-2002 and because only rural households are analyzed, it is reasonable to state, that the 'developing country' assumptions hold for the analyzed data set. And secondly, information about labor allocation and occupation are aggregated in the available data set at the household level.

The static household model developed by Singh et al. (1986) includes decisions of the household on production, consumption and supply. The key characteristic of such an agricultural household model is that it is recursive. Only market prices determine household's decision about production. On the other side the income derived from this production has an impact on household's decision about consumption and the supply of family labor. Singh et al. (1986) assume the farm household to be a price taker in all markets including food markets. Based on this assumption the household chooses the optimal production level independently of its decisions about the consumption of food and non-food commodities and leisure. Therefore the recursive model has one component that reflects the utility-maximization behavior of the agricultural household and one that includes the profit-maximization assumption. The concept behind such agricultural household models is not only useful for the assessment of farm households production and consumption decisions but they could also be used to analyze production and consumption decisions of households that run small scale enterprises, especially in developing countries (Bardhan and Uhdry, 1999).

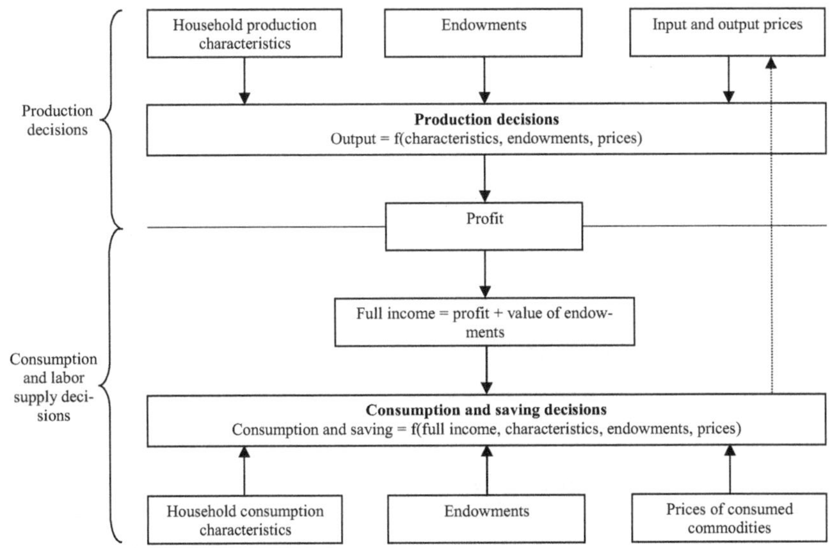

Source: Adapted from Kuiper (2005).

Figure 7: Production, labor supply and consumption decisions of agricultural households

Based on Singh et al. (1986) the following section provides a general agricultural household model. *Figure 7* provides a schematic overview of the links between an agricultural household's decisions about labor supply, production, consumption and savings.

A utility or welfare maximizing peasant household that is involved in own agricultural production but also provides resources (family labor) to off-farm occupations is expected to allocate labor in a way that the marginal utility to the household derived from off-farm income "is equal to the value of the marginal product of the individual worker" (Roll, 1980, p. 30). All markets, also intertemporal and insurance markets, are assumed to exist and to be competitive (Bardhan and Udry, 1999).

The following system of equations displays mathematically a basic static agricultural household model under the neoclassical assumption of well functioning land and labor markets that allows distinguishing between family on-farm and off-farm labor provision and hired farm labor, but where family and hired labor are assumed to be perfect substitutes (Singh et al., 1986; Kuiper, 2005). Land is assumed to be fixed. The household is assumed to maximize its utility with respect to the consumption of one own produced output (C_a) and leisure (C_l):

$$\max_{C_a, C_l, L_f, L_h} U(C_a, C_l) \tag{16}$$

s.t.

$$Q_a = f\left(L_f, L_h, \bar{q}\right) \tag{17}$$

$$L_f + L_o + C_l = \bar{T} \tag{18}$$

$$pQ_a + wL_o = pC_a + wL_h \tag{19}$$

The production constraint (17) indicates that the production Q_a of the crop produced at the family farm depends on the available amounts of family L_f and hired L_h labor and a fixed input $\bar{q}$ as for example the amount of arable land. The time budget $\bar{T}$ (18) of the household cannot be exceeded and is used to supply labor to the family farm, to supply family labor to off-farm activities L_o or to enjoy leisure, whereas leisure in this case includes the time for recovering. An agricultural household is also constrained in the amount of money it can spend. So in (19) the sum of income earned from selling Q_a for a price of p and wage income by supplying the amount of L_o with a wage rate of w equals the expenditures that occur from consuming some amount of the produced good C_a valued by the same (market) price p and from hiring labor L_h applying the same wage rate w.

The three constraints (17)-(19) can be combined to the full income constraint:

$$p\left[f\left(L_f, L_h, \bar{q}\right) - C_a\right] = w\left[L_h - \left(\bar{T} - L_f - C_l\right)\right] \quad (20).$$

Demand, consumption and supply decisions of the household are derived from maximizing (16) subject to the single constraint (20).

Lee (1965) indicates that individuals living in the household differ in their skills and opportunities to earn income off the family farm. They are also likely to differ in terms of their perceptions as to which utility levels they consider as satisfactory. But the assessment of such differences with the use of household models is rather difficult because it requires knowledge about the comparison of satisfaction levels among household members (Lee, 1965). This would result also in differences in their reservation wage (Gebauer, 1996). In difference to the preference determined reservation wage the market wage is determined by individual criteria (as age and qualifications) and by the overall market supply of labor. An individual household member would supply labor off the own family farm if the (market) wage is higher than the value of marginal product of labor time or in other words it exceeds the individuals' reservation wage. So if individuals are sovereign in deciding about their time allocation then the labor allocation decision is two dimensional: as a first step the decision is made to supply labor or not (based on the comparison of reservation and market wage) and secondly if the individual has made the decision to supply it decides about the amount of time to be supplied (Gebauer, 1996). Those considerations result in a two step decision calculus rather than in a recursive household model.

Following Wu and Meng (1997) the profit maximization of Chinese farmers was and partly still is constrained by policies like the household registration system (*hukou*), (grain) quotas and a social security system, that still excludes the rural population from most of the benefits that are granted to the urban population such as unemployment or retirement insurances.

4.3.2 Separability of households' labor decisions

According to the 'separation property' of agricultural household models, production decisions of the household do only depend on plot specific characteristics and prices but not on the factor endowment of the household (Bardhan and Udry, 1999). As Deolalikar and Vijverberg (1987) emphasize, separability of agricultural households' consumption and production decisions is build on the assumption of perfect competitive markets and perfect substitutability between family and hired labor. If markets are non-existent, are incomplete or if commodities are not fully substitutable because they differ in their properties like e.g. family labor and hired labor, then supply and demand prices will differ. In these cases non-separability of rural households' labor supply and demand decisions applies (Singh et al., 1986). In difference to household decisions in the context of economic assessments in developed countries, household decisions about labor supply, production and household consumption can hardly be assessed separately under the conditions that exist in developing countries where the economy is dominated by the agricultural sector (Kuiper, 2005). Non-separability is linked to the existence of "virtual prices" (Singh et al., 1986, p. 155) which are influenced by household's consumption and production decisions and by this are not fixed. This is in opposition to the assumptions regarding market prices used in the general agricultural household model above (see the dashed arrow in Figure 7). Following Kuiper (2005) the agricultural household model can no longer be solved in a recursive way if the prices of inputs and production outputs are affected by the consumption decisions. Also if family-specific variables (e.g. gender composition of the labor force) determine the labor allocation decisions of the household non-recursive models would have to be applied for the assessment of agricultural household decisions (Bollman, 1991). The model of Glauben et al. (2008) holds for both situations, for the case of non-separability as well as for the case when household's labor supply and demand decisions are separable because well-functioning labor markets exist.

As Bowlus and Sicular (2003) state, if a surplus of labor exists in an economy then non-separability is of relevance. In this situation the households don't maximize their utility anymore and households' preferences and factor endowments determine the production decisions (Bardhan and Udry, 1999). Bowlus and Sicular (2003) provide procedures to test for the separability of agricultural household decisions and make use of the panel data available to them by applying fixed effects estimations to remove the omitted variable bias that could result from time-invariant unobserved household characteristics. Wooldridge (2002) also uses the term 'omitted variables inconsistency' to describe the problem that arises in most empirical applications if estimations are influenced by unobserved factors. The author names the intuitive example of the relationship between education, ability and wages. Wages depend to a large extend on individual abilities but often only years of schooling are observable. Therefore estimation procedures have to be applied that take the unobserved effect of abilities on individual's wage earnings into account.

The following empirical model (in reduced form) is used in the analysis described in chapter 7.1.1 to test for separability of the household's labor decisions:

$$\ln L_{jt} = \alpha + \gamma \ln A_{jt} + \delta_0 \ln n_{jt} + \sum_{i=1}^{D} \delta_i \frac{n^i_{jt}}{n_{jt}} + \sum_{i=1}^{K} \theta_i D_{it} + \sum_{i=1}^{M} \xi_i X_{it} + \eta_j + \varepsilon_{jt} \qquad (21)$$

$j = 1,...,J; t = 1,...,T$ (Bowlus and Sicular, 2003 and Kuiper, 2005).

In this model L refers to the total agricultural household demand of labor given as the amount of total person-days used on cultivated or sown area, A is the amount of sown area, n is the size of the household, n^i are variables about household structural characteristics (number of females and dependents per household), D_{it} are village, year and village*year dummies, X_{it} are additional variables that control for differences in human capital of the household head[12], land characteristics and other observable household and farm characteristics, η_j is a component for unobserved household characteristics and held fixed over time, and ε_{jt} is an error term. The number of time periods is indicated by T and J indicates the number of households. The empirical test of Bowlus and Sicular (2003) is based on changes in the size and composition of the analyzed households where δ_0 is the elasticity of household's labor demand with respect to the number of household members and the δ_i's reflect the response of household's labor demand to changes in the household structure. The null hypothesis is that the labor decisions are separable. If the coefficients of the structural parameters are significantly jointly zero ($\delta_0 = \delta_i = 0$), the null hypothesis would have to be rejected and this would imply non-separability of household's labor decisions.

Bowlus and Sicular (2003) decide to follow the results from the fixed effect estimation because this estimation procedure provides unbiased results in the case that household unobservable characteristics are correlated with the regressors. In chapter 7.1.1 the separability is tested for the data set at hand to decide if recursive or non-recursive agricultural household models are applicable to the recent data set and to assess if imperfections in the rural labor market in Hebei province exist.

12 Bowlus and Sicular (2003) and Kuiper (2005) possess information about individuals which allows them to differentiate between the education and age of different household members. For the data set at hand this is not possible because education and age variables are only available for the main laborer in the household.

4.3.3 Theoretical model for the assessment of a household's labor allocation

In the studies of Glauben et al. (2005 and 2008) a theoretical unitary model about household labor market decisions is developed that is static and ignores risk attitude of farmers, proportional and fixed transaction costs (Key et al., 2000) on product and input markets and credit constraints. Also the role of intra-household labor allocation decisions to cope with stochastic (external) production shocks (see e.g. Halliday, 2010) is not covered by the model applied here. The reason for this is that there is just one household level utility function for the whole household modeled and not two or more additively combined individual utility functions.

Another aspect of modeling household decisions is that the composition of households changes over time (Kuiper, 2005). Glauben et al. (2008) apply the model to household data collected in Zhejiang province between 1986 and 2002 to analyze the transition of households into and out of off-farm activities. They define four different regimes regarding the labor supply and demand decision of rural households with agricultural production. If the household uses only family labor for farming and does not supply any family labor to off-farm occupations, the household is considered as acting in autarky. In a second scenario the household supplies some part or all of its family labor to off-farm activities. The third regime represents cases in which the household decides to hire labor for family farm production. The fourth possible regime is the case where the household participates on both sides at the labor market and supplies family labor and hires non-family labor at the same time.

Key et al. (2000) name several reasons for the existence of the fourth regime. Three of those reasons might also be relevant for labor market participation decisions of agricultural households in rural Hebei and can be considered in the empirical model: (1) agricultural households differentiate between diverse kinds of labor, for example based on qualification necessary to fulfill the work. Glauben et al. (2005) state that family and hired labor are not always perfect substitutes due to specific knowledge owned by the family e.g. about local environmental conditions. (2) Labor prices or the respective shadow wages follow seasonal patterns (Benjamin and Brandt, 2002) so that depending on the season it might be rational for the household to hire labor for one agricultural production activity while it supplies labor for an other occupation. (3) Uchida et al. (2007) discuss the off-farm labor provision of households participating in the Grain for Green program. They find that the program relaxes liquidity constraints that otherwise reduce rural households' provision of off-farm labor. So, if there is no liquidity constraint then the household can provide some family labor outside the farm.

The following agricultural household model is suitable for the analysis carried out later in the work at hand because the interest is on factors that determine the choice of labor market participation based on family and farm characteristics. Following Benjamin and Kimhi (2006) it is assumed that farm and household decisions cannot be separated from each other. The model as such is applicable to the situation of perfect markets but also to situations with market imperfections. Wang (2007) explains that this model can be applied for the situation of either increasing or decreasing per-unit costs of accessing the labor market. So, backward- or upward-sloping prices for hired labor or the respective wage for off-farm provided family labor can be incorporated into the model framework. Wang (2007) lists search or monitoring costs for hired labor and the limited substitutability between family and hired labor, due to land specific experience of family laborers, as factors leading to increasing per unit-costs. On the other side one could argue with Wang (2007) that familiarity and trust between hired and family laborers, which increases over time, could lead to lower supervision costs and by this to decreasing marginal costs for hired labor.

Chen et al. (2004) apply panel data models to assess labor market participation of rural households in China. In contrast, the available RCRE data set will here be used in a cross-section manner, which allows including household or farm characteristics that do not vary over time, such as the amount of arable land per capita of the household, if there is no land reallocation or land renting activity.

Agricultural households are assumed to maximize their utility according to the following maximization problem (Glauben et al., 2008):

$$\max_{c,x} U(c; z_u) \tag{22}$$

s.t.

$$G(x, r; z_G) = 0 \tag{23}$$

$$T_l + X_l + D_l^h X_l^h - D_l^s X_l^s - C_l \geq 0 \tag{24}$$

$$P_m C_m \leq P_c X_c + P_V X_V - D_l^h g(X_l^h; z_g) + D_l^s f(X_l^s; z_f) + E \quad (25).$$

Where (23) represents the technology constraint, (24) is the time constraint and (25) the budget constraint.

The utility function (22) of the agricultural household is assumed to be monotonic, continuous, quasi-concave and globally non-satiated. The vector c contains marketed commodities C_m and leisure C_l. Z_u is a vector of unobserved household characteristics and other exogenous utility shifters. The production technology as represented by G is assumed to be monotonic and convex. Production goods are included in (23) as vector x, quasi-fixed factors, land and capital, are shown by vector r, and household and farm characteristics that are considered to be exogenous drivers of the production are summarized in vector z_G. Agricultural products $(X_C > 0)$ are produced using the quasi-fixed factors, labor $(X_l < 0)$, and variable inputs $(X_v < 0)$. In household's time constraint (24) T_l stands for the total household time available, the absolute value of X_l indicates the total amount of on-farm labor that is the sum of hired labor time X_l^h and family on-farm labor X_l^f. X_l^s is family labor supplied to off-farm work. The household is also constrained in its budget as is expressed in (25) where the consumption expenditures $(P_m C_m)$ are not allowed to exceed the monetary income of the household (the right hand side of (25)). P_i, where $i = a, m, c, v$, indicates the prices for consumers and producers that are assumed to be exogenous.

The revenue that the household derives from farm production $\sum P_i X_i - g(X_l^h; z_g)$ depends on the household's labor allocation decision according to the specified regimes of labor market participation. The costs for hiring farm labor are indicated by the increasing and strictly convex function $g\ (\partial g(\cdot)/\partial X_l^h > 0; \partial^2 g(\cdot)/\partial X_l^{h2} > 0)$ depending on a function for hired labor (X_l^h) and a vector of exogenous factors like e.g. wage rates and transaction costs z_g. Family income derived from off-farm labor supply $f(X_l^s; z_f)$ is increasing and strictly concave $(\partial f(\cdot)/\partial X_l^s > 0; \partial^2 f(\cdot)/\partial X_l^{s2} < 0)$ and depends also on exogenous factors z_f, which could be for example laborer skills and a function of supplied labor (X_l^s). The non-linear properties of $g(\cdot)$ and $f(\cdot)$ indicate, that the price of leisure and labor (P_l) is endogenous due to labor market imperfections. So the model is non-separable and has to be solved in two steps. Transfers are represented by E and can either be a positive monetary amount, e.g. transfers from the state or from relatives, or can be negative in the case that the household provides transfers to others (Glauben et al., 2008).

The dummies D_l^j, (where $j = s, h$), in (24) and (25) indicate the labor market participation regimes:

autarky $^{(a)}$	if	$D_l^h = D_l^s = 0$,
hire $^{(h)}$	if	$D_l^h = 1$ and $D_l^s = 0$,
supply $^{(s)}$	if	$D_l^h = 0$ and $D_l^s = 1$, and
supply and hire $^{(sh)}$	if	$D_l^h = 1$ and $D_l^s = 1$.

In a first step of solving the model, one has to apply the Lagrangian approach to derive with the first order conditions from the utility maximization problem (22)-(25). The stationary solutions depend on the specific labor market participation regime and underlie the assumption that the interior solutions exist. While λ is the Lagrangian multiplier of the budget constraint, μ is the multiplier for the time constraint and ϕ the one for the technology constraint ($\lambda, \phi, \mu > 0$ and $c, x > 0$) (Glauben et al., 2005). Lagrangian multipliers are generally interpreted in economics as shadow prices of the factors included in the respective constraint. As the maximization problem above, also the system of first order conditions is presented in the notation of Glauben et al. (2005). The first order conditions provide the basis for the deviation of regime specific shadow prices, especially for labor, that are relevant for the second step of determining the labor market participation decisions of the households.

The Lagrangian here is:

$$L(\lambda,\phi,\mu,c,x)=U(c;z_U)+\lambda\left[P_C X_C + P_V X_V - D_l^h g\left(X_l^h;z_g\right)+D_l^s f\left(X_l^s;z_f\right)+E-P_m C_m\right]$$
$$+\phi\left[G(x,r;z_G)\right]+\mu\left[T_l + X_l + D_l^h X_l^h - D_l^s X_l^s - C_l\right] \tag{26}$$

The resulting first order conditions are:

$$\frac{\partial L(\cdot)}{\partial C_i}=\frac{\partial U(c;z_U)}{\partial C_i}-\lambda P_i=0 \qquad i\in\{m,l\} \quad \text{(Consumption goods)} \tag{27}$$

$$\frac{\partial L(\cdot)}{\partial X_i}=\lambda P_i+\phi\frac{\partial G(x,r;z_G)}{\partial X_i}=0 \qquad i\in\{c,v,l\} \quad \text{(Production goods)} \tag{28}$$

$$\frac{\partial L(\cdot)}{\partial X_l^h}=-\lambda D_l^h g(\cdot)+\mu=-D_l^h g(\cdot)+P_l=0 \qquad P_l=\frac{\mu}{\lambda}; \tag{29}$$

$$\frac{\partial L(\cdot)}{\partial X_l^s}=\lambda D_l^s f(\cdot)-\mu=D_l^s f(\cdot)-P_l=0 \qquad D_l^s, D_l^h\in\{0;1\} \tag{30}$$

$$\frac{\partial L(\cdot)}{\partial \lambda}=\sum_{i=c,v}P_i X_i-D_l^h g\left(X_l^h;z_g\right)+D_l^s f\left(X_l^s;z_f\right)+E-P_m C_m=0 \tag{31}$$

$$\frac{\partial L(\cdot)}{\partial \phi}=G(x,r;z_G)=0 \tag{32}$$

$$\frac{\partial L(\cdot)}{\partial \mu} = T_l + X_l + D_l^h X_l^h - D_l^s X_l^s - C_l = 0 \qquad (33).$$

The price for labor and leisure P_l is endogenous and can be different between the labor market participation regimes. From (31) one can see that the shadow prices $P_l^j = \chi(p, r, T_l, E, z)$ for every market regime $j \in \{a, h, s, sh\}$ depend on all exogenous variables which are: the production and consumption prices (p), the amount of fixed resources (r), the overall available family time (T_l), and other characteristics (z) of the labor market, the farm and the household.

One can either base the second step in the solution of the household's labor market participation decision on the comparison of alternative indirect utilities associated with the regimes or on the comparison of regime specific wage rates (Glauben et al., 2008). The price of labor is the decision price in the recent context and this price is one of the decision factors included in the indirect utility function according to Key et al. (2000).

The present study follows the argumentation of Glauben et al. (2008), according to which higher regime specific wage rates result in higher utility levels achieved by the respective households. Therefore the following regime wage rates have to be compared:

$$P_l^a = \chi(p, r, T_l, E, z_U, z_G) \qquad (34)$$

$$P_l^h = \chi(p, r, T_l, E, z_U, z_G, z_g) \qquad (35)$$

$$P_l^s = \chi(p, r, T_l, E, z_U, z_G, z_f) \qquad (36)$$

$$P_l^{sh} = \chi(p, r, T_l, E, z_U, z_G, z_f, z_g). \qquad (37)$$

The household achieves the highest (indirect) utility level if it acts according to the labor market regime that yields the highest endogenous wage rate (Glauben et al., 2008):

$$P_l^j = \max(P_l^a, P_l^h, P_l^s, P_l^{sh}). \qquad (38)$$

Because labor market decisions are assessed from a static point of view in this study, the effects that past decisions of households' might have on the present state of labor market participation are not analyzed.

Alternatively to the described approach by Glauben et al. (2008), Chen et al. (2004) apply a dynamic discrete choice model to RCRE panel data covering around 600 households in 9 Chinese provinces. They focus on the determinants of migration in rural China. Chen et al. (2004) emphasize that models which use pooled estimation methods for choice models on data sets with panel characteristics ignore the problem of initial condition and are likely to produce biased results due to the fact that decisions of previous periods can affect present decisions. Instead, they follow the approach of Wooldridge (2002) to integrate and estimate dynamic state dependence. Unobserved effects are modeled conditional on the initial value and a set of exogenous explanatory variables (Chen et al., 2004). If household characteristics do not vary over time they cannot be included as variables into dynamic panel data models (Chen et al., 2004).

Because Chen et al. (2004) are interested in the effects of local social networks on off-farm and migration decisions they include the percentage of off-farm labor in the village as explanatory variable of a household's labor market participation choice. Also they use village level income in their set of explanatories. Unfortunately, especially this village level information is not available in the analyzed data set of the present study.

Analogue to the discussion about family labor supply with individualized consumption of leisure time presented in chapter 4.2 one could also model the labor market participation decisions of farm households as utility maximization with disaggregated amounts of leisure as in Findeis and Lass (1994), but again such disaggregated information is not available in the assessed data set.

4.3.4 Theoretical model for the assessment of farm structure persistence

Rigg (2006) presents studies which find that rural households in some (developing) countries like Thailand develop a widespread part-time farming system while other countries (e.g. San Jose) have households that are full-time agricultural producers and households that leave the agricultural sector completely side by side. In rural Hebei province, like in rural China in general, people hardly ever completely abandon their agricultural production activities. One reason for this might be that land and labor markets as well as the social security system are not fully developed so that land is still considered as a social security net for the rural population (Piotrowski, 2009). Even if this topic was raised regularly in discussions and interviews during field surveys (Böber, 2008 and 2009) it would require detailed information about households' coverage by social security systems especially about their entitlement to pensions to include measures that might change individual and households' labor decisions into quantitative models. Time dummies to control for such policy changes are not always suited due to the lack of transmission of new regulations into practical application and an additional time lag until individual (labor market) behavior of labor market participation adapts to those changes. Also the mixed impact of different policy decisions and macroeconomic conditions complicates the distinction of effects stemming from one specific policy measure.

The use of hazard models allows considering dynamic aspects (Wang, 2007). So for the case here, it is of interest how the length of staying in a previous state, full-time or part-time farming, influences the probability to shift to the respective alternative regime. If state dependence exists then the probability of being in the present state depends on the state the household experienced before (Corsi and Findeis, 2000). Weiss (1997) finds in his panel study on Austrian farm households that participation of farm households in off-farm activities depends on a previous participation in off-farm activities. Chen et al. (2004) also confirm this phenomenon of state dependence. Depending on the kind of state dependence that is observed different recommendations to policy makers have to be provided. If state dependence is due to job-specific accumulated knowledge then the provision of respective specific training is appropriate. If search or transaction costs for alternative activities are too high and lead to the situation that the household/ laborers remain(s) in a state instead of changing it, then those costs or entry/exit barriers would have to be reduced (Corsi and Findeis, 2000).

As Wooldridge (2002) states, survival analysis allows testing to how far the probability of exiting a status or entering a new status depends on the length of time that the individual observation unit, in our case the farm household, spends in the previous status. Using time series or panel data, one can test and control for unobserved heterogeneity. It is important to control for unobservable individual effects that are stable over time. If this so called frailty is significant the empirical model has to control for it (Jenkins, 2008) otherwise it would not be possible to distinguish between the effect of frailty and the effect of the duration dependence. The estimation procedures available in Stata allow testing for different frailty distributions. This is necessary if frailty is of relevance for the data set in use because than the assumed distribution has an impact on the interpretation of the relative hazard rates (Cleves et al., 2002) that result from the estimation of the persistence model.

The analysis of the persistence of farming structures is also important with respect to considerations about the efficiency of the agricultural production in the study region. Presently, in most of the locations visited in Hebei, land use rights are allocated to the households based on the number of residents registered as members of this household. From the available panel data set one can see that the average size of arable land per capita is around 1.7 mu (min.: 0 mu, max.: 7.5 mu, SD: 0.91 mu). This is in line with results from interviews conducted in other villages in Hebei (Böber, 2008 and 2009). But such a distribution rule might not always result in allocative efficiency. In case a household prefers to abandon farming and to rent out the allocated land to other households that would like to increase their production area and to specialize in farming then the overall utility of the involved actors could be increased due to the fact that households would concentrate their labor and capital resources on activities where they have comparative advantages. Existing legal measures to exchange or rent land among households within a village or between villages are hardly executed. This is because either local administration hinders the enforcement of land renting activities or because the lessors do not trust the tenants, because the tenants are assumed not to invest resources into appropriate farming practices to keep the land fertility at a sustainable level (Piotrowski, 2009).

Especially a graphical representation of the results from the persistence or time failure analysis is an appropriate tool to explain the results of the analysis to policy makers or other interested stakeholders (Nevell, 2000).

As for the choice between four different labor market occupations described in part 4.2.3, a household in rural Hebei is assumed to base its decision to either be a part-time or full-time farming household on the principle of utility maximization. Brosig et al. (2009) define the following indirect utility functions:

$$\psi_{t*}^{FF} = \int V_t^{FF}\left(p_t, Y_t^{FF}, Z_t, DUR_t\right)e^{-rt}\,dt \qquad (39)$$

$$\psi_{t*}^{PF} = \int V_t^{PF}\left(p_t, Y_t^{PF}, Z_t, DUR_t\right)e^{-rt}\,dt \qquad (40)$$

where: Ψ^j = discounted working time utility
j {FF (full-time farming); *PF* (part-time farming)}
r = discount rate
$V^j(p,Y,Z)$ = indirect utility depending on:
p = vector of consumption prices,
Y = income,
Z = vector of household or localities specific characteristics,
DUR = duration.

The aim of the model presented here, is to predict movements between the two states part-time and full-time farming. Households are assumed to change between these two exclusive occupations if the net utility gain H_{t*}^{ji} of changing the occupation is positive:

$$H_{t*}^{ji} = \Psi_{t*}^{i} - \Psi_{t*}^{j} - TC_{t*}^{ji} \qquad (41)$$

where TC_{t*}^{ji} represents the disutility or transfer cost associated with the occupation change. Because agricultural households in rural China only possess use rights in land but no property rights these transfer costs could also be the fear to loose the use right (Jacoby et al., 2002) if the household decides to rent out all or some part of the allocated land and to supply labor to off-farm activities.

This model of household behavior on the choice between part- and full-time farming is based on the proposition that the indirect utility of the household depends on variables that might change in relation to the time the household spends in one of the two alternative states (Brosig et al., 2009). Thereby it is implied that the probability of changing between the states depends on the amount of time that the household already remained in one of the states (duration).

The basic concept of the time failure analysis as applied here is the hazard function. This hazard function is a specialized representation of the distribution of a random variable which displays the failure time, the point in time when a status change occurs, for an observation unit (Kalbfleisch and Prentice, 1980). Brosig et al. (2009) specify the following hazard function:

$$\lambda(t) = \lim_{\Delta t \to 0} \frac{\Pr(T \geq t)}{\Delta t}. \qquad (42)$$

Where $\lambda(t)$ is the spell completion rate at duration t, provided the spells last until t.

As derived from the hazard function the duration dependence can be positive at t if $d\lambda(t)/dt > 0$ or negative at t if $d\lambda(t)/dt < 0$ (Brosig et al., 2009). Positive duration dependence is interpreted as: the longer a farm household was in a specific state until t the higher the probability that it will change to the alternative state. The opposite holds for the negative duration dependence, where the hazard would be decreasing and the farm household would have a lower risk (probability) to leave its present state the longer it already was in this state.

Following Brosig et al. (2009) and allowing for time-varying covariates by using a proportional hazard model, the empirical hazard function is specified as:

$$\lambda_k^{ji}\left(t, z_k, \beta^{ji}, \theta^{ji}\right) = \lambda_0^{ji}\left(t, \theta^{ji}\right) \exp\left[z_k(t), \beta^{ji}\right] \qquad (43)$$

where: $\lambda_k^{ji}\left(t, z_k, \beta^{ji}, \theta^{ji}\right)$ = transition hazard between the states j and i for household k,

$\lambda_0^{ji}\left(t, \theta^{ji}\right)$ = hazard if no heterogeneity exists among the individuals (baseline hazard),

θ^{ji} = frailty variance,

β^{ji} = parameter for the impact of covariates, and

z_k = observed characteristics of the household (varying over time (t)).

The individual hazard might be changed by the heterogeneity of individual (or household) behavior. This is partly controlled for by the z_k's, which are scaled. So, $\exp[z_k(t), \beta^{ji}]=1$ at the mean value of the observed characteristics (Brosig et al., 2009). There could also be an "unobserved spell-specific random effect" (Brosig et al., 2009, p. 365), which might change the hazard if no heterogeneity exits among the individual households. To control for this, the parameter θ^{ji} is included in the estimations and by this it is assumed to avoid estimation bias from frailty (Brosig et al., 2009).

It is necessary to apply estimation techniques for discrete duration data if the length of each time period (here one year) is relatively long compared with the duration of the spells (here a maximum of eight years) (Kalbfleisch and Prentice, 1980). Brosig et al. (2009) group the spell length of the annual data using the amount of years a spell lasted as the grouping variable. Then they apply an estimation approach for grouped data that allows controlling for frailty. Brosig et al. (2009) use a complementary log-log link function to parameterize the estimation approach as provided by Jenkins (1995b). Jenkins (2008) explains that in the Stata procedures for the estimation of models with discrete time frailty the model specifications consider shared frailty instead of observation specific frailty. One has to interpret shared frailty as a single value of the unobserved differences that is common to a group of observations.

4.4 Summary

A societal assessment of welfare should not only focus on the sum of individual welfares but also on the distribution of welfare among the individual members of the society. In the microeconomic analysis of inequality of rural households in well-being and poverty one has to appropriately value own produced consumption goods. The coefficient of variation and the Shorrocks approach as methods for the decomposition of income inequality, e.g. by sources, are presented in this chapter. Poverty indices are presented in this chapter and two different approaches of decomposing poverty into its transient and chronic component by population sub-groups are introduced.

The poverty decomposition approaches of Jalan and Ravallion (1998) (JR) and the approach of equally distributed equivalent (EDE) poverty gap by Duclos et al. (2008) differ in terms of what is the basis of the analysis. In the JR approach chronic poverty is linked to an average of welfare experienced by the observation unit (here the household). In contrast Duclos et al. (2008) link chronic poverty with their EDE approach to an average of ill-fare states experienced by the household. This allows considering also households as being poor whose average welfare is always above the poverty line but who experienced poverty at one or several points in time over the assessed period. Another advantage of the EDE approach is the fact that the results can be interpreted in a cardinal way. Since the results using both approaches are likely to differ strongly both methods will be applied in chapter 6.1 to show the extent of difference when estimating the relation between chronic and transient poverty.

Different theoretical models to assess individual and household labor supply or allocation decisions are evaluated in this chapter. Besides the distinction between a maximization of individual utility or joint utility of a household one can also classify labor supply models into static and dynamic ones. Labor supply and allocation models are of importance for the assessment of policy measures such as tax changes, subsidy or welfare programs. Due to numerous changes in the tax and welfare system over the last two decades in China those models offer the possibility to assess impacts on household labor allocation decisions by including time dummies as explanatory variables as done in chapter 7.2.

Because households do not necessarily follow the behavior of utility maximization if consumption and production decisions are non-separable, it is important to assess the separabiltiy of agricultural households' demand and supply of labor. Also the prevalence of non-separability might indicate constraints in the labor market. It is important to test for separability of agricultural households' production and consumption decisions to decide about the application of either recursive or non-recursive models to estimate the impact of factors determining these household decisions. A model is presented that can be applied to the available data set to test the hypothesis of non-separability.

After a graphical and mathematical presentation of a general agricultural household model, a specific static model, developed by Glauben et al. (2008), is presented and explained. This model allows distinguishing between different labor market participation regimes when assessing rural households' labor allocation decisions. The introduced model can be solved when households' labor demand and supply decisions are separable but also in the case of non-separability. So, this model is chosen for the analysis in chapter 7.2 because it can be solved non-recursively and by this is applicable in cases where the hypothesis that household's labor demand and supply decisions are separable is rejected.

In addition a hazard model is described that will be used in chapter 7.3 to assess the persistence of part- and full-time farm structures. Hazard models can be used to assess dynamic aspects of farm households' labor market participation decisions. Such methods, which are commonly applied in survival analysis, allow analyzing to what extend the probability of remaining in a specific state or changing it depends on the time that the household already remained in the state. So, the application of models adapted from the survival analysis is relevant, because it is one of the research aims of this study to assess the stability (with respect to time) of part- and full-time farm households.

5 Data

The data used is a panel data set by survey design. The next section shortly explains features of panel data and highlights requirements when working with them.

5.1 Working with panel data

For econometric analyses quantitative micro- and/ or macro-level data are needed. Three types of data can be differentiated and used: time series, cross-sectional and panel data. Time series data reflect the measurement of one or more variables at different points in time over the same unit(s) of observation, e.g. individuals, households or firms. In contrast collecting cross-section data means that the same variables are asked from different observation units at one point in time, which of course in practical field work can be a time span like a week during which households in different villages are interviewed. As a kind of combination of these two methods, the collection of panel data is motivated by raising information from the same observation units at different points in time as done in the surveys of the Research Center for Rural Economy (RCRE). The data set received from the RCRE and used in this study will be explained in more detail in chapter 5.2.

Baltagi (2008) depicts in a clear overview the pros and cons of using panel data. Relevant for the study at hand could be the influence of individual heterogeneity, where in this case 'individual' could refer to land as the main input factor for agricultural production in rural Hebei.

A clear advantage of using panel data for this study is that they offer more degrees of freedom in order to deal with endogeneity between off-farm employment and on-farm investment and production decisions (Ahituv and Kimhi, 2006; Phimister and Roberts, 2006; Weiss, 1999). Besides offering more possibilities to detect unobserved heterogeneity, panel data also provide more information and variability (in information) than e.g. cross-section data. Normally there is also less colinearity found between variables. Panel data also provide information on adjustment dynamics of the observed units so it is possible to asses the adjustment of household behavior over time, e.g. with respect to macroeconomic and economic policy changes. This kind of data also allows us to draw conclusions about dynamics at the individual level (Deaton, 1997) and to augment across-household information with variation within households (Bowlus and Sicular, 2003). As Shi et al. (2007) point out, panel data sets allow for the proper estimation of life cycle effects that influence migration and off-farm activities which are both individual based decisions.

Baltagi (2008) suggests that random effect models are well suited for household panel studies where N observation units have been drawn from a large population. As long as the panel was drawn randomly, this type of models allows estimating individual effects that are characterized as random and inference pertains to the population. If omitted variables seem to exist, panel data can be used to obtain consistent estimators (Wooldridge, 2002). Following Deaton (1997) the "quality of land" is in most cases an omitted variable, e.g. if the data collection is not combined with an analysis of soil samples or plot level climatic data.

Following Wooldridge (2002) unobserved effects on the individual level could be the cognitive ability or personal motivation. Also personal preferences or their change can usually not be directly observed. If we think of a household level model, such unobserved effects can be trust or mistrust and altruistic behavior between household members or between neighboring households. Sometimes, such unobserved effects can also exists on the village level as shown by Piotrowski (2009). The author conducted interviews in Quzhou County where village heads revealed, that they mistrust neighboring villages and therefore do not exchange land with them.

As Corsi and Findeis (2000) emphasize, panel data are also very useful to distinguish between the reasons of state dependence.

5.2 The household data set

The data set available and used for the analysis is part of a large comprehensive study conducted by the Research Center for Rural Economy (RCRE) since 1986. The full RCRE sample for 31 provinces and administrative regions in China covers 300 villages and over 22.000 households (Duclos et al., 2008). For the study at hand a data set for Hebei province is used. The annual household survey includes only rural households. Because the variables contain information about households and individuals, this data set is a micro panel data set but the survey follows only households and not individuals over time. Responding households have to keep a daily dairy of all activities, e.g. farming or other household production, as well as income and expenditures. The information is collected once a month by an administrator that is resident to this region and living at the town or township that is the county seat (Duclos et al., 2008). In addition to the household level data, information about the village is collected every year but for the present work only the household level data set is available. It covers the period

1986 to 2006. The survey was not conducted in 1992 and 1994 due to financial reasons. Consequently 19 years with observations are available to construct a panel data set. Depending on the village size the sample covering Hebei province contains between 100 and 120 households randomly chosen per village. There are 4 different versions of household and village survey questionnaires – one for the years 1986 to 1991, one for 1993, one for 1995 through 2002 and a fourth one which is in use science 2003. Since 2003 the data set also contains information, e.g. regarding education and labor occupations, about every member living in the household.

The number of villages in the mentioned data set for Hebei is 6, for 1987 to 2003, and 11, for 1986 and the years from 2004 onwards. In the first year there are 1100 households in the data set. For the later years this changes to between 600 (1988) and 1091 households (2005 and 2006).

The household sampling procedure is described by Benjamin et al. (2005). On province level the RCRE selected counties from the lower, middle and upper income tercile. Villages are chosen from those county groups based on geographic criteria (village in plain, hilly or mountainous area), location (rural, suburban or urban), and according to main economic activities such as fishery or forestry (Glauben et al., 2008). So only the households interviewed in the chosen villages are selected randomly.

To derive with appropriate statistical and econometric conclusions samples have to be drawn as representative as possible. However, the data set has some shortcomings that need to be pointed out because they influence the selection of analysis methods and the quality of the results.

The data set lacks a detailed household roster (Duclos et al., 2008) and no household sampling weights are available. According to Chen et al. (2004) the sample shows slight attrition over time. But Benjamin et al. (2007) state, that they observed some attrition especially after the years when the survey was not conducted. Yet, it can be assumed that households lost through attrition have been replaced by new households based on random sampling (Benjamin et al., 2007).

Since the survey round conducted in 1993 the RCRE data set contains a variable classifying the household based on generations. This multivariate variable also allows to identify extended families (including relatives) or broken families (e.g. due to divorce). Sometimes the size of households, which remained in the sample for several survey rounds, drops sharply from one year to the next and on first sight there seems to be no reason for this pattern. But one has to have in mind that in China sons leave their parents' household once they get married (Jia, 2010). If this happens (and this can not be identified for the years before 1993), the sons (and their new household) are no longer included in the sample, which might cause some loss of information, e.g. on the composition of the original households' labor force and income. Based on the household IDs 537 households have been identified to stay in the sample over all survey years. This is a valid statement if the household ID is really a unique identifier.

However, it is possible that the ID of a household which dropped from the survey was used for a household that was included as a replacement (see Chen et al., 2003). Using the information from the variable "was this household surveyed last year?" and comparing the number of permanent residents and the age of main laborers between years were the household stated being surveyed a year before and those years were the household states not being surveyed in the previous year up to 27 IDs are identified, which might suffer from the described problem that the same ID is assigned to different cases. Without access to the original questionnaires, it is not possible to further cross check if this was a mistake in data processing or if the cases are really different but the same IDs are used. According to Jia (2010) the RCRE did not document cases of using old IDs for new observation units. An explanation might be that the RCRE was not aware of the difficulties that evolve for long term (panel) assessments from using the same IDs. The RCRE might have put a greater emphasis on replacing households that dropped out of the sample by "comparable" ones to keep the sample as such representative instead of tracking the same observation units over time. Such inaccurateness occurs in statistical data sets and has to be controlled for, if possible, but by and large official Chinese statistics seem not to suffer from falsification due to political influence on statisticians (Chow, 2006).

In future rounds of the survey there might also be the problem that areas which have been classified as rural will be defined as sub-urban or urban due to urbanization and infrastructure development, administrative mergers of villages into townships or towns or the new classification of towns according to population size (Yang and Zhou, 1999). This would also affect the possibility to track households and individuals if villages were dropped from the sample.

No refusal rates are reported for the RCRE data (Benjamin et al., 2005). Benjamin et al. (2007) raise the doubt that some households of the low end of the income distribution are excluded. They argue that this could be the case because the survey protocol requires keeping a diary of e.g. income and expenditures and this could lead to excluding illiterate (low income) households. Also the survey procedure is putting high costs on rich households. In general households with relatively high opportunity costs of time can be expected to be more likely to refuse (Benjamin et al., 2005). As further potential pitfalls of the design of the RCRE survey Benjamin et al. (2005) mention the possibility of inaccurateness in asking for income from household-run business and problems in distinguishing variable and fixed (production) costs during the enumeration. However, for the data set available it is not possible to check, if it is influenced by such tendencies because of the secondary nature. Since only the data set as such is available and no information about how the data have been collected it has to be assumed that the data were collected following a statistically sound sampling design.

For the RCRE surveys since 1993 farm households are asked to specify their time allocation. So they can state that they are either: full-time agriculture, mainly agriculture, mainly non-agriculture, or full-time non-agriculture households or allocate their time in another way. For the calculation of poverty incidence and differences in poverty inequality, as done in chapter 6, this self-classification variable is used to separate the observations in two sub samples: full-time farm households (full-time and mainly agriculture) and part-time (mainly non-agriculture and full-time non-agriculture).

Detailed information about all working household member's time allocation to farming and non-farming activities would allow a clearer differentiation between the degrees to which the household provides labor hours to farming activities. However such data about the individual allocation of working time of farm household members are only available from 2003 onward.

5.3 Summary

Panel data sets provide the possibility to track individuals and their behavior and decisions over relatively long time spans. This offers the chance to distinguish between time-variant and time-invariant individual effects such as individual preference sets or unobservable land characteristics.

By survey design the available RCRE data set for Hebei province is a micro panel data set where households rather than individuals are followed over time. The information provided is used in a cross-section manner for some part of the analyses and its panel data characteristics are utilized in other parts. The data set is representative for the rural areas of Hebei between 1986 and 2006 but due to changes in the variables contents and due to problems in uniquely identifying observation units only those parts of the observations will be used for the empirical assessments in chapter 6 and chapter 7 which can be correctly identified.

6 The trend of poverty and income decomposition for Hebei – Results

Building on the theoretical concepts presented in chapter 4.1 and using the data set described before, the following chapter presents and discusses the results of the assessment of poverty development and the income decomposition.

6.1 Poverty trend

For the assessment of poverty, the analysis focuses on consumption expenditures. Subsistence consumption expenditures as for food, housing or clothing as well as for non-subsistence components as for living or cultural components are distinguished in the data set for the years 1986-91. Since 1993 expenditures for living, including medical expenditures, and cultural services are also considered as subsistence consumption. This makes sense if one thinks of expenditures for medicine and schooling to improve the ability of household members to work or earn higher income and by this to improve their well-being. For the years up to 2002 no household rosters are provided. For this reason, variables that contain individual characteristics are related to the household head.

If the composition of the household is known with respect to e.g. gender or age of all individuals belonging to the household the concept of equivalent units can be applied (Milanovic, 2002). A factor of 0.5 could for example be assigned to a child reflecting that children contribute less to consumption expenditures than adults. Milanovic (2002) shows that the standard method to calculate poverty gaps would have to be adjusted if equivalent units are used instead of per capita measures of households consumption expenditures.

Because besides the household head no age, gender, and work occupation information about individuals living in the household are available per capita household expenditures are used in the poverty analyses as in Duclos et al. (2008). For the years from 1986 to 1991 and from 1995 to 2002 the variable that is available to determine the household size is the number of permanent residents by the end of the year. The data for 1993 contain only the number of permanent residents in the beginning of the year, so this information is used for this year to calculate per capita variables. As long as the households included in the sample are drawn from the population in a representative way there is no need to weight the observations. Because Benjamin et al. (2005) assume that there is some doubt that poor and rich household are under represented in the RCRE, sample weighting would be needed to make inferences about the population.

However, no sampling weights are provided with the data set. It is not possible to generate weights related to the households from the available data, because no information about the stratification procedures is available. Therefore no weighting procedures can be applied for the poverty analysis.

To take account of agricultural products that are produced and consumed by the household itself the consumed amounts have to be valued. The data set available here does not provide regional (market) price information for agricultural products but for grain the quantity sold and its total value are given. From this one can calculate a selling price for 1 kg of grain. The village mean of this price can be used as approximation of the value of household own consumption of grain if it is multiplied with the amount of grain that households produced and consumed on their own. A problem associated with this method is that it could not be distinguished which type of grain is considered. Only aggregated numbers for "grain" are provided for all years. Also there might be some portion of grain put into stock or it is possible, especially for those years where grain quotas where still relevant, that some grain was sold in a black or grey market system that was at least prevailing in the beginning of the 1980s and violating the rules of grain delivery to state purchase stations (Chan and Unger, 1982).

Brandt and Holz (2006) calculate the value of self-produced and consumed on-farm grain directly from the available data for amount of grain consumed and expenditures for purchased grain in markets. Benjamin et al. (2005) value the grain in stock and the self-produced-own-consumed grain at average village market prices because they state that the RCRE data for the value of own consumption of grain or grain in stock are biased downwards because these values are calculated till the mid 1990s using grain quota prices.

Due to land and climatic conditions in the Hebei province the dominating cropping system is winter-wheat summer-maize double cropping. So the dominating grain crops in Hebei province are wheat and maize. When using this method also quality differences across households are averaged out. An alternative way to calculate a proxy price per kg of grain to valuate the self produced grain consumption would be to divide the "value of grain in stock (Yuan)" by "the quantity of grain in stock (kg)". However, this was not done here because these variables are just available from 1993 onwards.

Only for grain it is possible to calculate the self-produced consumption because the amount consumed and the amount of consumption that was purchased in the market are provided. For other agricultural products no market purchased amounts are given. So multiplying the difference in amounts between purchased and consumed grain by the approximated value of 1 kg of grain should yield a monetary measure for the consumption of grain that was produced by the household itself. According to Chen and Ravallion (1996) already the re-valuation of grain is an important improvement in the consumption calculation because, especially for rural households, grain is the most important component of consumption. Zhou and Tian (2005) state that around 60% of the grain produced in rural China is still consumed on-farm. Not taking into account the value of consumption from own production would result in an underestimation of the well-being of the household or an overestimation of poverty levels respectively.

Duclos et al. (2008) include the expenditures for nondurable goods and expenditures for housing and a flow of services from household durable goods. They assume that the consumption of housing investments in every period takes place over 20 years and that consumption of durable goods lasts over 7 years. Following these assumptions the expenditures that are related to housing and durable goods will be converted into expenditure flows for the data set at hand. Based on Brandt and Holz (2005 and 2006) and the adjusted CPI values they provide for Chinese Provinces between 1986-2002 deflators are calculated to deflate expenditure values into real prices using 1990 as base year. Brandt and Holz (2006) argue for adjustments of the rural CPI because in defining the consumer price index the Chinese expression for "purchase" (*guomai*) (only monetary spending) is used instead of the Chinese equivalent for "expenses" (*zhichu*) (which would also include self-produced-self-consumed living expenditures). Based on recalculations of the CPI for 1997 they (Brandt and Holz, 2006) figure out that there is a discrepancy between the official CPI and real living expenditures due to exclusion of expenditures for self-produced-self-consumed goods, which are mainly foods and within those cereals.

Ravallion and Chen (2007) use different levels of the rural poverty line in China. First they apply the official poverty line of 300 Yuan (in 1990 prices) per person per year. The second poverty line they use is adjusted to better represent regional differences in living costs. As an average of the regional means this new poverty line can be set on national level for rural areas in China at 850 Yuan per year per person (in 2002 prices) (Ravallion and Chen, 2007). Following Duclos et al. (2008) this poverty line represents a diet of 2100 calorie per day per person (food component) plus per capita expenditures of individuals close to the poverty line for housing and durable goods (non food component). This nationally averaged poverty line of 850 Yuan is deflated to 1990 prices using the price deflator as described before and so results in a (rounded) poverty line of 498 Yuan per person per year which is used here for the calculation of the poverty indices. This procedure of applying the same, CPI adjusted, poverty line for assessing poverty development over time has the advantage that a fixed bundle of goods is used as basis of comparison, but the poverty calculations might be affected by changes in the consumption bundle due to institutional changes or changes in relative prices (Meng et al., 2005).

In *Table 3* some common indices for measuring poverty are presented for rural Hebei based on the RCRE data. First the headcount index (H) is calculated, which gives the percentage of people of the (underlying) population that live in households with per capita consumption expenditures below the poverty line. Second the mean distance below the poverty line as a proportion of the poverty line is displayed by the poverty gap index (PG). And thirdly the squared poverty gap index (SPG) that provides a measure of inequality amongst the poor by weighting the individual poverty gaps by the gaps themselves and puts more weight on those observations far below the poverty line (Foster et al., 1984).

Table 3: Poverty in rural areas of Hebei province, 1986 - 2002

Poverty measures (%)									
Year	**Headcount Index**			**Poverty Gap Ratio**			**Squared Poverty Gap**		
	Total sample	Full-time	Part-time	Total sample	Full-time	Part-time	Total sample	Full-time	Part-time
1986	17.33	-	-	2.38	-	-	1.10	-	-
1987	14.31	-	-	1.53	-	-	0.64	-	-
1988	21.85	-	-	3.56	-	-	1.73	-	-
1989	35.22	-	-	5.86	-	-	2.86	-	-
1990	32.39	-	-	5.48	-	-	2.67	-	-
1991	28.63	-	-	4.35	-	-	2.06	-	-
1993	19.40	19.68	15.39	2.48	2.58	0.72	1.10	1.14	0.19
1995	9.04	9.84	0.00	0.98	1.06	0.00	0.43	0.47	0.00
1996	8.48	9.24	0.00	0.77	0.84	0.00	0.28	0.31	0.00
1997	9.42	9.84	7.14	1.24	1.14	3.62	0.60	0.45	3.50
1998	3.77	3.98	2.70	0.45	0.30	2.66	0.27	0.10	2.63
1999	5.27	5.01	7.84	1.05	0.72	4.18	0.76	0.44	3.88
2000	4.71	4.57	3.92	0.47	0.45	0.23	0.18	0.18	0.06
2001	4.14	4.32	0.00	0.47	0.46	0.00	0.21	0.20	0.00
2002	3.01	3.27	0.00	0.33	0.37	0.00	0.13	0.15	0.00

Notes: Poverty line 498 Yuan per capita expenditures in 1990 prices, following Ravallion and Chen (2007) and using own deflators based on the consumer price index (CPI) for rural Hebei.
N differs for the sub samples because household's labor occupation might change between years.

Source: Own computations based on RCRE survey data for Hebei, 1986-2002, N=531 (total sample).

Poverty rose as expressed by the presented measures from 1987 to 1989 (*Table 3*). At this time there has been some political turbulence at national level with probable economic effects that also affected the well-being of the population. Again there is a rise in the poverty levels from 1996 to 1997, a time of overall financial and economic crisis in Asia. Those findings are in line with the results of Ravallion and Chen (2007) and Benjamin et al. (2005). The drop from 1997 to 1998 is rather large even in comparison to the results of Ravallion and Chen (2007). This can be explained either by discontinuities in the data used here or as a problem stemming from the valuation method used to value the self-produced consumption of grain.

Dividing the overall sample in two sub samples based on the degree of non-farm activities shows that even if poverty is expected to be less severe among households that are involved in non-farm activities still for some years, 1997, 1998 and 1999, they seem to be poorer than full-time farm households.

Table 4 shows the estimations for the chronic and transient poverty component with respect to per capita consumption for the total sample. Those results are derived by using the EDE approach.

Table 4: Transient and chronic poverty applying the EDE approach to RCRE data for Hebei province, 1986-2002

Components	without bias corrections	with bias corrections	
		analytical	bootstrap
Average gap $\Gamma_1(g)$	0.021	0.021	0.021
	(0.002)	(0.002)	(0.002)
Cost of inequality between households $C_\alpha(\gamma_\alpha)$	0.03	0.028	0.027
	(0.003)	(0.002)	(0.002)
Transient poverty (cost of inequality within households)	0.022	0.025	0.026
	(0.001)	(0.001)	(0.001)
Chronic poverty $\Gamma_\alpha^T(g)$	0.052	0.049	0.048
	(0.004)	(0.004)	(0.004)
Total poverty $\Gamma_\alpha(g)$	0.074	0.074	0.074
	(0.005)	(0.005)	(0.005)

Note: Asymptotic standard errors in parentheses.
The analytical and bootstrap estimation results refer to calculations using estimators that correct for a potential statistical bias that could occur if only a small number of time observations are available.

Source: Own computations based on RCRE survey data for Hebei, 1986-2002, N=531.

The total poverty over the period of 1986 to 2002 is estimated to be 0.074 with $\alpha = 2$, whereas the average poverty gap (α=1) is 0.021. Considering the bias corrected values, around 66% of this estimated poverty can be devoted to the component of chronic poverty. So, transient poverty accounts for around one third of the overall poverty level of the analyzed rural households. This means that a social decision or policy maker that wants to remove intra-individual inequality in ill-fare status would be willing to accept the equivalent of an increase of around 33% in the total poverty gap. Because the chronic component is found to be larger than the transient component of poverty policies that are intended to improve the well-being of people should concentrate on targeting and improving the situation of the chronic poor first. But as Li et al. (2007) aruge, this consumption oriented measure might suffer from the risk, that it underestimates the extend of poverty because savings could be used in periods of lower income to fund the consumption. So, Li et al. (2007) find that income based measure result in higher estimates for the share of transient poverty. The authors also confirm that the ratio between the chronic and transient component strongly depends on the chosen poverty line. In their study they find that, for low poverty lines the share of transient poverty as share of total poverty is relatively higher than the share of transient poverty if higher poverty lines are defined.

Using the JR approach and setting $\alpha = 2$ provides totally different results, as 100% of the estimated poverty would be devoted to transient poverty (*Table 5*). In comparison, Jalan and Ravallion (1998) state in their study chronic poverty rates between around 20 up to nearly 60%.

Table 5: Transient and chronic poverty applying the approach of Jalan and Ravallion to RCRE data for Hebei province, 1986-2002, $\alpha = 2$

Components	without bias corrections	with bias corrections	
		analytical	**bootstrap**
Transient	0.005	0.005	0.005
	(0.001)	(0.000)	(0.000)
Chronic	0.000	0.000	0.000
	(0.000)	(0.000)	(0.000)
Total	0.005	0.005	0.005
	(0.001)	(0.001)	(0.001)

Note: Asymptotic standard errors in parentheses.
Source: Own computations based on RCRE survey data for Hebei, 1986-2002, N=531.

To some part this shift in the ratio of transient to chronic poverty can be explained by some limitations in the underlying data set as like the mentioned non-availability of weights. But as such, this higher ratio of transient poverty when applying the JR approach to data for rural China is also confirmed by the comparison of the JR and EDE approaches in Duclos et al. (2008) and Muyanga (2008).

In the following part, differences in poverty elasticities that can be associated with either regional effects, human capital measured using levels of education achieved by the household head or effects from differences in labor time allocation of households are evaluated. This assessment provides a basis for a better understanding of the reasons behind poverty. As Rigg (2006) emphasizes the link between the holding of farm land and poverty became weaker during the transition of many societies that have been dominated by the agricultural sector. So, household characteristics less related to land holding might be helpful for the explanation of differences in poverty characteristics between the assessed households, even though only information about rural households is available.

First the question is which marginal impact the regional variable (village) has on poverty, poverty inequality and the elasticity of poverty with respect to inequality especially comparing the within and between components of the marginal impact on inequality (MII), the marginal impact on poverty (MIP), and the elasticity of poverty with respect to inequality (ELS). Secondly, the same numbers are calculated using a variable representing human capital: education of household head. And as a third part the marginal impacts and associated elasticities are assessed with respect to an economic variable: labor occupation of the household. Due to the actuality of results with respect to the time of analysis only the results of the elasticity and marginal impact analysis for 2002 are presented here.

The S-Gini index is changed by 1% in the calculations. The poverty line is set at the 498 Yuan for per capita expenditures of the household in 1990 prices. α is set to 0 for the headcount index and $\alpha = 1$ to calculate the estimates related to the average poverty gap index. Because the number of residents living in the household is used as a weighting factor the results are computed at individual level.

Table 6: Elasticity of poverty with respect to within- and between equality for "village"

		ρ = 2			
		α = 0		α = 1	
Group g	MII	MIP	ELS	MIP	ELS
Village 1	0.000274	0.000351	7.464437	0.000055	12.553526
Village 2	0.000273	0.000483	10.352505	0.000061	14.065746
Village 3	0.000359	0.000357	5.796812	0.000066	11.447813
Village 4	0.000273	0.000303	6.476967	0.000000	0.000000
Village 5	0.000360	0.000245	3.963944	0.000014	2.499613
Village 6	0.000334	0.000569	9.946538	0.000120	22.440006
Within	0.001873	0.002307	7.190463	0.000316	10.561295
Between	0.000228	0.000030	0.761016	0.000004	1.160638
Whole sample	0.002083	0.002808	7.869483	0.000319	9.606565

Notes: MII: marginal impact on inequality, $\partial I(\rho)/\partial()$

MIP: marginal impact on poverty, $\partial P(z;\alpha)/\partial()$

ELS: elasticity of poverty with respect to inequality, $\varepsilon_0(z;\alpha;\rho)$

Source: Own computations based on RCRE survey data for Hebei, 2002, N=531.

Table 7: Elasticity of poverty with respect to within- and between equality for "education household head"

		ρ = 2			
		α = 0		α = 1	
Group g	MII	MIP	ELS	MIP	ELS
Illiterate	0.000058	0.000120	11.9877283	0.000051	54.727737
Elementary graduate	0.000616	0.000930	8.815389	0.000152	15.440973
Secondary graduate	0.001174	0.001438	7.152406	0.000098	5.240461
High school or above	0.000222	0.000261	6.869705	0.000000	0.000000
Within	0.002069	0.002749	7.753213	0.000301	9.109984
Between	0.000013	0.000021	9.243858	0.000010	48.251774
Whole sample	0.002083	0.002808	7.869483	0.000319	9.606565

Notes and Source: Same as in Table 6.

Table 8: Elasticity of poverty with respect to within- and between equality for "household time allocation"

		$\rho = 2$			
		$\alpha = 0$		$\alpha = 1$	
Group g	MII	MIP	ELS	MIP	ELS
Full-time agriculture	0.000776	0.000738	5.547792	0.000055	4.434353
Mainly agriculture	0.000963	0.001536	9.311152	0.000242	15.763857
Mainly non-agriculture	0.000098	0.000048	2.874173	0.000000	0.000000
Full-time non-agriculture	0.000098	0.000033	5.169385	0.000000	0.000000
Others	0.000097	0.000102	6.106178	0.000012	7.554927
Within	0.001972	0.002457	7.272657	0.000309	9.816250
Between	0.000099	0.000056	3.291541	0.000006	3.550741
Whole sample	0.002083	0.002808	7.869483	0.000319	9.606565

Notes and source: Same as in Table 6.

The sign and the size of the elasticities presented in *Tables 6, 7* and *8* are highly sensitive to the choice of the absolute value of the poverty line and of the poverty aversion parameter (Araar and Duclos, 2007a). Therefore the interpretation focuses on relative differences between specific values of the estimated elasticities. Because the values for both the marginal impacts on poverty and the elasticity of poverty with respect to inequality are always positive, poverty increases with an increase in inequality.

The same poverty and poverty aversion parameters are applied in the estimations to all subgroups, therefore the heterogeneity in the estimates for the marginal impacts and the elasticities across the lines in *Tables 6, 7* and *8*, or in other words the variability in the distributive impacts, stems from differences in the distributions of well-being of the initial subgroups (Araar and Duclos, 2007a).

For the underlying data set the within-group estimates for the elasticity of poverty with respect to inequality are numerically higher than the between-group estimates for the grouping by villages and by labor occupations. This indicates that for the explanation of poverty inequality the inequality component stemming from dispersions and inequality changes within those specific groups is more important than the component that is related to between group differences. This means that policy measures that are designed to reduce within-group inequality should yield higher returns, in the sense of a more equalized well-being, than policies that focus on the reduction of between-group inequality. For the case of different locations the result that village effects matter in explaining inequality differences among the rural population is in line with the findings of Benjamin et al. (2005).

The results with respect to grouping the observations by the school grade achieved by the household head differ for the elasticity estimates. They are numerically higher for the between group effect. From this finding it follows that policies that aim to reduce between-group inequality would seem to be more effective than policies that concentrate on reducing within-group inequality, if inequality in well-being is assessed with respect to human capital.

When comparing different labor occupation groups the same pattern as for the village grouping is observed. Poverty inequality is mainly related to within group differences, even if the ratio of the two effects is smaller here than in the comparison based on the grouping by villages. But it is worth to mention that the MII for individuals living in households which are mainly or full-time non-agricultural households is lower than for those who are full-time or mainly involved in agriculture (*Table 8*). So inequality is more prevalent in the groups of households being full-time or mainly agriculture producers.

De Janvry et al. (2005) find that the effect of off-farm income on absolute poverty reduction is stronger than the effect of farm income. An intuitive next step of analysis would be to figure out the determinants of poverty and respective inequality by exploiting the richness of information of the available panel data set by estimating multivariate regression models to assess the determinants of both poverty components; chronic and transient (Li et al., 2007). This was not done here, because the data set provided does not contain a sufficient amount of independent variables on regional, household and individual scale. Especially variables related to individual characteristics like age or gender of the household head but also the educational level attained by every household member are not available.

6.2 Income decomposition

6.2.1 Decomposition of income for 1986 and 2002

More than 90% of all studied RCRE households earned income from agricultural production in 2002. As can be seen from columns 4 and 7 in *Table 9* that show the percentage of households that derive income from the respective source. *Table 9* also reveals that rural households derived around 46% of their income from agricultural production in 1986. Over the observation period this share dropped by around 50% and in 2002 only 24% of household income stem from agricultural production income. Still more than 90% of all studied households earn income from agricultural production. Income from grain contributes the biggest share to total income. But especially wage income closed the gap and now also contributes around 20% to total income whereby local wage income (6%) became less important relative to income earned by migrant workers (14%). The highest annual increases in the share of total income are found for income from transportation family business (12%) and from fruits production (14%). Only the income from agricultural sideline activities declines absolutely. One should not interpret the calculated per annum growth as shown in *Table 9* as a linear growth trend. There are fluctuations in the contribution of the different income components to the total income of households, e.g. income from grain production is influenced by variations in grain output and prices.

Benjamin et al. (2005) reported absolute declines also for agricultural production and grain cropping. The difference between their findings and the results here can be explained by the difference in provinces analyzed, the use of different base years and the different time span. Especially the last factor might lead to a lower influence of strong price fluctuations in some years on the development of agricultural income over the whole period from 1986 to 2002.

Table 9: Composition of income in 1986 compared to 2002

	1986			2002			
	Mean	Share	%>0	Mean	Share	%>0	Growth
Total Income	1024	1.000	1.000	2035	1.000	1.000	0.043
Agricultural income	475	0.464	0.987	488	0.240	0.938	0.002
Grain income	375	0.366	0.985	414	0.203	0.936	0.006
Cash crop income	97	0.095	0.960	45	0.022	0.426	0.012
Fruits, tea and silkworm cocoon	3	0.003	0.130	29	0.014	0.043	0.142
Agricultural sidelines income	107	0.104	0.889	98	0.048	0.458	-0.005
Forest products	15	0.015	0.158	36	0.018	0.141	0.055
Livestock	32	0.031	0.823	62	0.030	0.341	0.041
Aquaculture	0	0.000	0.011	0	0.000	0.000	0.000
Other family businesses income	137	0.134	0.315	470	0.231	0.360	0.077
Household industry	13	0.013	0.035	0	0.000	0.000	0.000
Construction	19	0.019	0.064	20	0.010	0.017	0.003
Transportation	26	0.025	0.021	172	0.085	0.064	0.118
Retailing, restaurants, and other services	58	0.057	0.077	172	0.085	0.149	0.068
Others	20	0.020	0.154	106	0.052	0.162	0.104
Wage income	181	0.177	0.663	406	0.200	0.591	0.050
Local wage income	99	0.097	0.431	112	0.055	0.269	0.008
Temporary migrant	82	0.080	0.362	294	0.144	0.363	0.080
Local government employment	24	0.023	0.079	70	0.034	0.056	0.067
Family transfers	25	0.024	0.512	45	0.022	0.550	0.037
Government transfers	6	0.006	1.000	9	0.004	0.936	0.025
Other income	11	0.011	0.081	31	0.015	0.064	0.065

Note: All income means are in 1990 prices.
Source: Own computations based on RCRE survey data for Hebei, 1986 and 2002, N=531.

The income shares presented in *Tables 9* and *10* do not sum up to 100%. This is due to the fact that only those income variables that provided the same information in 1986 and 2002 have been analyzed here. There are changes in the level of aggregation of information. Some income categories are not recorded anymore in 2002 such as income from township and village enterprises or from economic cooperatives. New categories that were not considered in 1986 are for example income from shareholding or private enterprises.

6.2.2 Inequality in income

The results of decomposing different sources of household per capita income in 1990 prices based on the coefficient of variation are presented in *Table 10*. Some income sources are slightly negatively correlated to total per capita household income. If the concentration indices of these income sources are weighted by their share in overall income it follows that these sources of income in absolute terms neither decrease nor increase per capita household income inequality among the sample population.

Based on the concentration index all sources of income from farm households' agricultural production reduce income inequality because the concentration index is smaller than one. The largest contribution from agricultural production to income inequality stems from grain production income with a share of 19% and 28% of inequality stemming from this source in 1986 and 2002 respectively.

Income earned from transportation business increases income inequality in both analyzed years. In 2002 it contributes around 63% to total per capita income inequality among households. By this it is the source of income contributing relatively strongest to inequality. Because only around 6% of households are involved in this business in 2002 the overall absolute contribution from this source to income inequality in the analyzed villages should not be too high. Besides transportation, only income from household construction business has a relative concentration coefficient larger than one ($c_i = 1.04$) and by this has an increasing effect on total inequality. Income from operating a restaurant is of lower importance in explaining income inequality among the analyzed households in 2002 than it was in 1986. This is mainly due to the lower variation of this income source.

Table 10: Income decomposition by coefficient of variation, 1986 and 2002

	1986						2002					
	w_i	CV_i	r_i	CV_i/CV	c_i^a	w_i*c_i	w_i	CV_i	r_i	CV_i/CV	c_i^a	w_i*c_i
Total Income	1.000	71.32	1.00	1.00	1.00	1.00	1.000	72.57	1.00	1.00	1.00	1.00
Agricultural income	0.464	46.33	0.27	0.65	0.18	0.08	0.240	72.96	0.25	1.01	0.26	0.06
Grain income	0.366	44.51	0.31	0.62	0.19	0.07	0.203	69.45	0.29	0.96	0.28	0.06
Cash crop income	0.036	94.58	0.11	1.33	0.15	0.01	0.022	208.27	0.07	2.87	0.19	0.00
Fruits, tea and silkworm cocoon	0.003	736.15	-0.04	10.32	-0.39	-0.00	0.014	550.65	0.01	7.59	0.04	0.00
Agricultural sidelines	0.104	90.55	0.21	1.27	0.26	0.03	0.048	190.15	-0.04	2.62	-0.10	0.00
Forest products	0.015	266.71	-0.16	3.74	-0.60	-0.01	0.018	273.17	-0.07	3.76	-0.27	0.00
Livestock	0.031	104.30	0.27	1.46	0.40	0.01	0.030	273.47	0.00	3.77	-0.01	0.00
Aquaculture	0.000	1482.30	0.02	20.78	0.42	0.00	0.000	0.00			0.00	0.00
Other family businesses	0.134	458.72	0.83	6.43	5.32	0.71	0.231	291.76	0.75	4.02	3.00	0.69
Household industry	0.013	714.31	0.15	10.02	1.49	0.02	0.000	0.00			0.00	0.00
Construction	0.019	555.23	0.07	7.79	0.58	0.01	0.010	1074.62	0.07	14.81	1.04	0.01
Transportation	0.025	956.06	0.36	13.41	4.82	0.12	0.085	725.043	0.74	9.99	7.43	0.63
Retailing, restaurants, other services	0.057	962.81	0.72	13.50	9.70	0.55	0.085	327.02	0.16	4.51	0.73	0.06
Other family business income	0.020	352.09	0.06	4.94	0.28	0.01	0.052	282.35	-0.04	3.89	-0.16	-0.01

Table 10 continued

Wage income	0.177	140.12	0.32	1.96	0.63	0.11	0.200	137.36	0.09	1.89	0.16	0.03
Local wage income	0.097	203.81	0.22	2.86	0.63	0.06	0.055	315.35	-0.04	4.35	-0.17	-0.01
Temporary migrant	0.080	220.53	0.20	3.09	0.62	0.05	0.144	168.46	0.13	2.32	0.29	0.04
Local government employment	0.023	379.43	0.06	5.32	0.31	0.01	0.034	506.97	0.08	6.99	0.57	0.02
Family transfers	0.024	267.54	0.12	3.75	0.46	0.01	0.022	488.51	0.08	6.73	0.50	0.01
Government transfers	0.006	343.00	0.03	4.81	0.14	0.01	0.004	737.97	-0.02	10.17	-0.22	0.00
Other income	0.011	673.17	0.21	9.44	1.97	0.02	0.015	471.01	-0.12	6.49	-0.80	-0.01

Note: [a] $c_i = r_i * CV_i / CV$

Source: Own computations based on RCRE survey data for Hebei, 1986-2002, N=531.

The comparison of the estimated contributions of variations in different income sources between 1986 and 2002 to overall income variation based on the Shorrocks decomposition is presented in *Table 11*. Columns (1) and (4) show the OLS estimates for the regression of household per capita income by source on total per capita income. To control for potential measurement error in income, per capita income is instrumented by the deflated per capita consumption expenditures in columns (2) and (5). In columns (3) and (6) also two step least squares estimates with per capita expenditures as instrument are presented but with village dummies as additional exogenous regressors to control for location effects on income inequality (Village 2 is the omitted category).

A standard Hausman test using per capita total expenditures as instrumental variable test is performed to compare estimates in column (1) with those in (2) and estimates of column (4) with those in (5) H_0: difference in coefficients OLS and 2SLS are not systematic. Based on the Hausman test the two stage least squares estimator (2SLS) is preferred over the ordinary least squares estimator (OLS).

The strength of the instrument variable "total per capita expenditures" is assessed applying the tests of Stock and Yogo (Cameron and Trivedi, 2009). For the instrument variable used here the null hypothesis that "total per capita expenditures" is a weak instrument can be rejected.

Also the results from the Shorrocks decomposition show that income from agriculture is in 2002 less important in explaining inequality among households in Hebei province than it was in 1986.

For 1986 the disequalizing effect of agricultural income (around 10%) is lower then it's share in total income (around 46%). Even with the decline in the absolute share of agricultural income of total income this holds. Non-farm family businesses contributed in 1986 and 2002 around 68% to the inequality in households' total income. Because this income source has only a share in total income of around 13% in 1986 and 36% in 2002 it clearly contributes over proportionally to income inequality. Whereas in 1986 variations in the income from retailing and other sources had the highest contribution to income inequality this role was taken over in 2002 by variations in income from transportation (around 80% if excluding the village dummies). The disequalizing effect of income from household transportation business is lower when village effects are controlled for, around 63%, and that is the same result as found when using the decomposition based on the coefficient of variation. Wage income is not contributing much to income inequality for the data set at hand in the years 1986 to 2002. This might be explained by either relative equal wages earned by the rural households because of working in same occupations or equal amounts of labor devoted to wage earning or a combination of both effects.

The 2SLS estimates including village dummies to control for location effects are more different from the 2SLS estimation without dummies for 1986 than for 2002. So in 1986 a higher part of households' income inequality seems to stem from inequality between villages or regions. In other words the across village effect is less relevant in explaining inequality in rural households income in Hebei in 2002 than in 1986. Also Benjamin et al. (2005) confirm that inequality is higher among neighboring households in the same village than between households in different locations. Because no further village level information are available it cannot be assessed which differences in village institutions could explain the share of income inequality that is related to village effects.

Table 11: Shorrocks income decomposition, 1986 and 2002

	1986			**2002**		
	OLS	2SLS	2SLS	OLS	2SLS	2SLS
	(1)	(2)	(3)	(4)	(5)	(6)
Village dummies?	No	No	Yes	No	No	Yes
Agricultural income	0.082	0.122 [a]	0.103	0.061	0.053	0.100
Grain income	0.070	0.098 [a]	0.087	0.057	0.058	0.093
Cash crop income	0.014	0.025	0.018	0.004	-0.003 [a]	0.008
Fruits, tea and silkworm cocoon	-0.001	-0.001	-0.002	0.001	-0.002	-0.001
Agricultural sidelines	0.027	0.020	0.031	-0.005	-0.008	-0.005
Forest products	-0.009	-0.014 [a]	-0.014	-0.005	-0.009	-0.010
Livestock	0.036	0.034	0.046	0.000	0.001	0.005
Aquaculture	0.000	0.000	0.000	[b]		
Other family businesses	0.711	0.713	0.680	0.693	0.843 [a]	0.672
Household industry	0.019	0.007 [a]	0.014	[b]		
Construction	0.011	-0.007 [a]	-0.001	0.010	0.003	0.004
Transportation	0.124	0.133	0.119	0.629	0.795 [a]	0.637
Retailing, restaurants, and other services	0.552	0.574	0.542	0.062	0.044 [a]	0.038
Other family business income	0.006	0.006	0.005	-0.008	0.001 [a]	-0.008
Wage income	0.110	0.087 [a]	0.109	0.033	0.010	0.000
Local wage income	0.060	0.039 [a]	0.051	-0.010	-0.022	-0.042

Table 11 continued						
Temporary migrant	0.050	0.049	0.059	0.042	0.032	0.042
Local government employment	0.007	0.005	0.013	0.020	-0.006 [a]	-0.010
Family transfers	0.011	0.017	0.013	0.011	0.046 [a]	0.039
Government transfers	0.001	0.000	0.001	-0.001	-0.001	-0.001
Other income	0.022	0.011	0.015	-0.012	-0.009	-0.012

Notes: The table shows the decomposition of income following Shorrocks (1983) and Benjamin et al. (2005).
a indicates where the OLS and 2SLS coefficients are significantly different (using a standard Hausman test) and thus the 2SLS coefficients are to be preferred.
b variable dropped during the estimation.

Source: Own computations based on RCRE survey data for Hebei, 1986-2002, N=531.

It seems plausible to assume that with a rising development of the Chinese economy the importance of the tertiary or service sector for total income but also for differences in income equality will increase. Therefore comparison of the findings above with the most recent income figures (2008 and 2009) for the sample households could provide a closer insight in the changes in the income structure for rural Chinese households over the last 20 years. These data are not available to the author.

6.2.3 Empirical Lorenz Curves

The comparison of the normalized Lorenz Curves for per capita income between 1986 and 2002 (*Figure 8*) reveals that the curve for 2002 is always outside of the one for 1986. This means that for all measures of inequality that would be applied the distribution of household per capita income is more unequal in 2002 than it was in 1986. This is in line with the results of Benjamin et al. (2005).

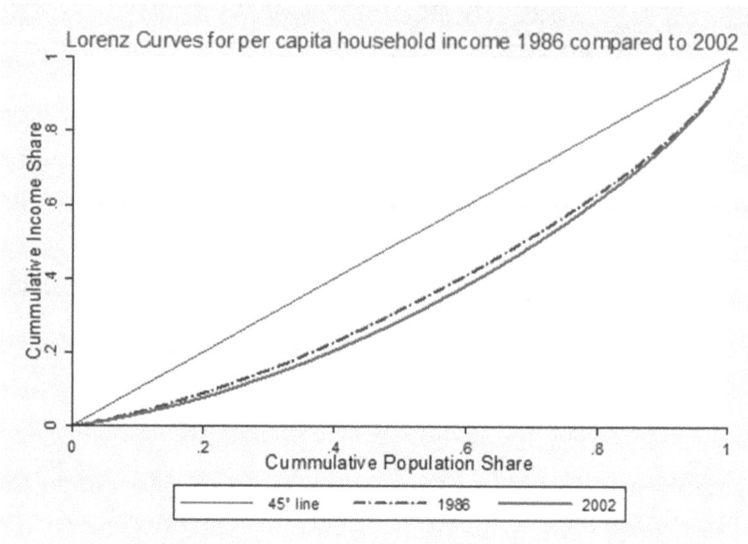

Source: Own computations based on RCRE survey data for Hebei, 1986-2002, N=531.

Figure 8: Lorenz curves for per capita household income 1986 compared to 2002

From the generalized Lorenz Curves (*Figure 9*) one can see that the curve for 2002 lies above the one for 1986. Because this is the case for all population shares one can say that the income distribution from 2002 dominates the one for 1986.

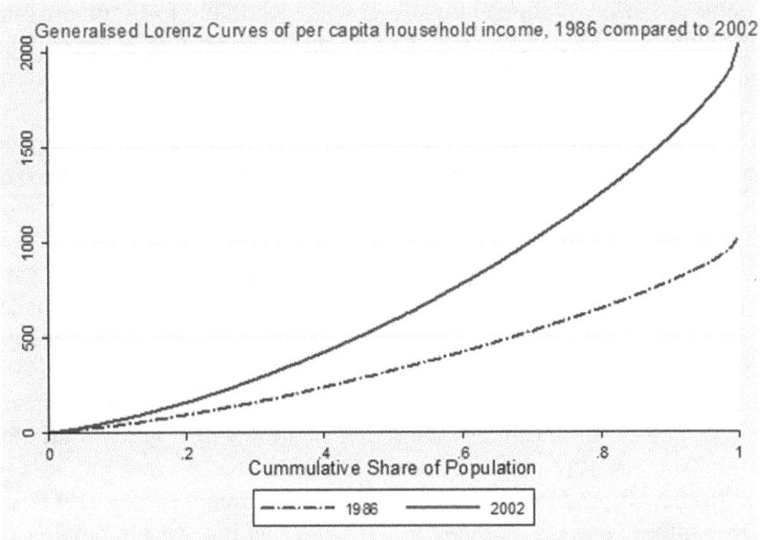

Source: Own computations based on RCRE survey data for Hebei, 1986-2002, N=531.

Figure 9: Generalized Lorenz Curves of per capita household income, 1986 to 2002

6.3 Summary

In this chapter different poverty indices are calculated based on household expenditures and applying an adjusted poverty line of 498 Yuan per person and year in 1990 prices. To reflect the relative high share of self produced and own consumed agricultural products, especially in the case of grain, subsistence consumption is considered in the expenditures. This procedure reduces the risk of overestimating poverty in rural areas that are dominated by subsistence farms. Also long term expenditures for housing and non-durable goods are included in the analysis by calculating deflated expenditure streams for those items.

Besides a slight increase in poverty during 1988 and 1990 poverty declined during the period 1986 to 2002. Measures to further lower poverty rates have to be designed to best address the causes of poverty. Therefore it is helpful to decompose poverty in its chronic and transient component. Two approaches to do this are discussed in this chapter. The application of the EDE approach to the data for Hebei yields that the major part of overall poverty is explained as chronic poverty. In addition the assessment of differences in poverty elasticities within or between different population sub-groups (according to location of the village and labor time allocation of the household) indicates that poverty inequality within a specific subgroup is more important in explaining overall poverty inequality than the between group inequality component. The opposite result is found for the assessment of poverty elasticities by distinguishing population sub-groups according to the education achieved by the household head. This indicates that with respect to human capital policies which are designed to reduce poverty should focus on between group inequalities.

The decomposition of households' income using the coefficient of variation and Shorrocks decomposition methods show that agricultural income made up a lower share in total income in 2002 than in 1986 but was also less relevant in explaining income inequality among households. The share of wage income increased, especially the wage income from working outside the own village/ county. Migratory income shows the fourth highest annual growth rate (8%) of all income sources over the period 1986 to 2002. The per year growth rates of income from fruit production (14%), income from transportation (12%) and income from other family businesses (10%) are higher but less households receive income from those sources than from migratory wage income. It is also worth to mention that the share of households that earn migratory income is constant and is in both years 36%. The biggest contribution to income inequality between the assessed rural households stems from inequality in non-farm family businesses. The inclusion of dummy variables that control for village effects results in less relevance of the geographical location in explaining income inequality in 2002 than in 1986.

From the comparison of the distribution of household income using Lorenz Curves it is found that per capita household income was less equal distributed in 2002 than in 1986 and that this is the case for all population shares.

7 Empirical specifications and econometric testing of separability, agricultural household and farm structure persistence models

In the first part of this chapter it is tested if farm households' decisions about the demand and supply of labor are separable from each other for the whole sample but also for sub-samples that only include part- or full-time farm households respectively. The choice of variables to explain households' labor market participation and their impact on the probability to belong to one of the distinct labor market regimes are explained and assessed in section 7.2. Section 7.3 contains the chosen variables set for the assessment of farm structure persistence and the respective regression results.

7.1 Separability of households' labor demand and supply decisions

7.1.1 Variable set for testing separability

Reasonable and accurate information about wage rates and prices are crucial to the analysis of households' labor allocation decision (Bowlus and Sicular, 2003, see also Sikei et al., 2009). Bowlus and Sicular (2003) do not have such accurate data on prices and only a small amount of households in their sample participate in off-farm work. Because wage rates are not available for self-employed labor (Sumner and Frazao, 1989), Bowlus and Sicular (2003) assume that prices for goods and wage rates for the same quality of labor are identical at the same location at one point in time. Consequently, they use year, village and the dummy out of the product year*village to capture price and wage effects on households' labor demand. In addition they argue that the control for unobserved heterogeneity on household level in the fixed-effects regression captures differences in households' labor quality. Following this argumentation and because there are no household or village level wage rates provided in the RCRE data set there will be no wage variable included in the fixed-effects estimation. Instead, time, location as well as the product of time*location will be included. Alternatively Kuiper (2005) calculated an average wage rate from the data available from her cross section analysis. However, this option was not feasible in the recent analysis because of a lack of the necessary data.

For the structural components used in the study at hand the number of female laborers is calculated as the difference between the total number of household laborers and the number of male laborers. Because the data set does not contain variables about the number of children and elderly persons living in the household, the number of dependents is approximated as the difference between the number of persons living in the household (household size) and the total number of laborers in the household. To do so, it is assumed (1) that the number of laborers is smaller than the number of persons living in the household and (2) that all persons that are non-laborers are dependents. The first condition holds for the underlying data set because there is no observation where the number of laborers in the household is larger than the household size. Unfortunately, the lack of original data about numbers of children and elderly persons hampers the identification of the core reasons for changes in the number of laborers or the household size as was demonstrated by Bowlus and Sicular (2003) or Kuiper (2005). In their analysis, it is possible to track the individual household members and identify where changes in the labor force of the household occur as for example a child entering the labor force or an older household member going to retirement.

Kuiper (2005) includes variables related to farming technologies such as the prices for fertilizer and herbicides in the empirical model because she argues that both of them could be substitutes for labor in agricultural production. However, there is no substitution effect between human labor and urea in agricultural production in the study region (Böber and Zeller, 2009). An explanation for this might be that farming in Hebei province was only to a small degree mechanized in the assessed period (1995 to 2002). Especially the application of fertilizer is done by hand (Böber, 2008 and 2009). Therefore a higher amount of urea fertilizer applied would require more labor. In addition to this, the application of more fertilizer results in higher yields. Higher yields would again require more labor for harvesting if farming is not much mechanized. Heady (1963) argues the opposite way in the case of the highly mechanized agricultural production in the United States. Because also no village level price information about fertilizers is available no fertilizer technology variable is included in the model. As another difference to Kuiper (2005) and Bowlus and Sicular (2003) also no variable indicating the amount of irrigated land can be included because that information is not available from the RCRE data for the period 1995-2002.

From 2003 onwards the RCRE data set clearly indicates which person is the household head. Up to 2002 education and age information are only provided for the main laborer of the household. For the years until 2000 the age of the main laborer of the household is not provided in years, but as a multinomial variable (see also Chen et al., 2003). Therefore the variable "age of main laborer given in years" for 2001 and 2002 is also converted into the same multinomial variable: 1: up to 30 years old, 2: 31-40 years old, 3: 41-50 years old, 4: 51-60 years old, 5: 61 years or older. It is not possible to change the multinomial variable for the age of the main laborer into years of age because there are changes in the person that is considered as main laborer that are evident e.g. in the case of household with the id 1301014 for which the age of main laborer is stated in 2000 as being in the range between 51 and 60 years (value 4 for the multinomial variable) but is given with 25 years in 2001 (which would be value 1 for the multinomial variable). The highest level of education of the main laborer is stated as: 1 if the main laborer is illiterate, 2 for elementary school graduates, 3 in case of completion of secondary school and 4 if the main laborer earned a high school degree or above. According to Benjamin (1992) the education of the household head is likely to have an impact on the management of the family farm household. For both variables dummies representing the respective classification will be included in the estimations.

Glauben et al. (2008) argue that membership in the communist party influences the labor allocation decisions of rural households in China. Therefore a dummy variable capturing household member's association with the Chinese Communist Party (CCP) is included in the model. Because the area of land allocated to the household is quite fragmented in the study region, as can be seen from the summary statistics in *Table 12*, the number of plots is included in the variables representing observable farm characteristics. If available farm land is quite fragmented and some of the plots are located further away from the household's place of living then it is assumed that more labor (time) is required to reach these fields and so more of the household's labor available will be devoted to agricultural production.

Because there are no plot level variables available that allow controlling for the quality of arable land or other environmental variables that provide information about cropping conditions those effects are assumed to be included in the village dummy variables.

The number of labor days used for agricultural production is the dependent variable in the regressions to test for separability. This variable contains the total input of labor in days that the household devotes to agricultural crop production. For the years 1995-2002 no distinction between different types of human labor (e.g. male vs. female or with respect to age) is possible because the RCRE labor input data have been aggregated on household level. Therefore the discussion regarding different levels of efficiency of different kinds of labor as in Bowlus and Sicular (2003) and an assessment to how far the regression estimates are biased due to this limitation in substitutability among different labor inputs is not possible. Households are sometimes active in crop and animal production, and for around 2.3% of the observations labor input in husbandry is even larger than in cropping. Therefore, the whole amount of labor in agricultural production is considered here as dependent not as in Bowlus and Sicular (2003) only the amount of labor days for crop cultivation. To control for the effect of animal production a dummy variable is included in the regression that equals 1 if the household is mainly engaged in husbandry or is zero otherwise. Another alternative to control for the effect of non-crop agricultural production on households' labor decisions is to include the share of income from non-cropping agricultural production.

The following *Table 12* provides the variables used to test for separability of households' labor demand and supply, with the summary statistics for the full sample of 4,231 observations for the years 1995 to 2002 (excluding 1997 due to duplicities in the data for 1996 and 1997).

Table 12: Variables and their summary statistics used for modeling separability in labor demand and supply

Household characteristics	Variable	Mean	SD	Min.	Max.
Log of hh size [persons]	LN_HHSIZE	4.19	1.518	1	13
Share of females among family laborers	FEM_LAB	0.46	0.223	0	1
Share of dependents	DEPENDENTS	0.60	0.221	0	1
Age of hh head (up to 30 yrs old) [1/0]	AGEMAINLAB_1	0.05	0.217	0	1
Age of hh head (31-40 yrs old) [1/0]	AGEMAINLAB_2	0.23	0.418	0	1
Age of hh head (41-50 yrs old) [1/0]	AGEMAINLAB_3	0.24	0.425	0	1
Age of hh head (51-60 yrs old) [1/0]	AGEMAINLAB_4	0.12	0.323	0	1
Age of hh head (60 yrs or older) [1/0]	AGEMAINLAB_5	0.06	0.240	0	1
Educational level attained by hh head (1=illiterate) [1/0]	EDUMAINLAB_1	0.05	0.221	0	1
Educational level attained by hh head (2=elementary school graduate) [1/0]	EDUMAINLAB_2	0.38	0.485	0	1
Educational level attained by hh head (3=secondary school graduate) [1/0]	EDUMAINLAB_3	0.45	0.498	0	1
Educational level attained by hh head (4=high school graduate and above) [1/0]	EDUMAINLAB_4	0.12	0.323	0	1
Communist party member (=1 if hh has a member belonging to the CCP, 0 otherwise) [% of households]	PARTY	0.19	0.392	0	1
Household mainly active in animal production (=1 if labor devoted by hh to husbandry is larger than labor devoted to planting, 0 otherwise)	ANIMAL	0.02	0.140	0	1
Farm characteristics					
Log of sown area [mu]	LN_AREA	11.93	8.116	0	58.1
Number of plots at the end of the year	NUMPLOTSEND	4.70	3.098	0	15
Village Dummies					
Village 1 [1/0]	V1	0.165	0.371	0	1
Village 2 [1/0]	V2	0.149	0.356	0	1
Village 3 [1/0]	V3	0.147	0.354	0	1
Village 4 [1/0]	V4	0.099	0.299	0	1
Village 5 [1/0]	V5	0.229	0.420	0	1
Village 6 [1/0]	V6	0.212	0.408	0	1
Year Dummies					
Dummy 1995 [1/0]	D_1995	0.143	0.350	0	1
Dummy 1996 [1/0]	D_1996	0.139	0.346	0	1

Table 12 continued					
Dummy 1998 [1/0]	D_1998	0.139	0.346	0	1
Dummy 1999 [1/0]	D_1999	0.145	0.353	0	1
Dummy 2000 [1/0]	D_2000	0.145	0.352	0	1
Dummy 2001 [1/0]	D_2001	0.145	0.352	0	1
Dummy 2002 [1/0]	D_2002	0.144	0.351	0	1

Notes: Summary statistics refer to the non-logged variables. The summary statistics for the interaction terms between the village and year dummies are provided in Appendix B.

Source: Own computations based on RCRE survey data for Hebei 1995-2002.

As de Janvry and Sadoulet (2003) indicate most models that assess separability of agricultural households' decisions neglect the heterogeneity of households. Also Kuiper (2005) states, that global separability tests are not well suited for assessing the labor market participation of rural households. She suggests applying separabiltiy to distinguishable sets of households. In the context of the present study these groups are part-time and full-time farm households.

7.1.2 Results of testing for separability

The next table summarizes the results of the fixed effect model estimation. These results are the basis for the separability tests for which the results are also contained in this table. Part- and full-time observations are distinguished based on the definition provided in chapter 3.5.2. The omitted dummy variables are: AGEMAINLAB_5, EDUMAINLAB_1, D_2002 and all of the dummies that combine the village and time effect which are related to the year 2002. All of the location and some of the time and location*time dummy variables have been dropped during the estimation because they do not vary within the households as observation units.

Table 13: Demand for labor in agricultural production – Fixed Effects results

Dependent Variable: ln of household labor days used in agricultural production	Full Sample			Part-time			Full-time		
	Parameter		Standard Error	Parameter		Standard Error	Parameter		Standard Error
LN_HHSIZE	0.236	***	(0.031)	0.165	***	(0.040)	0.445	***	(0.061)
FEM_LAB	0.021		(0.027)	0.054		(0.037)	-0.038		(0.044)
DEPENDENTS	0.177	***	(0.036)	0.149	***	(0.048)	0.264	***	(0.063)
AGEMAINLAB_1	0.020		(0.038)	0.074		(0.049)	-0.170	**	(0.068)
AGEMAINLAB_2	-0.008		(0.032)	0.005		(0.042)	-0.145	***	(0.052)
AGEMAINLAB_3	0.002		(0.031)	0.006		(0.040)	-0.128	**	(0.057)
AGEMAINLAB_4	0.040		(0.032)	0.077	*	(0.042)	-0.101	*	(0.056)
EDUMAINLAB_2	0.010		(0.035)	0.104	**	(0.052)	-0.023		(0.052)
EDUMAINLAB_3	-0.025		(0.036)	0.055		(0.053)	-0.065		(0.054)
EDUMAINLAB_4	-0.042		(0.043)	0.019		(0.060)	-0.139	**	(0.071)
PARTY	-0.051	**	(0.027)	-0.034		(0.035)	-0.059		(0.048)
ANIMAL	0.338	***	(0.036)	0.312	***	(0.042)	0.347	***	(0.071)
LN_AREA	0.672	***	(0.026)	0.568	***	(0.034)	0.668	***	(0.051)
NUMPLOTSEND	-0.002		(0.005)	-0.004		(0.005)	0.006		(0.011)
D_1995	0.109	**	(0.048)	0.124	**	(0.056)	0.156		(0.183)
D_1996	0.172	***	(0.042)	0.182	***	(0.049)	0.028		(0.137)
D_1998	0.198	***	(0.052)	0.184	***	(0.060)	0.132		(0.128)
D_1999	0.033		(0.047)	0.049		(0.055)	-0.078		(0.134)
D_2000	0.128	***	(0.030)	0.216	***	(0.050)	0.069	**	(0.035)
D_2001	-0.029		(0.036)	-0.025		(0.038)	-0.049		(0.095)

Table 13: continued

V1_D_1995	0.603	***	(0.053)	0.561	***	(0.061)	0.522	**	(0.206)
V1_D_1996	0.103	**	(0.049)	0.028		(0.056)	0.291	*	(0.169)
V1_D_1998	-0.050		(0.056)	-0.016		(0.063)	-0.044		(0.155)
V1_D_1999	-0.127	**	(0.052)	-0.119	**	(0.056)	-0.008		(0.170)
V1_D_2000	-0.259	***	(0.053)	-0.351	***	(0.074)	-0.175		(0.114)
V2_D_1996	-0.110	**	(0.050)	-0.101	*	(0.052)	-0.105		(0.258)
V2_D_1998	-0.166	***	(0.058)	-0.131	**	(0.062)	-0.145		(0.175)
V2_D_2000	-0.142	***	(0.054)	-0.235	***	(0.073)	0.169		(0.148)
V2_D_2001	-0.001		(0.051)	0.004		(0.054)	-0.024		(0.154)
V3_D_1995	0.258	***	(0.058)	0.303	***	(0.062)	-0.106		(0.222)
V3_D_1996	0.300	***	(0.054)	0.305	***	(0.059)	0.255		(0.186)
V3_D_1999	0.103	*	(0.058)	0.103	*	(0.063)	0.167		(0.179)
V3_D_2000	-0.094		(0.058)	-0.177	**	(0.078)	-0.056		(0.130)
V3_D_2001	0.005		(0.056)	-0.031		(0.061)	0.112		(0.154)
V4_D_1995	-0.084		(0.060)	-0.084		(0.071)	0.038		(0.213)
V4_D_1996	-0.119	**	(0.056)	-0.160	***	(0.061)	0.218		(0.185)
V4_D_1998	-0.124	**	(0.063)	-0.125	*	(0.073)	0.120		(0.165)
V4_D_1999	0.030		(0.060)	0.002		(0.064)	0.265		(0.182)
V4_D_2000	-0.070		(0.061)	-0.192	**	(0.080)	0.162		(0.132)
V4_D_2001	0.059		(0.058)	0.056		(0.062)	0.042		(0.153)
V5_D_1995	-0.238	***	(0.049)	-0.073		(0.068)	-0.284		(0.184)
V5_D_1996	-0.210	***	(0.044)	-0.088		(0.072)	-0.021		(0.144)
V5_D_1999	-0.076		(0.049)	0.015		(0.062)	0.051		(0.138)
V5_D_2001	-0.035		(0.046)	-0.094		(0.062)	-0.009		(0.101)

Table 13 continued

V6_D_1995	0.008	(0.049)	-0.010	(0.051)	-0.058	(0.263)
V6_D_1998	-0.262 ***	(0.053)	-0.261 ***	(0.057)	-0.072	(0.177)
V6_D_1999	-0.148 ***	(0.049)	-0.176 ***	(0.051)	0.069	(0.179)
V6_D_2000	-0.134 ***	(0.049)	-0.235 ***	(0.069)	-0.027	(0.130)
V6_D_2001	0.057	(0.047)	0.051	(0.049)	0.132	(0.155)
Constant	3.573 ***	(0.062)	3.743 ***	(0.093)	3.602 ***	(0.098)
R-square: within	0.4839		0.3991		0.6382	
Between	0.4462		0.4492		0.6305	
Overall	0.4203		0.3859		0.6785	
Test of null hypothesis of separability	F(3, 3337) = 22.59		F(3, 2324) = 8.12		F(3, 673) = 19.79	
Number of observations / households	4008 / 621		2963 / 589		1045 / 322	

Notes: ***: significant at 1% level of error probability, **: significant at 5% level of error probability,*: significant at 10% level of error probability.

Source: Own computations based on RCRE survey data for Hebei 1995-2002.

Testing the full sample for the joint significance of household size and the structural parameters share of female labor and share of dependents, as discussed in the methodological part of this work, reveals that they are not jointly zero as can be seen from the bottom of *Table 13*. The null hypothesis of separability can be rejected. The same holds if the sample is split into subsets of observations for part-time and full-time farm households. So, only agricultural household models that can be solved non-recursively are applicable to the data set.

The coefficients of household size and the share of dependents belonging to the household are both positive and highly significant in all three estimations. The positive coefficient for household size indicates that larger households use more household labor in their own agricultural production, what is expected for the case of non-separability (Bowlus and Sicular, 2003) and could be a hint to restrictions in the possibility to supply off-farm labor (Kuiper, 2005).

The coefficient for dependents is positive. A higher number of dependent persons living in the household goes along with a higher supply of household labor. This result confirms that it is important not only to consider the household size as such for the interpretation of household's labor demand and supply decisions but also to take the composition of the household into account. In difference to the results of Bowlus and Sicular (2003), there is no significant effect of the share of female laborers in the household. The coefficients of the structural variables like the share of female labor or the number of dependents cannot be interpreted directly but instead one would have to calculate implied elasticities as in Bowlus and Sicular (2003). This is not done here because the main interest of the present study is on testing for spearability.

None of the variables of education show a significant effect in the whole and part-time sample. But the variable for high school education of the household head is significant in the sample for full-time farm households. Hence, agricultural labor demand of the household is reduced if the household head received high school education or above. This is in line with the results of Kuiper (2005) who argues that better educated households are either more efficient in production and therefore less labor time is required or better educated household members are more likely to provide labor off the farm. Another possible explanation would be that households with better educated household heads are more likely to run a non-agricultural household business.

For the age of the main laborer the dummy for the age group 4 (between 51 to 60 years) is positive and slightly significant for the part-time sample indicating that older laborers might be less efficient than younger ones. Alternatively, if the main laborer is older he or she might be faced with more difficulties to find off-farm work and thereby increasing the amount of labor provided to household agricultural production (see also Kuiper, 2005). The inverse relation between age and efficiency in farm labor is confirmed by the significant negative effects of the age dummy for younger household members in the full-time farm household sub sample. Younger household members are expected to be more productive and therefore the household demands less labor for agricultural production.

The effect of the amount of productive land is positive and highly significant. This means that the more land the household can cultivate, the more of its labor force is devoted to agricultural production. The number of plots and thus land fragmentation does not have an effect on the separability between labor demand and supply. In conclusion, demand, production and supply decisions of rural households in Hebei are strongly related to the amount of land available for agricultural production. Animal production is also positively influencing households' on-farm labor provision.

Party membership negatively influences the decision of households to use family labor in own agricultural production suggesting that party members might have a better access to off-farm employment.

Most of the dummies that control for time and location*time effects are highly significant for the total sample and for part-time farm households. This indicates that location and time effects are especially important in the explanation of part-time farm households' labor allocation decisions. Because the location*time variables have been included in the analysis to compensate for missing information about wages it can be concluded that those hidden wage rates are relevant for explaining rural households' labor allocation.

From this section it can be summarized that the labor demand and supply decisions of rural households in Hebei province are not separable. This holds for the whole sample but also for sub-samples that either contain the observations for part-time or full-time farm households.

7.2 Labor market participation of farm households

7.2.1 Empirical model and choice of variables

As discussed in chapter 4.2.3 a household k is assumed to choose among the four distinct labor market participation regimes the one that yields the highest internal wage rate P_{lk}^{j}. Because P_{lk}^{j} cannot be observed a dichotomous choice variable $Part_{1k}^{j}$ is defined as in Glauben et al. (2008) that is equal to 1 if $P_{1k}^{j} = \left(P_{1k}^{h}, P_{1k}^{s}, P_{1k}^{sh}, P_{1k}^{a}\right)$ or 0 otherwise (see also Key et al., 2000). Consequently the probability that a household k chooses one of the participation states can be expressed as in Glauben et al. (2008, p. 334) by:

$$prob_k^j = prob(Part_{1k}^j = 1) = prob[(\beta_j' - \beta_i')z_k > e_k^i - e_k^j]\forall i \neq j.$$

The probabilities of different household choices are estimated based on a function that represents a set of explanatory variables (Theeuwes, 1981) related to household and farm characteristics and time effects. As in Glauben et al. (2008) the error terms are assumed to have identical and independent Weibull distributions. Thus $e_k^i - e_k^j$ is distributed logistically and therefore the model of households labor choice discussed here is multinomial logit (Glauben et al., 2008).

With multinomial logit models only relative probabilities between different choices can be estimated (Wooldridge, 2002). If one of the choice categories is chosen as a base category then "this normalization implies that the estimated model reduces to three log-odds ratios of the form: $\ln(prob_k^j / prob_k^a) = \beta_j' z_k$; $j = h, s, sh$." (Glauben et al., 2008, p. 334).

In the following paragraphs the generation of the dependent and the choice of independent variables will be described.

The information about labor market occupation is aggregated at the household level for the period 1986 to 2002. Therefore it is not possible to classify households in the four different labor market regimes based on the occupation status of individual household members. To derive with the classification of the households into the four different labor market participation regimes two dummy variables D_l^h and D_l^s are generated. The dummy for the supply of family labor to non-agricultural activities also contains the provision of family labor to non-agricultural family business. Out of these two variables four combinations are possible as described in chapter 4.2.2 to distinguish the respective labor market participation regimes.

From the total of 8,551 observations for the period 1986-2002 2,511 households can be classified as belonging to the regime *a*, 33 households belong to *h*, 5,907 households supply labor (*s*) and 100 households hire and supply labor at the same time (*sh*). This distribution of observations between the different labor market regimes differs strongly from the one reported by Glauben et al. (2008), which indicates that the sectoral composition of production and labor force for Hebei differs from that one of Zhejiang province that is analyzed in Glauben et al. (2008).

In general, not only the amount of human capital accumulated by individuals should determine their participation in the labor market but also the kind of human capital acquired (Polachek, 1981). Also Barro (2001) explains, that for the macroeconomic assessment of impacts from education on the well-being of a society in the long run, it is important to distinguish not only between the amount of education received by individuals but also to account for differences in the quality of education.

Because human capital is considered as being more productive in off-farm employment (Ahituv and Kimhi, 2006) and a higher education associated with higher earnings (de Janvry and Sadoulet, 2001) the education variables ELEMENTS, SECONDS and HIGHS should be positively related to the probability to supply family labor to off-farm activities. In addition, investment in human capital should enhance the labor productivity and by this increase the mobility of rural labor (Zhang and Fan, 2004). But Glauben et al. (2008) state, that it is not clear whether the net effect of higher educational level achieved on the probability that the household participates in off-farm activities is positive or negative because higher levels of education could also increase the productivity of farm labor and by this reduce the probability to provide labor off the farm. One explanation for this is offered by Gould and Saupe (1989). They indicate that there might be positive or negative spillover effects from the labor decisions of a better educated member on those of other household members. In Gold and Saupe's (1989) study the probability that a spouse of a farm operator participates in off-farm activities is lower the higher the number of years of formal education completed by the farm operator is, under the condition that the formal education increases the productivity of the on-farm labor. But Gold and Saupe (1989) indicate that there is mixed empirical evidence for these positive or negative spillovers in the relationship between educational level and the participation in off-farm labor markets of husband and spouse, since other studies show no significance for both effects.

For the present data set regimes *a* and *s* show the highest share of laborers that completed elementary schooling. Besides that the amount of observations for *h* and *sh* is rather low, the share of high school graduates among the labor force is higher than for *a* and *s* (*Table 14*).

Related to education also special training received by one or more family members might explain the labor allocation of households. Gould and Saupe (1989) show a higher probability for the uptake of off-farm labor if the laborer received training relevant for manufacturing or service employments. Similar to this, specific agricultural or farm management training is expected to increase the productivity of family labor on the own farm. According to the different regimes the sign of SKILLS can therefore be either positive or negative. It should increase the probability of supplying labor if one or more household members are specially trained for non-farm work. But it might also discourage the household to hire additional on-farm labor force if the household members already run the farming activity productively due to training that increased farming knowledge, e.g. about newly available varieties with better adaptation to pests or droughts. However, because every kind of specific training received by one or more household members is aggregated in the data set within the variable SKILLS, positive and negative effects might compensate each other. The share of skilled laborers is highest for the supply and hire regime.

There is some debate to how gender differences influence the labor market participation of rural laborers (de Brauw et al., 2002). In his work on the feminization of farm work in China, de Brauw (2003) hypothesizes that the share of female labor in agricultural production of family farms is rising. De Janvry and Sadoulet (2001) find in their study on Mexican farm households that married women and women in the reproductive age are participating less in off-farm activities than men of the same age.

The variable FEM_LABOR shows the share of female laborers among the total labor force of the household and is included in the model to control for the effect of female laborers. With exception of the regime *h* the share of women in the labor force of rural households in Hebei is below 50% (*Table 14*).

As discussed in chapter 7.1 the number of dependent household members is calculated as the difference between the total number of permanent residents and the number of laborers living in the household. DEPENDENTS as the share of dependent household members to the total household size is included in the set of explanatory variables because women are considered to be mainly responsible to take care of those dependents. So the additional work load stemming from care taking would hinder women to provide labor to the market (Glauben et al., 2008). Therefore especially for regime *s* the sign DEPENDENTS is expected to be negative.

Glauben et al. (2008) follow Chen et al. (2004) and argue that if one considers the membership in the Chinese Communist Party as being a participation of the household in a social network that helps improving the access to information and off-farm job opportunities then the effect of PARTY on the probability of taking up off-farm work is expected to be positive.

It is assumed that agricultural income is endogenous to the labor market participation decisions of the household (Glauben et al., 2008). Therefore in a first step a linear model is estimated and predicted values for AGRI_INC are used in a second step for the multinomial logit estimation.[13]

Currently (see e.g. Zhang, 2010) subsidies are discussed in the Chinese public to be a feasible way to reduce urban-rural income inequality and political support is devoted to this topic to outbalance the discrimination against agricultural production by heavy taxation over centuries (Gale et al., 2005). The net TRANSFER rural households received from the state as fiscal subsidiary in-

[13] See Appendix D for the first step estimation.

come or from relatives as donations is included to reflect the influence of unearned income on labor market decisions. The term unearned income used here is different from what is sometimes referred to as nonearned income, which includes rents, interests or such like incomes. Those income components are partly related to individual life cycle decisions and by this reflect personal behavior and past decisions about factor allocation (Schultz, 1990). Pensions and other retirement payments are also not included in the definition of transfers as applied here. There is even no question in the survey that asks for such payments. Adjusted consumer price index (CPI) deflators for Hebei are calculated based on Brandt and Holz (2005) and used to value the monetary variable TRANSFER at 1990 constant prices.

It is expected that the higher the transfers are the less likely it is that the household participates in the labor market. Glauben et al. (2008) indicate that this might be the case because unearned income would increase the demand of leisure, if leisure is seen as a normal good.

All the variables mentioned up to now reflect household characteristics. The following ones are related to the characteristics of the farm as production basis.

If there are more per capita productive assets available the household should be more productive in labor and therefore hiring labor is expected to be more likely (Glauben et al., 2008). The above mentioned adjusted CPI deflators for Hebei are also used to value the monetary variable ASSETS at 1990 constant prices.

Arable land is the main input for agricultural production. The variable LAND represents the per capita amount of land available for cultivation (crop land and orchards) that the household possesses by the end of the respective year. If more agricultural land is available to the household it should reduce the possibilities to supply family labor outside the own farm because more labor is needed in family farming (see the results in 7.1.2) if it is not compensated by intensification in capital use, such e.g. as mechanization via the use of tractors. So a higher amount of per capita land should increase the probability that non-family labor is hired by the household (Glauben et al., 2008).

A dummy variable for LIVESTOCK is included to control for differences in production systems among farm households. The value of LIVESTOCK is 1 if the household produces pigs, cattle or sheep.

The time dummies included for every year should reflect the effects of changes in overall economic conditions but also policy changes (as discussed in chapter 3.3) that might have different impacts on rural and urban areas (Glauben et al., 2008). But also within the rural areas of one province the direction of the effect that changing policies have on farm households' labor allocation decisions is not clear. The reasons for this are de facto diversified rural institutions. Land renting (Piotrowski, 2009) or water use decisions (Böber, 2009) are made in regulatory settings that differ from the legal framework and are different even between villages in the same county.

Previous studies (Benjamin and Brandt, 1997; Kung, 2002; Wang, 2007) emphasize the impact of the existence and functioning of land markets and the interlinkages between land and labor markets on the labor market participation decisions. Since land renting has an impact on agricultural productivity this also influences labor time allocation. Benjamin and Brandt (1997) show that the allocation of households' land and labor resources is optimized for the market that functions best of both markets, but the degree of market development differs significantly between villages. In their neoclassical model to explain the distribution of land and income the possibility for the households to fully utilize land and labor enhances the welfare at the village level, because well functioning land and labor markets have an equalizing effect on the distribution of incomes within the village (Benjamin and Brandt, 1997). The share of households in a village that rent out land, as one measure for a functioning land market, is used by Wang (2007) as an additional explanatory variable. This variable and the other village level variables, unemployment rate and the average per capita income in the village are not available for the present assessment. Including this village level information might increase the explanatory power of the chosen labor allocation decision model.

Irrigation water use and the institutional set up of ground and surface water use would be an important factor to test for. Also irrigated land should provide higher agricultural income to the household (de Janvry and Sadoulet, 2001). But relevant information about the share of irrigated land, irrigation water use, differences in water associations between villages or water pricing are not available from the data set for the analyzed period.

Table 14 provides the explanatory variables with respective summary statistics for the different labor market regimes. The codes provided in the second, third and fourth column are the variables included in the RCRE household survey that are needed to calculate the respective values for the explanatory variables/ dummies. They are consistent with the variable codes provided by Giles (2010).

Table 14: Variable set labor market participation

Variable	Code 1986-1991	Code 1993	Code 1995-2002	Regime	Hire (h) (n = 33)	Supply (s) (n = 5,907)	Supply and hire (sh) (n = 100)	Autarky (a) (n = 2,511)
				Variable	Mean (Std. Dev.)			
Household charackteristics								
Share of laborer graduated from elementary school	024 to 020	022 to 018	022 to 018	ELEMENTS	0.308 (0.337)	0.397 (0.340)	0.283 (0.285)	0.397 (0.365)
Share of laborer graduated from secondary school	025 to 020	023 to 018	023 to 018	SECONDS	0.448 (0.396)	0.379 (0.321)	0.431 (0.317)	0.352 (0.347)
Share of laborer graduated from high school and above	026 to 020	024 to 018	024 to 018	HIGHS	0.150 (0.233)	0.100 (0.221)	0.163 (0.259)	0.065 (0.184)
Share of laborer with special skills	027 to 020	026 to 018	025 to 018	SKILLS	0 (0)	0.071 (0.172)	0.152 (0.214)	0.043 (0.140)
Share of female labor force on rural labor force	(020-022) to 020	(018-020) to 020	(018-020) to 020	FEM_LABOR	0.52 (0.178)	0.465 (0.190)	0.442 (0.181)	0.486 (0.258)
Share of dependents	(018-020) to 018	(016-018) to 016	(016-018) to 016	DEPENDENTS	0.526 (0.238)	0.400 (0.188)	0.420 (0.197)	0.468 (0.241)
Communist party membership	013	012	012	PARTY	0.061 (0.242)	0.196 (0.397)	0.250 (0.435)	0.157 (0.364)

Table 14 continued

Net transfer per capita at 1990 constant prices[1] [1000 Yuan/capita]	(187+189+191)-218	(311+313+315)-349	(328+330+332)-367	TRANSFER	-0.145 (0.396)	-0.003 (0.553)	-0.052 (0.546)	0.075 (0.509)
Ln (Household's agricultural income per capita at 1990 constant prices) [1000 Yuan/ capita][2]				AGRI_INC	1.222 (1.598)	-0.026 (0.998)	0.088 (1.241)	0.235 (1.280)
Farm characteristics								
Ln(Household's agricultural productive assets per capita at 1990 constant prices) [1000 Yuan/ capita]	072/018 (durable goods in Yuan) (deflated to 1990)	106/016 (durable goods in Yuan) (deflated to 1990)	106/016 (durable goods in Yuan) (deflated to 1990)	ASSETS	0.661 (0.983)	-0.923 (1.593)	0.860 (2.003)	0.240 (1.492)
Ln(Total land per capita) [mu/capita]	043/018 (Land at year end)	057/ 016 (Land at year end)	057/ 016 (Land at year end)	LAND	0.775 (0.646)	0.380 (0.600)	0.503 (0.508)	0.516 (0.564)
Dummy for pigs, cattle, and sheep	092 > 0	138 and/or 139 > 0	140 and/or 141 > 0	LIVESTOCK	0.394 (0.496)	0.322 (0.467)	0.300 (0.461)	0.377 (0.485)
Dummy for 1986				D_1986	0.152 (0.364)	0.069 (0.253)	0.040 (0.197)	0.082 (0.274)
Dummy for 1987				D_1987	0 (0)	0.072 (0.258)	0.100 (0.302)	0.074 (0.262)
Dummy for 1988				D_1988	0 (0)	0.073 (0.260)	0.060 (0.239)	0.065 (0.246)
Dummy for 1989				D_1989	0 (0)	0.071 (0.257)	0.080 (0.273)	0.076 (0.266)
Dummy for 1990				D_1990	0 (0)	0.070 (0.254)	0.020 (0.141)	0.082 (0.275)

Table 14 continued

Dummy for 1991	D_1991	0.030 (0.174)	0.067 (0.250)	0.030 (0.171)	0.087 (0.282)
Dummy for 1993	D_1993	0 (0)	0.075 (0.264)	0.010 (0.100)	0.069 (0.254)
Dummy for 1995	D_1995	0 (0)	0.068 (0.251)	0.050 (0.219)	0.080 (0.272)
Dummy for 1996	D_1996	0.061 (0.242)	0.066 (0.249)	0.060 (0.239)	0.074 (0.263)
Dummy for 1998	D_1998	0.212 (0.415)	0.070 (0.254)	0.100 (0.302)	0.063 (0.244)
Dummy for 1999	D_1999	0.212 (0.415)	0.077 (0.267)	0.095 (0.295)	0.056 (0.230)
Dummy for 2000	D_2000	0.151 (0.364)	0.073 (0.260)	0.130 (0.338)	0.066 (0.249)
Dummy for 2001	D_2001	0.121 (0.331)	0.073 (0.261)	0.110 (0.314)	0.066 (0.248)
Dummy for 2002	D_2002	0.061 (0.242)	0.076 (0.266)	0.110 (0.314)	0.058 (0.234)

Notes: [1] Deflated prices based on deflators calculated using official CPI's for Hebei province as provided by Brandt and Holz (2005) with 1990 as base year.
[2] The summary statistics are provided for the real per capita agricultural income instead of the summaries for the predicted values from the first step estimation.

Source: Own computations based on RCRE survey data for Hebei 1986-2002.

7.2.2 Estimation procedure, measures of model fit and calculation of predicted probabilities

The -mlogit- procedure is used in Stata to estimate the multinomial choice model of household labor allocation as developed in Chapter 4.2.2.

According to the measures of model fit as presented in the lower part of *Table 15* the model performs good in estimating the effects that the independent variables have on the probabilities that one of the respective labor market regimes is chosen relative to the autarky regime. The reported standard errors are robust to misspecification and are tolerant to correlation within the specific labor market regimes. Regarding the model diagnostics there is still a debate which indicator to choose if the multinomial logit specification is appropriate for a specific choice models (Brüderl, 2010).

In multinomial logit models it is assumed that the response categories, in this case, the different labor market participation regimes, are independent of each other and not ordered (Wooldridge, 2002; Hilbe, 2009). Consequently the error terms are supposed to be distributed independently over all regimes (Grilli and Rampichini, 2007).[14]

Multinomial logit models are sensitive to the independence of irrelevant alternatives assumption (IIA). As described in Wooldridge (2002) and Hilbe (2009) it is possible to check this assumption by estimating first a full model. Then a model is fitted that is reduced by one level. Afterwards a Hausman-McFadden test of the assumption above is employed. The null hypothesis for this test is H_0: there is no systematic difference in the estimates of parameters between the full and the reduced model.

The model here seems not to meet the asymptotic assumptions that underlie the specification of the Hausman test for the IIA. Even if H_0 is reported as not being rejected for all participation states the χ^2 statistic is <0 for the regimes hire and supply and hire. Also Benjamin and Kimhi (2006) cannot test the IIA for all labor allocation regimes because the test statistic χ^2 is negative for six out of their 15 equations. This is especially the case if the different states are in a substitution relation to each other (Brüderl, 2010). Also the fact that there are relatively few observations in the regimes *h* and *sh* causes problems in testing the IIA assumption.

As Haan (2004) indicates, the IIA property hardly holds for discrete choice models of labor supply, because it is quite likely that the introduction of a new

14 If this assumption is violated one could apply models that are more flexible in the assumptions about the distribution of the error terms such as multinomial probit or nested logit models (Wooldridge, 2002).

alternative of labor time use changes the odds ratios of the former alternatives. Even if the estimation results using a conditional choice rather than a random coefficient model might be biased they are favorable if the differences between both specifications are not significant because the computational burden for the more flexible random coefficient model is much higher (Haan, 2004).

As described by Hilbe (2009) studies that compared multinomial logit and multinomial probit models over various simulations of choice models concluded that multinomial logit yield more accurate results than multinomial probit even in cases where the IIA is violated. In general the procedures proposed to test for IIA do not prove to be overall valid. Especially in the case of labor market decisions of rural households in Hebei were there are unobserved variables such as the seasonal cropping structure or a high share of subsistence agriculture the labor market participation regimes are not fully complements but substitution relations can be assumed.

So, even if the data set utilized here does not fulfill all assumptions underlying the application of multinomial logit models, those models are chosen for the recent analysis, since the differences between the logit and probit estimations are generally not significant and the logit estimates are more accurate.

Based on the results of the likelihood ratio test (LR) presented in the bottom of *Table 15* the model is significant at the 1% level of error probability or better.

The outcome that has the highest estimated probability is the predicted outcome for the respective observation. So from a comparison of the predicted outcomes and the observed regimes the percentage of correct predictions is calculated (Wooldridge, 2002). In total 74% of the observations used in the estimations are correctly classified by the model.

The estimated coefficients of the explanatory variables can be interpreted as the marginal change of the logarithm of the odds if the respective independent variable changes marginally (Glauben et al., 2008). This is the case for each of the three states s, h and sh in relation to the base regime or category a. The odds ratio describes the change in the probability, to be in one regime relative to the base category, which is related to a change in the respective independent variable by one empirical unit (Rese, 2000). So, if the odds ratio is 3 and the probability of the household to be in category s against a was 3:1 before a one unit chane in the explanatory variable it will be 9:1 after the one unit change. For continuous explanatory variables the exposed value of the coefficient is the factor of change in the odds to be in one of the states *h*, *s* or *sh* alternative to *a*, due to an increase in the explanatory variable by one unit. So if $\exp(\beta'_{jk})$, $j = h$, s, or sh; $k =$ ELEMENTS,..., D_2001, is higher than 1 it follows that the odds ratio increases $\exp(\beta'_{jk})$ times if the explanatory variable is increased by one unit. If the covariate is increased by one unit and $\exp(\beta'_{jk})$ is smaller than 1, then the odds ratio will decrease $\exp(\beta'_{jk})$ times (De la Mothe and Foray, 2001). So "for dummy variables the calculated change in probability occurs when the value of the dummy variable switches from 0 to 1." (Theeuwes, 1981, p. 488). Because the odds as such is still a ratio and not intuitively informative (Theeuwes, 1981) it requires a further step to calculate the change in the probability to be in a respective state compared to autarky caused by a marginal change in a specific explanatory variable. The predicted change in the probability can be calculated as:

$$dprob_k^j = prob_k^j \left(\beta'_{jk} - \sum_{j=h}^{sh} prob_k^j \beta'_{jk} \right) dz_k , \qquad (44)$$

where $dprob_k^j$ is the predicted change in the probability to be in regime j if the explanatory variable k is changed marginally and the other variables are the same as explained before.

Because the predicted changes in probabilities have to sum up to 0 the results for changes in the probabilities of the base category *a* are derived from the difference between 0 and the sum of the other three probabilities.

7.2.3 Results of estimating farm households' labor market participation

The comparison of the self-classification of farm households regarding their labor time allocation with variables about agricultural production and income derived from various sources partly confirms the disadvantages of a distinction between farm types based on working hours.

In *Table 15* the results from the estimation of the multinomial logit model are provided. The results can not be directly interpreted as marginal effects. But they indicate which variables allow for a significant differentiation between the four labor market participation regimes (Sarkisian, 2010). The signs of the coefficients indicate the relationship between alternative regimes and the base category (Rese, 2000). If the coefficient β'_{jk} is negative, then it is more likely that the household belongs to autarky if the value of the respective explanatory variable increases. For the same increase in the explanatory variable value a positive coefficient β'_{jk} indicates a rising probability that *h*, *s* or *sh* respectively are chosen against *a*. A graphical illustration of the logistic relationship, which is behind this interpretation, can be seen in *Figure 10* for the case of a binomial logistic regression where *a* is the base category and *s* would be the only alternative regime that a household could be in (compare: Rese, 2000, p. 121).

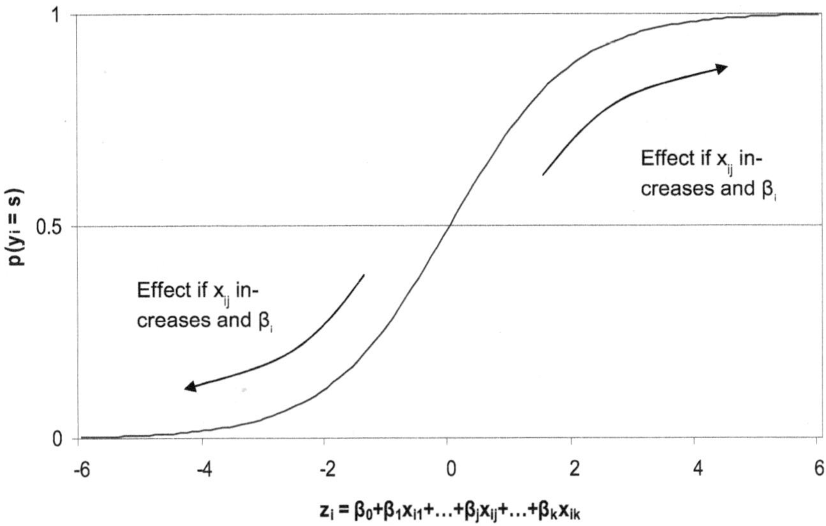

Source: Own illustration following Rese (2000, p. 121).

Figure 10: The effect of a negative or positive β_i on the probability that $y_i = s$

Table 15: Multinomial logit estimation of household's labor regime choices, 1986-2002

Variable	Hire (h)		Supply (s)		Supply and hire (sh)	
	Parameter	z-value	Parameter	z-value	Parameter	z-value
Household characteristics						
ELEMENTS	-0.266	(-0.24)	1.145 ***	(8.62)	-0.902	(-1.31)
SECONDS	0.446	(0.44)	0.742 ***	(5.59)	-0.681	(-1.04)
HIGHS	2.135	(1.55)	1.300 ***	(7.08)	0.196	(0.24)
SKILLS	-140.737 ***	(-24.88)	1.032 ***	(5.34)	2.650 ***	(5.28)
FEM_LABOR	0.091	(0.09)	-0.877 ***	(-6.21)	-1.078 *	(-1.79)
DEPENDENTS	2.961 *	(1.74)	-2.282 ***	(-12.45)	-2.039 ***	(-2.60)
PARTY	-1.769	(-1.29)	0.151 **	(2.02)	0.384	(1.54)
TRANSFER	-0.605 *	(-1.74)	-0.263 *	(-1.94)	-0.331	(-1.04)
AGR_INC	-0.170	(-0.63)	-0.729 ***	(-14.11)	-2.195 ***	(-8.22)
Farm characteristics						
ASSESTS	0.656 ***	(5.59)	0.150 ***	(6.00)	1.177 ***	(8.73)
LN_LAND	2.494 ***	(3.11)	-0.766 ***	(-13.21)	-0.077	(-0.29)
LIVESTOCK	1.797 ***	(3.80)	-0.398 ***	(-6.68)	0.386	(1.27)
Time dummies						
D_1986	-0.034	(-0.03)	-0.504 ***	(-2.91)	0.017	(0.02)
D_1987	-31.69 ***	(-35.87)	-0.344 **	(-1.99)	1.098	(1.61)
D_1988	-31.607 ***	(-39.14)	-0.230	(-1.34)	0.587	(0.91)

Table 15 continued

D_1989	-31.875	***	(-39.98)	-0.424	**	(-2.54)	0.391		(0.63)
D_1990	-32.531	***	(-41.43)	-0.629	***	(-3.85)	-1.879	*	(-1.65)
D_1991	-0.674		(-0.51)	-0.751	***	(-4.66)	-1.187		(-1.37)
D_1993	-31.783	***	(-39.16)	-0.188		(-1.14)	-1.239		(-1.13)
D_1995	-32.359	***	(-40.48)	-0.593	***	(-3.86)	-1.529	**	(-2.10)
D_1996	-0.189		(-0.17)	-0.573	***	(-3.67)	-1.114		(-1.62)
D_1998	1.402		(1.50)	-0.387	**	(-2.46)	-0.438		(-0.83)
D_1999	1.244		(1.29)	0.048		(0.29)	0.002		(0.00)
D_2000	0.783		(0.81)	-0.248		(-1.57)	-0.108		(-0.22)
D_2001	0.663		(0.71)	-0.315	**	(-1.97)	-0.170		(-0.36)
CONSTANT	-8.024	***	(-3.92)	3.943	***	(15.85)	2.945	***	(3.42)
Log L			-4998.19		R^2_{MF}				0.106
LR (df)			1220.01	(75)	RLogL				-4388.19
Prob > LR			0.000		N				7,332
Wald χ^2 (df)			29420.66	(75)	AIC				1.218

Notes: z-statistics (based on robust standard errors) in parentheses.
***: significant at 1% level of error probability,**: significant at 5% level of error probability,
*: significant at 10% level of error probability.
Autarky is chosen as the base category. The dummy for 2002 is the omitted time dummy variable.

Source: Own computations based on RCRE survey data for Hebei 1986-2002.

As explained above one cannot directly see the quantitative effect of a marginal change in the explanatory variables on changes in the probabilities of being in the respective regime *h*, *s* or *sh* relative to the base category *a*.

Table 16: Predicted changes in regime participation probabilities if explanatory variables are changed marginally

Independent variable	Predicted change in the probability of [1]			
(unit of measure)	*h*	*s*	*sh*	*a*
ELEMENTS (%)	-0.0285	2.5418	0.0000	-2.5132
SECONDS (%)	0.0000	0.0017	0.0000	-0.0017
HIGHS (%)	0.0470	2.8326	-0.0009	-2.8787
SKILLS (%)	-5.2545	5.5930	0.1555	-0.4940
FEM_LABOR (%)	0.0005	0.0793	-0.0391	-0.0407
DEPENDENTS (%)	0.1676	-4.9856	-0.0753	4.8932
PARTY (d)[2]	-0.0657	0.0443	0.0008	0.0206
TRANSFER (1000 Yuan/ capita)	0.0000	-0.0005	0.0000	0.0006
AGR_INC (ln (1000 Yuan/ capita))	0.0009	0.1639	-0.0797	-0.0851
ASSESTS (ln (1000 Yuan/ capita))	-0.0005	-0.0884	0.0427	0.0462
LN_LAND (mu/ capita)	0.0927	-0.0638	-0.0011	-0.0279
LIVESTOCK (d)	0.0668	-0.0456	-0.0007	-0.0204
D_1986 (d)	0.0000	-0.0011	0.0000	0.0011
D_1987 (d)	-0.0016	-0.0828	0.0399	0.0445
D_1988 (d)	-1.1740	0.7859	0.0133	0.3748
D_1989 (d)	-1.1840	0.7922	0.0134	0.3784
D_1990 (d)	-1.2076	0.9497	-0.0545	0.3123
D_1991 (d)	0.0005	0.0879	-0.0431	-0.0453
D_1993 (d)	-1.1801	0.8839	-0.0316	0.3278
D_1995 (d)	-1.2013	0.9192	-0.0419	0.3240
D_1996 (d)	0.0005	0.0827	-0.0404	-0.0428
D_1998 (d)	0.0521	-0.0357	-0.0006	-0.0158
D_1999 (d)	0.0462	-0.0308	-0.0005	-0.0148
D_2000 (d)	0.0000	-0.0006	0.0000	0.0005
D_2001 (d)	0.0000	-0.0007	0.0000	0.0007

Notes: [1] Calculation of the predicted changes in probabilities based on equation (44) and using the results from the estimation of the logit coefficients in Table 15 and the sample frequencies of the labor regimes which are: 0.0037 for *h*, 0.6674 for *s*, 0.0113 for *sh*, and 0.3176 for *a*.

[2] (d) indicates a dummy variable and "For dummy variables the calculated change in probability occurs when the value of the dummy variable switches from 0 to 1." (Theeuwes, 1981, p. 488).

If one compares two specific values of one explanatory variable (e.g. the values for ELEMENTS in regime *h* and *s*) then the difference between those values is a measure of the change in the conditional probability between both labor market participation regimes.

Source: Own computations based on RCRE survey data for Hebei 1986-2002.

When interpreting the predicted changes in probabilities as presented in *Table 16* one should have in mind that these are changes of probabilities that are given in percent. So even if some of the numerical values in *Table 16* seem to be high, the probability of some scenarios as such is quite low due to relative low numbers of observations in two of the four regimes.

Some of the coefficient values in the regimes *h* and *sh* are very high. This is mainly due to the fact that there are not many observations for both categories (Sarkisian, 2010). A solution would be to define new categories, which would have more observations. This is not done here but it is one of the reasons why in part 7.3 only two categories, full- and part-time farming, are assessed.

All effects of education variables are highly significant for the regime *s*. This confirms that higher education levels of the household or higher education levels attained by its members lead to a higher probability that the household participates in the labor market compared to the alternative autarky (Glauben et al., 2008) and to more off-farm employment activities of the household (Ahituv and Kimhi, 2006). In comparison to Glauben et al. (2008) and Zhang et al. (2002) the almost 4 times increase in the probability to supply labor found here is a much higher quantitative effect of a 1% increase in the share of laborers with high school education. This might indicate that returns to education in Hebei are not only limited to agricultural occupations. Another explanation would be that there are less people completing high school in Hebei than in the provinces assessed by the other authors and therefore those people with high school degrees are almost fully employed by the industry or service sector. Sikei et al. (2009) argue that a higher educational level obtained by laborers is a signal of higher productivity to employers. This might explain the absolute highest value of the marginal effects of HIGHS in all regimes and especially for *s* which is also in line with the suggestions of Tuan et al. (2000). Benjamin and Brandt (1997) have shown that education is one of the main factors contributing to inequality among the Chinese rural population.

The results for SKILLS are very interesting. For alternative *h* the coefficient is highly significant and negative. This means the smaller the share of skilled household members is, the more likely it will be, that the household chooses to hire non-family labor for agricultural production. The expectation that specialization in the skills of laborers leads to a sector specific supply of labor is confirmed by the positive and significant effect of SKILLS with respect to *s* and *sh*. So households that have received special training or acquired specific knowledge for other purposes than for agricultural production will supply labor to those non-farm activities. The marginal effect is highest in *s*. An increase in the share of skilled laborers by 1% leads to a more than 6 times higher probability that the household supplies labor compared to autarky if all other variables are held constant. That the sign of the coefficient is different between *h* and the alternatives *s* and *sh* can be explained by the fact that SKILLS does not only refer to special abilities required for agricultural production but that it also covers skills which are beneficial for non-agricultural jobs.

Given that a 1% higher share of female laborers among household's working force increases household's probability to supply labor by around 8% relative to *a*, it seems that off-farm work in Hebei is favorable and accessible for women besides the fact that women are contributing a large share to farm work. During own surveys (Böber, 2008 and 2009) it was observed, that especially labor intensive activities such as weeding or harvesting of cotton and maize are done by women. Why a 1% higher share of female laborers among household's working force reduces the probability to be in regime *sh* by 4% even though at a low level of significance, cannot be further assessed based on the available variables. It could be hypothesized that the possibilities to substitute female household labor with hired labor are limited due to differing characteristics of both types of labor. To assess this, information on the exact type of labor hired and the labor provided would be needed.

In the regimes *s* and *sh* a higher share of dependent household members reduces the probability that a household is found in one of these regimes by 6 times and by around 8% respectively. The opposite effect of DEPENDENTS is found for the regime *h* with an increase of the probability to be in this regime of 17% if the share of dependents in the household increases by 1%. So a higher share of non-working household members requires the household to reduce supplying (female) labor (to take care of the dependents) and even seems to make it necessary to hire additional labor. The second possibility is likely if the dependents are a couple of retired and less productive persons who still possess land use rights and have to hire labor to cultivate the land. These results are in line with Kimhi (1994) who states, that a higher share of children in the household reduces the participation of both sexes but especially women in the farm and off-farm labor market. It is not possible to further decompose the variable DEPENDENTS here, but in theory especially for younger children, women's time costs are rather high and therefore discouraging women to supply labor outside the family especially because they might have a comparative advantage in housework compared to farm or non-farm work (Kimhi, 1994).

Households with members of the Chinese Communist Party are more likely to participate as suppliers in the off-farm labor market. This is in line with the results of Chen et al. (2004) that the access to social networks provides better access to off-farm employment. It is not possible to further assess if this better access is due to specific knowledge achieved via party education courses or due to closer personal relationships among party members.

TRANSFER is significant at the 10% level of error probability with a negative sign for the regimes *h* and *s*. For the supply regime this can be explained if one assumes leisure to be a normal good. Under this assumption an increase in non-labor income would lead to a reduction of labor supply and an increase in leisure time consumed (Theewues, 1981; Glauben et al., 2008). Explaining the negative coefficient of TRANSFER on hiring non-family labor, one could argue that received monetary transfers (unearned income) allow the household to produce less to meet its consumption needs and consequently it would not be required to hire any additional non-family labor from the market.

Interviews in Hebei (Böber, 2009) revealed a different behavior of farmers. Some of them stated that they don't change their supply of labor to off-farm occupations if per area subsidies for grain production are provided but instead they reduce labor input in grain cropping. So, there seems to be a conflict between increasing farmers' incomes and stabilizing grain output that needs further assessment.

A 1% higher per capita agricultural income reduces the probability to supply and hire labor at the same time relative to *a* by around 8%. But interestingly it increases the probability to supply labor by 16% relative to *a*. This is a good example for interpreting the coefficients of the multinomial logit estimation results. Even if is negative, the predicted change in the probability to be in a specific regime can be positive with respect to the reference regime. A calculation using equation (44) yields that also in Glauben et al. (2008) the coefficient of AGR-INC is negative for *sh* but the predicted change in the probability to simultaneously supply and hire labor is around 2%. If the increase in agricultural income is considered as an increase in overall wealth of the family, then the negative coefficient of income in the two regimes *s* and *sh* could be explained as the household's decision to shift from supplying labor to "purchasing" leisure time (Theeuwes, 1981). A similar line of thought was used above to explain the effect of the variable TRANSFER.

Jalan and Ravallion (1999) explain that the provision of more family labor to off-farm jobs can be a reaction of Chinese farm households to income shocks caused by bad harvests and the resulting decline in agricultural income. So not only wages or the shadow price of leisure influence households' labor allocation decisions in reality but also considerations to smooth income fluctuations stemming from the main income source for farm households in Hebei (as shown in chapter 6); agricultural income.

Almost all households in the data set possess use rights for agricultural land. If they have no skills in farming or if they have skills that would generate a higher utility by providing this skilled labor to production outside the family farm, then there are three possibilities for the farm household to decide about the use of the assigned land.

First, the household could give up the use right, abandon all agricultural activities or even physically migrate to an urban area. This behavior is hardly observed in reality because households fear that they might not be reassigned use rights in future land (re)allocations once they quit agriculture. The second option would be to rent out land and hence to liberate their labor force to be employed in other sectors or locations. Land renting possibilities increased over the last years but still in some regions land renting is prohibited or restricted e.g. by village heads (Piotrowski, 2009). As a third option, the farm household could hire labor that is sufficiently qualified to carry out all agricultural activities independently and could by this supply its own family labor to the market.

The coefficient for the LAND variable is significant and positive for the hiring regime and it is negative at the same level of significance for the regime where households supply off-farm labor. So as expected, a higher per capita amount of land decreases the probability to supply family labor off the farm and increases the probability to hire non-family labor.

For several years in the beginning and middle of the analyzed period the time dummies for regime *h* are statistically significant and negative. This result is different from Glauben et al. (2008) who found especially the dummy variables after 1993 to contribute negatively to the probability that a household is hiring labor. But in relation to the predicted probabilities of a household belonging to regime *h* it is obvious that the probability to hire labor is de facto 0 for the years up to 1995, whereas there is a slight increase in the probability to hire labor from 1995 onwards. It might be related to changes in the composition of sampled households that time dummy coefficients for the estimation of *h* after 1998 are not significant and totally different (positive) from the ones before 1995.

Regarding the supply regimes, almost all time dummies are negative and for most years statistically significant. This indicates that policy measures and macroeconomic conditions were not likely to stimulate participation of rural agricultural laborers in the off-farm labor market in those years. Even if it is difficult to distinguish policy and macroeconomic effects (Glauben et al., 2008) and despite the different speed of implementing policy changes in different regions, the absolute highest values of the time dummies for 1995 and 1996 might be explained by the mentioned changes in the grain procurement system in the end of 1994. In line with this, for 1995 and 1996 the lowest probability of farm households in Hebei to supply off-farm labor is predicted. So a change from market mechanisms in grain production to more state organization in grain purchase might have discouraged labor supply to non-farm activities.

Overall rural households in Hebei have a probability to supply labor outside the own farm of around 70% (*Table 17*). This underlines the results of the income analysis that the importance of agricultural income in total households' income is declining and consequently the distribution of labor time to the primary sector is lower than it would be if the households would have to be subsistence farms without access to labor markets.

Table 17: Predicted probabilities of households' choices of labor market regimes, 1986-2002

Year	Autarky (*a*)		Hire (*h*)		Supply (*s*)		Supply and hire (*sh*)	
	Mean	Std. Dev.	Mean	Std. Dev.	Mean	Std. Dev.	Mean	Std. Dev.
1986	0.324	(0.158)	0.002	(0.004)	0.669	(0.157)	0.005	(0.013)
1987	0.293	(0.145)	0.000	(0.000)	0.693	(0.143)	0.014	(0.030)
1988	0.264	(0.143)	0.000	(0.000)	0.725	(0.140)	0.011	(0.028)
1989	0.303	(0.176)	0.000	(0.000)	0.684	(0.171)	0.012	(0.028)
1990	0.333	(0.149)	0.000	(0.000)	0.665	(0.147)	0.002	(0.005)
1991	0.349	(0.154)	0.002	(0.007)	0.646	(0.154)	0.004	(0.009)
1993	0.250	(0.123)	0.000	(0.000)	0.748	(0.123)	0.002	(0.004)
1995	0.348	(0.155)	0.000	(0.000)	0.647	(0.151)	0.006	(0.025)
1996	0.339	(0.189)	0.004	(0.012)	0.649	(0.189)	0.008	(0.028)
1998	0.283	(0.151)	0.014	(0.028)	0.688	(0.152)	0.016	(0.048)
1999	0.201	(0.137)	0.012	(0.035)	0.767	(0.142)	0.020	(0.053)
2000	0.260	(0.162)	0.010	(0.038)	0.708	(0.162)	0.022	(0.056)
2001	0.251	(0.149)	0.008	(0.024)	0.720	(0.150)	0.021	(0.054)
2002	0.197	(0.126)	0.004	(0.013)	0.779	(0.127)	0.020	(0.054)
Average	0.287	(0.155)	0.004	(0.018)	0.698	(0.152)	0.011	(0.036)

Source: Own computations based on RCRE survey data for Hebei 1986-2002.

Labor allocation decisions of rural households depend not only on the existence and functioning of markets for agricultural and non-agricultural labor. Also constraints in or the non-existence of land and credit markets or insufficiencies in social security institutions can cause situations in which the household does not follow the seemingly rational behavior of only comparing marginal utilities of family labor with marginal wage rates. Instead it might be preferable for a household to use some portion of the available family labor, e.g. from the female labor force, as a buffer to compensate for market imperfections (Ilahi, 2000). Some of those effects might be hidden in the location and time dummies. On the basis of the RCRE household data set it is not possible to further assess potential constraints stemming from failure of other markets than the (rural) labor market.

In addition one should bear in mind, that for the assessment of policy interventions the intra-household decision process about the allocation of resources, including family labor time, matters. As Alderman et al. (1995) state, examples can be found where the introduction of new agricultural technologies failed because men have been addressed by policy makers whereas the de facto decision about the use of e.g. new crop varieties was made by women in the household, who did most of the related farm work.

The age of rural laborers that are involved in agricultural production is rising. Fan (2007) expects the median age of the agricultural population to be around 45 years in 2050 which would be more than double the median age of around 20 years in 1970. If the productivity of older laborers is considered as being lower, then this aging of the labor force has to be compensated by adjustments in the production technology to compensate the decreasing contribution of human labor. But as long as elderly individuals in rural areas are not covered by a sufficient old age security system it is quite likely that they continue to contribute labor to family farm production (Piotrowski, 2009, Böber 2008 and 2009). For this reason, the impact of the retirement payment system on labor decisions and incentives should be included in further assessments of labor allocation decisions in rural China and Hebei.

7.3 Persistence and transition of farming structures over time

To assess the persistence of the farm structure in Hebei, methods from survival analysis, sometimes referred to as time failure analysis or hazard analysis, are applied. Relatively few observations are found in the regimes *h* and *sh* and therefore only a few transitions between these states occur. For this reason, the following analysis uses a simpler classification of households namely full-time and part-time farms. Here the definition of part-time and full-time farm households of Brosig et al. (2009) is applied, where every farm household that still farms land but allocates some or all family labor time is considered to be a part-time farm household.

7.3.1 The independent variable and the choice of explanatory variables

The independent variable in the following model is a dichotomous variable , that is equal to 1 if the spell of participation in one of the states is completed in t. The independent is equal to 0 for spells that are not completed in t or for spells that are censored. This variable indicates the movements between the farming states and is regressed on the duration variable, on covariates that describe household and farm characteristics and on frailty.

Based on previous studies on the farming activity or labor market occupation of agricultural households in China (e.g. Kimhi, 2000; Brosig et al., 2009) the following explanatory variables are considered for the estimations. Their expected effect on the hazard to change between full-time and part-time farming or the other way around are discussed in the following parts and presented in *Table 20.*

The number of persons living in the household, HSIZE, includes the labor force and all dependents. The size of the family has effects on the demand for the time spent at home, overall consumption and on the amount of labor that is supplied to off-farm activities (Kimhi, 2000). It is assumed that this variable has a positive influence on the hazard in the case of the transition from full-time to part-time farming because it becomes more likely that one household member starts to supply labor off the farm if the family is larger (Brosig et al., 2009). The opposite should be the case for the switch from part-time to full-time farming. So the effect of the household size on the hazard rate is expected to be negative in the latter transition case.

Men and women in rural China differ in the degree and type of labor market participation (Maurer-Fazio et al., 2005; de Brauw et al., 2002). Therefore, the number of female laborers in the total household labor force is included to control for effects stemming from the gender composition of household's labor force. In general, women are assumed to be more likely to supply labor off the farm (Ahituv and Kimhi, 2006). Since the 1980s, this is also the case for China to the evolving rural village and township enterprises that demanded labor in e.g. textile manufacturing.[15] Based on several sets of variables included into the

---

[15] In 1995, around 18 % of laborers in Hebei were employed in manufacturing as compared to the national average of 16 % (NBS, 1996). In 2002, still 17 % of the laborers in Hebei have been employed in manufacturing compared to the national average of 11 % (NBS, 2003). In the same year, 43 % of the laborers employed in manufacturing on the national level were women and for wholesale and retailing this figure was 45 % (NBS, 2003). For Hebei there is no decomposition of the labor force by sector into male and female laborers available.

empirical model, the absolute number of female laborers is not included here because it never showed a significant contribution to the explanation of the hazard rate.

Zhang et al. (2002) analyze the impact of education on the supply of labor to off-farm activities in rural China and they show that laborers with higher education are more likely to participate in off-farm work. The farm household can benefit from comparative advantages and maximize its income, if it is able to provide labor to either on- or off-farm activities in function of the educational level of the household's labor force (Yang, 1997). So if one assumes that a laborer with a higher level of achieved human capital is more productive in off-farm than in farm work (Ahituv and Kimhi, 2006) then a higher share of household members that graduated from secondary school (EDUS) should positively contribute to the hazard rate of leaving full-time farming. Again the opposite effect should be found for the state change from part-time to full-time farming.

It is assumed that the membership in the Chinese Communist Party helps in creating informal social networks (McGuire et al., 2007; Knight and Yueh, 2002). Therefore it should have a positive effect on taking up off-farm work. At the same time, party membership in rural China might also provide better access to inputs necessary for farming (Brosig et al., 2009). Consequently, the effect of the dummy variable PARTY that reflects the number of party members belonging to the household is expected to be positive on both state changes.

The impact that hired farm labor might have on the hazard rate depends on the assumptions regarding the substitution between family and hired farm labor (Alasia et al., 2009; Kimhi, 2009). If farm size increases it might be more likely that family laborers specialize in management or supervision of the household agricultural production while employing labor for less sophisticated activities. In this case, the two kinds of labor would not be (perfect) substitutes (Kimhi, 2009). In addition, incentive issues (Swinnen, 2009), moral hazard and monitoring problems would suggest that family and non-family agricultural labor would not be perfect substitutes. Also the profitability of family labor might be higher than that of hired labor (Rosenzweig and Wolpin, 1985). However, because the farm size in the case of rural Hebei is rather small in the observation period, it is assumed here that family and non-family farm labor can be substituted, if not fully then at least to some extent. Brosig et al. (2007) argue that also land specific experience might decrease the substitutionality between hired and family labor. Especially for the rather scattered farm structure in Hebei this might hold, because farm households cultivate plots that sometimes differ strongly e.g. in the soil properties or the access to irrigation water (Böber, 2009).

The variable EMPLOY covers all non-family labor, so also non-agricultural hired labor is contained in it. Therefore, it is possible to argue with Brosig et al.

(2009), that families that run highly labor intensive agricultural production might not be able to provide off-farm labor. It might also be possible that hiring farm labor (for less sophisticated activities) might provide the possibility to supply (higher skilled) family labor to off-farm activities (Brosig et al., 2009). Based on these thoughts it is hypothesized that the coefficient of EMPLOY is positive for the shift from full- to part-time farming if family and non-family labor are almost substitutable and negative if they are not. So, also for the shift from part- to full-time farming both impacts from hired labor on the hazard rate can be thought of. If part-time farm households employ more non-family farm labor they might be specializing in farming activity and therefore the effect of EMPLOY is positive. On the other hand if the employed labor is only engaged in non-agricultural household activities it might have a negative effect on the probability that the household changes from part- to full-time farming.

In rural China, there is still a surplus of labor, so especially in agricultural production labor is used to a larger extent than what would be necessary under an optimal combination of input factors (Feng and Heerink, 2008). Effects of labor migration are included with the variable MIGRANT that provides the information if a household has any member that is working as a migrant laborer. In general men have a higher probability to be migrant workers than women in China (de Brauw, 2003). The migration of family labor in other regions has two effects (Brosig et al., 2009). First it affects the amount of family labor available for family farm agricultural production. And the second effect is the income effect stemming from the remittances that are sent home by the migrant workers. If there are one or more members of the household working as migrants this might increase the hazard that a household shifts away from full-time farming because less labor is available for farming, if not compensated by hired labor. One could argue that provision of migrant labor is a substitute to local off-farm labor (Brosig et al, 2009) and then newly up-taken or increased migrant labor provision of the household might also positively contribute to the hazard rate for the state change from full-time to part-time farming.

The possibilities to provide family labor off the farm and to earn income depend also on farm characteristics. The available arable land and also the type of agricultural production, e.g. plant versus animal production, have an impact on how the household uses its labor endowment (Brosig et al., 2009). Land is the core productive asset for farmers. Most of the farms in Hebei are rather small scale farms. For those farms the inverse productivity relationship literature argues that the family farmers farm their land more intensively (Benjamin and Brandt, 1997). The reason for this are imperfections in the labor or land rental market that restrict the amount of family labor provided on or off the own farm to be adjusted via changes in the amount of land holdings.[16] If land adjustments are restricted, then the effect that land holdings have on farm households' labor provision might be biased. The variable LAND contains the amount of arable land plus the amount of orchard area of the household per capita in mu. Based on Brosig et al. (2009), one can argue that the effect of the variable household's arable land per capita (LAND) is positive in both estimations of state change. This would imply that a larger amount of land provides more flexibility to the agricultural household to decide about the provision of family labor outside the own farm. If this holds, then allowing households to adjust in the farm size by transfer or rental would enable them to provide family labor to those occupations where it would be most productive.

The specialization of a household in animal or plant production has an impact on the ratio between on- and off-farm labor provision. Some kinds of animal production require a large amount of labor. To account for the effect of husbandry, the variable LIVES is included which represents the output of pork, beef, lamb, poultry, eggs, and milk production weighted by labor requirements (Brosig et al., 2009). It is most plausible to use weights relative to the mean value of 1 kg of pork produced, because for pork there are more observations in the data set than for the other husbandry products. Therefore the following weights are applied to generate LIVES (*Table 18*).

Table 18: Weighting factors for the husbandry output (LIVES)

Output	Mean labor days per kg	Weight
Milk	6.64	2.60
Eggs	2.87	1.12
Pork	2.56	1
Beef	2.00	0.78
Poultry	1.56	0.61

Source: Own computations based on RCRE data for Hebei, 1995-2002.

Even though the output of husbandry production is of less importance in the data set because grain and vegetable cultivation are the dominating agricultural production types of family farms in the study region (*Table 19*) husbandry is still included in the regressions to control for differences in agricultural production systems. It is assumed that larger amounts of animal products are based on

16 For the data set at hand no variable can be included that directly measures the effect of different institutional settings regarding land transfers or other restrictions in the land and labor market, beside the known limitation of labor migration because of the *hukou* system.

specialization17 of the household in animal production. As a consequence from this assumption, the effect of LIVES on the hazard rate is expected to be negative for the state change from full-time to part-time farming because some of the production specific knowledge might be of less use in off-farm employment. This means, that the household cannot achieve an adequate income from husbandry specific knowledge outside the own farm production and so is faced with a sunk costs constraint in its decision to provide labor off-farm. So, the household would still decide to provide labor time off the own farm, but the investment in husbandry specific knowledge could not be recovered.

Table19: Household income and farming activity, 1995-2002

Households in sample holding arable land [%]	95
Per capita net income rural households, 2002 [1000 RMB] [a]	2.7
Income share of household business in total income, 2002 [%] [b]	66
Average land endowment of household [mu]	7.1
Most common size class (arable land + orchard)	1.5-10
Share of farms with 1.5-10 mu [%]	61
Volume of annual agricultural production [1000 RMB, 2000 prices] [c]	5.4
Within this: share of home consumption	43.5
Main products (% in value of production) [d]	Vegetables (50), Wheat (41), Maize (30), Pork (25)

Notes: [a] NBS (2003), Statistical Yearbook 2003, p. 368, Tab 10-20.
[b] 74 % of household income stem from agricultural production.
[c] Value of production in prices of 2000. As in Brosig et al. (2009) mean (deflated) unit values of sales over the period 1995-2002 were used to compute average prices for each product. This method provides enough price information in the absence of (village or province level) price data for agricultural products.
[d] Mean values for the whole sample. Not all farmers produce all products.
Source: Own computations based on RCRE data for Hebei, 1995-2002.

The duration variable is expected to have a negative sign in both estimations. Because it is assumed that the longer a household already remained in either full- or part-time farming the less likely is it that it changes this occupation-

17 Pingali (1997) expects that the degree of specialization in husbandry production is raising in several Asian agricultural production systems under transformation (including rural China) despite the fact of the still quite high level of fragmentation.

al state due to transition costs or the achieved state specific knowledge (Rosenzweig and Wolpin, 1985).

Table 20: Household and farm characteristics by labor market participation state

Household characteristics	Variable	All households (N = 4,231)	Part-time farm households (N = 2,980)	Full-time farm households (N = 1,251)		Expected impact on the hazard rate $\lambda(t)$: Full-time to part-time	Expected impact on the hazard rate $\lambda(t)$: Part-time to full-time
Household size [persons]	HSIZE	4.21 (1.51)	4.41 (1.44)	3.66 (1.57)	*	+	-
Secondary school graduates among laborers [%]	EDUS	57.83 (34.52)	57.82 (33.38)	52.32 (39.42)		+	-
Communist party member [1/0]: % of households	PARTY	0.19 (0.39)	20.81 (40.6)	0.14 (0.35)	*	+	+
Employing hired labor [1/0]: % of households	EMPLOY	2.20 (14.66)	2.10 (14.28)	2.48 (15.55)		+/-	+/-
Any members working as migrants [1/0]: % of households	MIGRANT	20.21 (40.16)	28.42 (45.11)	0.64 (7.97)	*	+	+
Farm characteristics							
Agricultural land [mu per capita]	LAND	1.65 (0.91)	1.62 (0.83)	1.73 (1.08)	*	+	+
Animal production, weighted output [100 kg]	LIVES	44.90 (205.97)	39.45 (171.33)	57.88 (270.86)	*	-	+

Notes: Standard deviations in parentheses.
* Distributions differ significantly between full- and part-time farm households (see Appendix C).
+ Covariate expected to have a positive impact on the hazard rate
- Covariate expected to have a negative impact on the hazard rate

Source: Own computations based on RCRE survey data for Hebei 1995-2002.

Table 20 provides an overview of the explanatory variables, their respective summary statistics, the results for the test of significant differences between the two sub samples full-time and part-time farm households and the expected signs of the coefficients of those variables in the estimation of the respective hazard models.

Based on the analysis described in Appendix C (*Table 23*) most of the co-variates are found to be significantly different between the two sub samples of full-time and part-time farm households. Following Brosig et al. (2009) this confirms the relevance of distinguishing between both groups.

The independent variable ξ is generated separately for both samples.

7.3.2 Estimation procedure and model power

Two models are estimated separately, one for the change from full-time to part-time farming and one model for the change in the opposite direction. In both settings it is tested for frailty. With respect to frailty, the null-hypothesis is that the variance of frailty is zero. This is necessary to be able to distinguish between the effects of unobserved heterogeneity and duration dependence.

As in Brosig et al. (2009) the -pgmhaz8- procedure programmed by Jenkins (1997) is applied for the estimation of the hazard models in a first step. With this procedure it is possible to include the variance of unobserved heterogeneity (frailty) as parameter in the estimation of the hazard rate. Controlling for several possible distributions of the frailty parameter, gamma, mass-point and normal distribution (Jenkins, 2008) shows that this unobserved heterogeneity is not relevant. The null-hypothesis regarding frailty is rejected in both models (*Table 21*).

Based on this result the final models for both state changes are estimated using a generalized linear model with a complementary log-log link function (see Brosig et al., 2009, footnote 13). The Stata command is as follows: glm xi DUR HSIZE FEM EDUS PARTY EMPLOY MIGRANT LAND LIVES, family (binomial) link(cloglog), where xi is the respective independent variable indicating state changes either from full-time to part-time farming or from part-time to full-time farming.

The explanatory power of the models is tested by calculating the share of right predicted state changes and by comparing the full models (all covariates) with restricted models using the Likelihood Ratio test (LR test). The null hypothesis is that all parameters except the constant are equal to 0. As can be seen from *Table 21*, H_0 is rejected in both model settings. Consequently, the chosen covariates are of relevance for explaining the changes between the two farming states.

A state change is considered to be predicted right by the model if the value of the predicted movements between the states is larger than the relative frequency of a state change. Therefore as in Brosig et al. (2009) the predicted completion of participation state is set equal to one if the predicted probability of a state change exceeds the relative frequency of a status change in the original sample and zero otherwise. For the sample of 2,980 observations a total of 722 observed state changes occur for the state part-time farming, meaning 722 households change from part-time to full-time farming. Of these changes, 462 are correctly predicted by the model, which corresponds to 53%. For the changes from full- to part-time farming the model predicts 63% of the state changes correctly. Those results are satisfactory and in line with the findings by Brosig et al. (2009). But even if the frailty variance is not found to be significant, it is likely that there are variables that better explain the hazard of state changes than those available for the analysis here. For example, village effects could not be included, because the RCRE household data set does not contain sufficient information about the income or migration structure or the demographical composition of the population on village level.

7.3.3 Estimation results

The results of the duration estimations for both state changes, full-time to part-time farming and part-time to full-time farming, are presented in *Table 21*.

Besides the DUR variable (length of the period that a household remained in a previously occupied state) 3 out of the 7 covariates in the model have a significant effect on the hazard that a household leaves the currently occupied state for the state change from full- to part-time. For the state change from part- to full-time farming, 2 out of 7 covariates are significant.

The hazard ratio that provides the relative change of the hazard rate if the respective covariate changes by 1 unit is computed from the respective β as in Brosig et al. (2009): hazard ratio = $d \ln \lambda(z, \beta) / dz = \exp(\beta)$. First, the results for the estimations regarding model (1) are discussed. Against the expectation, the coefficient of HSIZE is negative. The value of -0.092 for this parameter implies a hazard ratio 0.912, which means that the hazard to start supplying off-farm labor decreases by 8.8% for a household with one more person than the average household in Hebei.

Table 21: Results from the estimation of duration models

	State change full-time to part-time farming (1)			State change part-time to full-time farming (2)		
	Parameter		Hazard ratio	Parameter		Hazard ratio
DUR	-1.76	***	0.172	-1.414	***	0.243
	(0.096)			(0.059)		
CONSTANT	1.460	***		0.964	***	
	(0.201)			(0.183)		
Household characteristics						
HSIZE	-0.092	**	0.912	-0.015		0.985
	(0.039)			(0.030)		
EDUS	-0.003	**	0.997	-0.002		0.998
	(0.001)			(0.001)		
PARTY	0.047		1.048	0.014		1.014
	(0.152)			(0.103)		
EMPLOY	0.398		1.489	0.011		1.011
	(0.372)			(0.292)		
MIGRANT	-0.681		0.506	-0.228	**	0.796
	(0.774)			(0.088)		
Farm characteristics						
LAND	0.044		1.045	0.089	*	1.093
	(0.056)			(0.047)		
LIVES	0.0004	***	1.000	0.0002		1.000
	(0.0002)			(0.0002)		
Model diagnostics						
H_0: All parameters except the constant = 0	LR-statistic		442.22		633.68	
	p-value		0.000		0.000	
Share of correct predictions			63%		53%	
State changes/ Observations			437/1,251		722/ 2,980	
H_0: Variance of frailty = 0	LR-statistic		-151.64		-146.99	
	p-value		0.5		0.5	

Notes: Standard errors in parentheses.
***: significant at 1% level of error probability,
**: significant at 5% level of error probability,
*: significant at 10% level of error probability.
Source: Own computations based on RCRE survey data for Hebei 1995-2002.

As Brosig et al. (2009) explain, it is more intuitive that larger households have a higher probability to supply (more) off-farm labor. But the picture looks different if larger households tend to employ more family labor full-time on the farm (Kimhi, 2000). One reason for this behavior could be specialization of family members and specific knowledge of them about the production processes on the family farm. Because only household level aggregated data are available, it is not possible to fully account for the specific labor market occupation of individuals.

Yang (1997) found that work specialization in agricultural households in China takes place especially with respect to education. Higher educated workers tend to supply more labor off-farm. Put differently, if a farm household supplies labor to other occupations than on-farm agricultural or non-agricultural household business, then it is more likely to provide the higher educated family members. But the coefficient of EDUS is unexpectedly negative. EDUS measures the share of household members with secondary education. Therefore, the absolute value of the coefficient results in a 0.3% lower hazard rate if the share of laborers who graduated from secondary school increases by one percentage point.

The weighted output of animal production (LIVES) is highly significant but with a small absolute value of the coefficient. This might be due to the fact that only a small amount of farm households produces animals or animal products. So, for the value of 0.0004 of the parameter LIVES in the model (1), this gives in a hazard ratio of 1.0004. This means that if a household produces 100 kg more of husbandry output per year, then it has a 0.04% higher hazard to change from full- to part-time farming independent form the duration. Even the sign of the coefficient is not as expected because a higher level of animal production seems to be related to a higher probability to leave full-time farming.

For the estimation of the model that estimates the state change from part-time to full-time farming (2) the following variables have a significant effect on the hazard rate.

The variable MIGRANT has a significant but negative effect of -0.228 on the hazard rate for the model that estimates the state change from part-time to full-time farming. For the dummy variables the parameter of the coefficient is interpreted as the hazard if the dummy takes the value 1 as in contrast to the hazard if the value of the dummy variable is 0 (Brosig et al., 2009). A household that has at least one member of the family working as a migrant has a hazard ratio of 0.80 and by this a 20% lower hazard to stop the supply of off-farm labor. This is an opposite result to what Brosig et al. (2009) found for Hubei province and indicates that there is no substitution relationship between the local supply of non-agricultural family labor outside the family farm and migratory labor supply for Hebei.

LAND shows a slightly significant positive effect on the hazard rate to stop off-farm labor supply. The hazard ratio for LAND is 1.103 (exp (0.098)). So, a household with 1 mu more of agricultural land per capita than the average household in the data set has a 10.3% higher hazard to change from part-time to full-time farming independent of the duration (the hazard rate is the same for every point in time). It was expected for LAND to have a positive effect in both state change estimations.

Because the other explanatory variables show no significant effect, they are not discussed in more detail here. Instead the interpretation of the predicted hazards reveals some insight to how far the probability that a household remains in a state depends on the length of this occupation. The parameter estimates for the variable DUR are used to calculate the predicted hazard rates for a hypothetical household (Brosig et al., 2009). The predicted hazard for a duration of t years

$$=1-\exp\left(-\exp\left(\sum_{k\neq DUR}\bar{x}^k\beta^k+\ln(t)\beta^{DUR}\right)\right),$$

where $\bar{x}^k$ is the mean of the k-th covariate (Brosig et al., 2009).[18]

In general, the hazard rate for the shift from part-time to full-time farming is lower than the one for the shift in the other direction (*Figure 11*).

For both estimations the coefficient of the duration variable is negative. So, the probability to change from one state of farming activity to the alternative one becomes less likely the longer the farm household remained in the current state (*Figure 11*). These findings are conform to the results of Brosig et al. (2009). For a spell length of one year being full-time farm household the hazard is 55%. After 3 years of being a full-time farm household the hazard to change the state is 11% and decreasing for longer durations: only 2% for a duration of 8 years. The decline in the hazard to leave full-time farming can be explained by specific knowledge gained during a longer occupation in family agricultural production and a resulting high efficiency in farming (Brosig et al., 2009). If the household started supplying off-farm labor some of this specific knowledge would get lost.

[18] This is computed in Stata, e.g. for the part-time to full-time model: mat b = e(b), mat score xb = b; sum xb if _end_Part_time==1; ge z0 = r(mean) + _b[DUR]*DUR; sort id duration_part_time; by id: gen p0 = 1-exp(-exp(z0)).

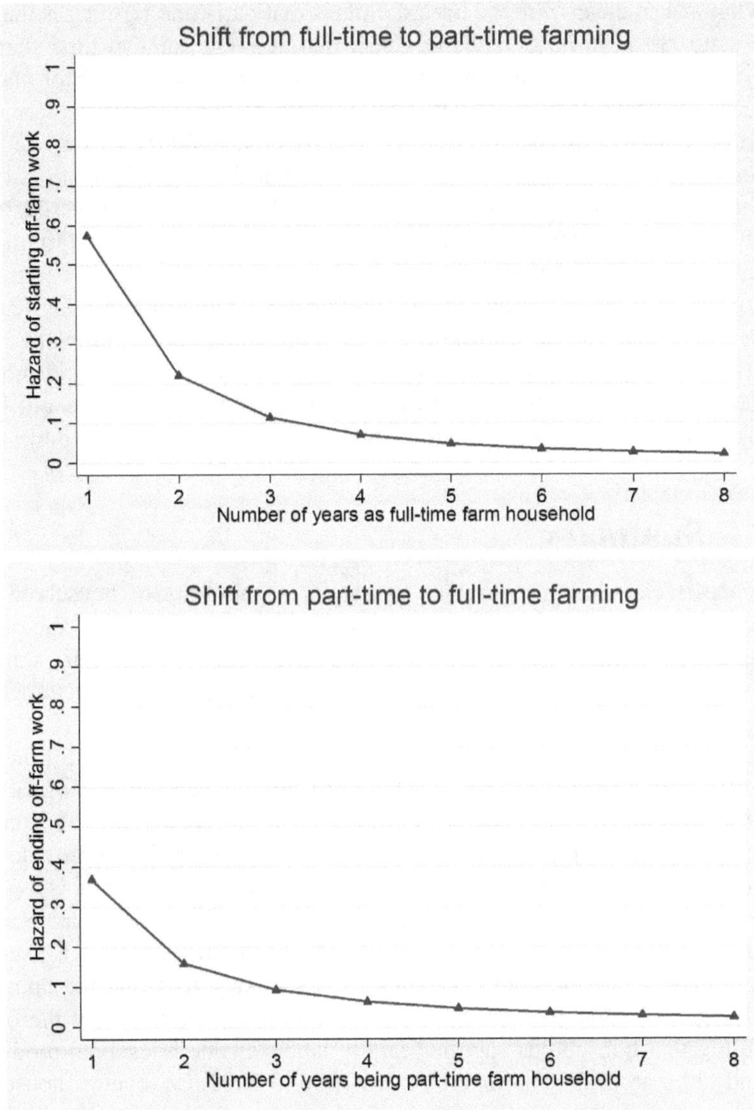

Source: Own computations based on RCRE survey data for Hebei 1995-2002.

Figure 11: Predicted hazards for state changes between full-time and part-time farming and between part-time and full-time farming

What is also clear from the hazard plots is that part-time farming is the more stable state. So farm households in Hebei that at some point in time started to supply labor off the farm hardly leave this state. If the spell lasted for one year the hazard to leave is 37%. Again after 3 years of being part-time farmer the hazard to change is lower than 10%. As Brosig et al. (2009) explain one has to be careful with the interpretation of movements from part-time to full-time farming when assessing those changes on household level. Two reasons might lead the change of a household from part-time farming to full-time farming (see Brosig et al. 2009). The first is that family members that supplied off-farm labor give up this activity and fully supply all their labor force to family agricultural production or that they stop working off-farm due to e.g. health problems. A second possibility is that the member(s) that formerly was (were) responsible for the classification of the household as being a part-time farm household leaves (leave) the household either by setting up an own household or dies (die).

7.4 Summary

This chapter explains the variables to test for separability of household labor demand and supply, for estimating households' labor allocation and for assessing the persistence of farm structures and provides their summary statistics. Fixed-effect regressions are applied to control for unobserved heterogeneity among the sample households.

The hypotheses of separability can be rejected. This is the case for the analysis of the whole sample but also for the test using the sub-samples of part- and full-time farm households. Larger households use relatively more labor in agricultural production which might indicate missing opportunities to provide family labor to off-farm occupations. Even though no wage information is available some variables that should contain wage influences on households' labor allocation are significant (e.g. some of the location*year dummy variables). The higher the amount of arable land per capita the less likely it is that the household provides family labor outside the own agricultural production. But the overall probability that households supplied family labor outside household production is found to be around 70% for the period 1986 to 2002. So, even if households are constrained in their possibilities to provide labor off the farm, they still supply labor to the market. As de Brauw et al. (2002) find, the reform of rural institutions in thc 1980s and 1990s increased the possibilities of rural households to provide labor to off-farm occupations and they estimate that the number of rural laborers providing labor time to these off-farm activities increased for overall China from 40 million in 1981 to 150 million laborers. For this reason, it is important to assess household and farm characteristics that might explain rural households' labor allocation decisions.

The longer a household in rural Hebei remained in the state of either being a part- or full-time farm household the less likely it is that it will change the state. But the state change from full-time to part-time farming is more likely to occur than the change from part- to full-time farming. Larger households are less likely to change from full- to part-time farming.

The assessment of labor market participation is done using the hazard model developed before. About 74% of all assessed observations of labor market participation states are correctly classified by the chosen static logit model specification to explain households' choices between 4 different labor market participation states (autarky, supply, supply and hire or hire). Significant and strong positive effects on households' labor allocation decisions are found for variables related to education and to individual skills of labor force members. In addition off-farm work is found to be accessible and also favorable for women. Transfer income reduces the overall probability that households participate in the labor market.

8 Conclusions

It was the aim of this study to assess the development of rural institutions, households' well-being and the labor market allocation decisions of farm households in Hebei province between 1986 and 2002.

General shortcomings of this work are the limited availability of individual and village level data, which restricted the power of the application of panel data models. There exist also some problems regarding the quality of the secondary data set like the use of the same IDs for different observations. Methodologically the study only applies static models. So, future research could focus on the application of dynamic models to assess agricultural households' labor allocation behavior.

Overall the assessment resulted in several implications for policy makers and further research which are presented separate for the specific topics addressed in the analysis chapters 6 and 7 in the following concluding sections.

Poverty development

With the first research question it was asked how poverty levels developed in Hebei province between 1986 and 2002 and it was hypothesized that absolute poverty declined over this period.

It is shown in this study that well-being improved and less people are considered being poor in rural Hebei province in 2002 than in 1986 besides the fact, that rural households might be more sensitive to fluctuations in productivity when comparing the new market oriented institutional systems with the former communist one (Benjamin et al., 2005). Although absolute poverty decreased in Hebei over this period, 1986 to 2002, the poverty decomposition indicates that if rural households in Hebei are poor then two thirds of poverty is explained as being chronic poverty. Using the approach developed by Duclos et al. (2008), transient poverty contributes less to total poverty in 2002 than estimated by Jalan and Ravallion (1998). The latter find, through their analysis of poverty in China over the years 1985 to 1990, that half of the squared poverty gap and more than one third of the mean poverty gap is found to be transient poverty. From this part of the analysis it can be concluded that the choice of instrument really matters when measuring the relative importance of chronic and transient poverty. For political and social decision makers it is worth to notice the difference in results of both methods. Depending on the poverty decomposition method used there are differing suggestions regarding policy programs to identify rural poor in China. The question is if policies for poverty elimination should concentrate on measures to improve permanent well-being of the rural households or if they should be oriented to lower the exposure to transient poverty or the exposure to uninsured income risk as proposed by Jalan and Ravallion (1998). It is recommended that investments in measures to reduce chronic poverty should be continued, since they proofed to be successful over the last three decades. In addition market oriented instruments such as crop insurances should be implemented to reduce severe fluctuations in agricultural income due to bad harvests and by this lower the probability that rural households experience periods, during which they can not cover their living expenditures from own production and income.

Poverty levels are more unequal between different villages. This means that poverty levels are more different when comparing villages with each other instead of comparing the level of poverty of households within one village. So the location of the household strongly affects its well-being. Therefore measures to prevent inequality in poverty should focus on the development of institutions at the village level (Benjamin et al., 2005) or community development (Liu and Sicular, 2008). But poverty levels are also more unequal among households which differ in their labor market participation. The impact on inequality is lower for households that are stronger involved in non-farm activities. This indicates that supporting rural families in diversifying their labor allocation might also be a way to prevent inequality in well-being in a specific location.

For future research, a more comprehensive data set of the RCRE including village, household and individual level information for the period 2003-2009 could be used to better distinguish between personal, family and location characteristics in explaining differences in poverty. Information about the development of market prices for grain or other agricultural inputs could be included into further poverty assessments because Benjamin et al. (2005) show that strong fluctuations in market prices for grain also let poverty rates vary strongly in rural China.

Income decomposition

Two of the research questions were devoted to the composition of agricultural households' income and the inequality in income among households.

It is found, that non-agricultural income contributes stronger to income inequality among rural households in the same location than income earned from agricultural production. So, even though on one side providing individual farm households an insurance against income fluctuations due to unforeseen yield and price changes for agricultural outputs by diversifying income, on the other side, non-agricultural income also contributes to differences in well-being especially within the same village. Currently the inequality increasing effect of non-farm income on household income inequality is stronger than the risk-insurance effect, which would make incomes between households more equal. There are several reasons why households are unequal with respect to their off-farm income. It can be assumed that off-farm wages are higher the better qualified laborers are. Individual characteristics and abilities of household members would therefore be a reason why income is distributed unequally. As discussed, inequality in qualification but also in income can be beneficiary for the whole economy, since it incaourages the laborers to compete for higher incomes and is by this promoting economic development. The approach to equalize income of rural laborers during the commune system was a failure because it provided no incentives to the individual workers to put more effort into work. Recently policy makers are concerned about rising inequality in well-being especially between rural and urban areas. If the rural areas can not keep speed with well-being improvements in urban areas then migration (legally or illegally) takes place, which challenges urban work and social institutions systems.

Because income inequality is mainly explained by individual or household characteristics, it should be addressed at this level. To some extent, educational differences could be balanced by providing equal schooling to children. Currently, education expenditures differ strongly between regions in China because provincial and local governments are responsible for education and they are likely to distribute financial resources for education depending on the local development stage (Liu and Sicular, 2008). But because also individual physical factors like for example differences in the nutrition of children (Luo et al., 2009) have an effect on human capital and future abilities to participate in highly productive occupations, it is not possible to reach full income equality by just providing education. Therefore, policy measures that address e.g. nutritional deficiencies of children, like the provision of information about linkages between sufficient nutrition and children's abilities to parents and teachers or the provision of sufficient meals, especially in boarding schools, have to be applied to equalize rural well-being in the long run. A better balanced nutrition might help especially poorer groups of the rural population to be able to increase their knowledge and skills. Up to now it was a policy aim to increase the well-being in rural areas in the sum, but more care should be taken on the distribution of well-being.

However, any measure to equalize income should be implemented with great care because equalizing income among a population could also decrease incentives to be more productive, as already discussed in the theoretical part of this work. In consequence, non-market measures (subsidies or other income support) to equalize income among the rural population might also be a danger for overall economic development of rural areas in Hebei especially compared to urban areas. During the period of the centrally planned socialist economy China already experienced problems arising from low incentives to work (efficiently), because of central redistribution. Policy makers should be aware that centrally planned measures of income support for the rural population reduce the possibilities of the rural economy to allocate production factors, in the present case especially labor, in the most efficient way. The agricultural and non-agricultural production in Hebei would not only be not Pareto optimal but also the potential to (re-) adjust input combinations to increase the agricultural output in a sustainable manner could hardly be fully utilized.

Separability of labor demand and supply

As hypothesized, separability is rejected for the data set at hand so that it can be concluded that labor market constraints existed in rural Hebei during the analyzed period. In contrast to Bowlus and Sicular (2003) and Kuiper (2005), no significant difference between households that are full-time farm households and those providing family labor for off-farm purposes is found. So, labor market constraints affect the two distinguished household groups to the same extent. Wang (2007) also confirms non-separability regarding households' decision to supply family labor off the farm and to hire agricultural labor instead.

Future research should further assess whether differences in separability of household decisions are found by including wage variables available, individual characteristics (age, education, skills) and exact (hourly) labor occupations, also for different agricultural activities such as manual work versus supervision activities, of each household laborer into the model.

Labor market participation of rural households

Based on the research questions which factors determine the labor allocation decisions of the assessed agricultural households it was hypothesized that education and the provision of specific training might enable laborers in farm households to better devote their labor to farm or off-farm occupations.

The results presented in section 7.2.3 confirm that rural households in Hebei are more likely to participate in off-farm labor markets if household members are better educated and receive training to acquire special skills. Better education provides better access to usually higher paid jobs. The highest return to education is found with respect to high schools. According to the statistical yearbook of Hebei, in 2008 around 30% of all school-age children enter institutions of higher learning, hence are enrolled in schools beyond senior secondary schools (ACMR 2010) but this number includes rural and urban children. For rural areas it can be assumed that high school enrollment rates are lower than for urban areas (Zhang et al., 2002). Hence, infrastructural investments in high schools in rural areas should be increased (see also Zhang et al., 2002) and high school enrollment rates of children in rural Hebei should be improved, to empower children to move out of agricultural production in their later work life. So, this positive externality of education should encourage local and central governmental bodies to invest in schooling, despite the ongoing debate about the decentralization of revenue raising and spending from the central to the provincial and even local administrative level (Zhang and Zou, 1998). Providing financial support to enable rural children to participate in higher education was also recommended by Liu and Sicular (2008) and would help to improve off-farm labor market participation of households in rural Hebei. Investment in the rural areas in Hebei province and in the agricultural sector should not only be seen as capital investment or money transfer. It is the investment in skills and knowledge that helps facilitating the transformation of agricultural traditional labor intensive production systems to modes of production that require less labor and by this offer the chance to allocate labor to industry and services (Schultz, 1964). Also Wang (2007) argues that improvements in education are likely to increase the heterogeneity among the rural labor force and by this encourage farm households to supply better educated family labor off the farm and to hire more farm labor as long as the marginal off-farm income is equal or higher than the marginal costs of hired labor. If policy makers in the future want to improve the possibilities for rural labor to migrate, then investment in human capital is one promising starting point.

It is found that unearned income (TRANFERS) reduces rural labor supply to non-farm agricultural activities. This confirms the conclusion of the income inequality assessment, that subsidies to increase rural household incomes need to be handled carefully. In the short run, an increase in income might satisfy people but might as well reduce their labor time spent in off-farm activities. Consequently, the respective off-farm labor productivity might decline due to a loss of work specific knowledge over time. So in the long run, a permanent and even increasing governmental income support, for example in the form of per area subsidies, might have a negative effect on the off-farm income earning potential of rural laborers and by this widen the inequality gap between urban and rural areas in Hebei. This result is very important considering current agricultural policy approaches of providing subsidies that are aimed to increase rural households' incomes. Even if per area subsidy for sowing wheat might provide income to the farmers in the short run, it discourages them to participate in off-farm labor markets. This was also confirmed by farmers who explained that they worked less outside the village after they received a fixed amount of Yuan per area land sown with wheat (Böber, 2009). They did not only reduce the labor supply to off-farm activities (less rural to urban labor migration) but they also reduce their efforts regarding agricultural production. So, wheat fields of those farmers showed a higher proportion of weeds, since weeding is a relatively labor intensive activity in wheat production in Hebei. The result is that the transfer (per area subsidy) that was earmarked as a contribution to increase the wheat production, was considered by the farmers as a kind of lump sum income transfer that they did not necessarily use for agricultural production purposes such as investment in mechanization. The farmers are aware that they are not monitored regarding the output of wheat.

For further research it would be especially interesting to use the most recent RCRE data (2003-2009) for investigating which impacts the mentioned changes in the agricultural tax and subsidy system had on off-farm labor market participation or labor supply decisions of farm households in Hebei. Since recent years, the RCRE survey also collected information on all individuals in the household. So, it would be interesting to apply multinomial models to assess the determinants of individuals' labor market participation as done in de Janvry and Sadoulet (2001) or to analyze more possible labor market participation regimes as done in Benjamin and Kimhi (2006). If possible, this data should also be used to assess the impact of seasonal effects or the composition of family labor in comparison to the composition of hired labor (Deolalikar and Vijverberg, 1987) on the labor allocation decisions of rural households.

The power of the chosen model to explain the labor allocation of the assessed households could be improved if additional information about the characteristics and extend of land rental markets could be included as well as information about the village level wage and unemployment rates. That information is available with the village level questionnaire of the RCRE surveys.

Persistence of farm structures

Regarding the persistence of the decision to be either a part-time or full-time farm household the hypothesis was that the longer the farm household remained in a specific state the less likely it will be, that it changes to the alternative state.

It is evident that farm households frequently supply (some) family labor outside the own farm. So, there is indication that secondary and tertiary labor markets are accessible. But a change in farm regime is less likely to happen the longer the household remained in the full-time farming state. This important insight should fuel programs that increase the degree of specialization in agricultural production so that the knowledge of experienced agricultural laborers is kept and is used to improve production efficiency. The existence and creation of off-farm employment possibilities might lead to a lower amount of rural labor fixed in agricultural production and might also increase overall household income and reduce poverty. But the land market restrictions might still be a reason that hinders this labor specialization process by keeping farm sizes small.

In comparison to the study of Brosig et al. (2009) the effects from the existence and intensity of land markets could not be assessed here. Because it was found during stakeholder interviews in Hebei (Böber, 2009) that the de facto regional and village level institutional set ups regarding land use and land renting differ between locations, it would be valuable to include village level land use rental patterns into the analysis of household's choice between full- and part-time farming.

For further assessments of the determinants of either full- or part-time farming persistence and for explaining which persons are more likely to be either a specialized agricultural or non-agricultural laborer, it is necessary to analyze individual level data about labor market occupations, as already discussed. Also the inclusion of the amount of income earned by individuals from different sources could be a promising variable to explain farm structures. Even if panel data on individual household members are available it might be difficult to assess individual preferences and tastes that are responsible for the choice to be either full-time or part-time involved in agricultural activities.

The institutional system in rural China in general, and Hebei in particular, is still subject to policy induced changes also due to the complexity of differing local economic and environmental conditions even within one province. Even if China is not a fully competitive market economy one could follow the constituting principles of economic policy formulated by Eucken (2004) and argue that the institutional or the policy framework should be kept stable for some time to allow economic agents, and especially farmers, to adjust their behavior to changing institutional conditions. For specific crop, per area or fertilizer subsidies to show their success or failure it might take at least two or three cultivation periods until farmers adjust their sown area or fertilization practice. That agricultural and social policies change and that those adjustments happen in response to changing world market or environmental conditions or the increasing inequality among societal groups is not a negative development as such. But policy makers should give the agents the time to react to the adjustments.

As the development in rural China since 1978 has shown, decentralized approaches to adjust rural institutions can be successful in improving the income and poverty situation of rural households, mainly because a central authority can hardly possess full information about the local requirements, e.g. of the labor market. Therefore, it might be beneficial for the future economic development of Hebei's rural economy to allow local decision makers to adjust the institutional framework (e.g. regarding the distribution of land-renting and water rights) to their needs. Such a decentralized course of action might also be better suited to find location specific solutions for the increasing environmental problems (e.g. nitrate leaching, declining groundwater tables) caused by the intensive agricultural production in Hebei and the North China Plain. Even if the negative externalities caused by environmental degradation affect usually more areas than just the region where the environment is degraded the measures to reduce these negative effects have to be adjusted in a way that preventive measures are accepted by the agents in the region where the negative effects originate from.

References

Abbott, M. and O. Ashenfelter (1976): Labour supply, commodity demand and the allocation of time, *The Review of Economic Studies*, 43 (3): 389-411.

ACMR (2010): China Data Online, http://chinadataonline.org, All China Marketing Research Co., Ltd (ACMR) [last accessed: 2010-02-22].

Adger, W.N. (2000): Social and ecological resilience: Are they related?, *Progress in Human Geography*, 24 (3): 347-64.

Ahearn, M., and J. Lee, Jr. (1991): Multiple job-holding among farm operator households in the United States, in: Hallberg, M., J. Findeis and D. Lass (eds.): Multiple job-holding among farm families, Ames: Iowa State University Press: 3-30.

Ahituv, A. and A. Kimhi (2006): Simultaneous estimation of work choices and the level of farm activity using panel data, *European Review of Agricultural Economics*, 33 (1): 49-71.

Ahituv, A. and A. Kimhi (2001): Off-farm work and capital accumulation decisions of farmers over the life-cycle: The role of heterogeneity and state-dependence, *Journal of Development Economics*, 68 (2): 329-53.

Alasia, A., A. Weersink, R.D. Bollman and J. Cranfield (2009): Off-farm labour decision of Canadian farm operators: Urbanization effects and rural labour market linkages, *Journal of Rural Studies*, 25: 12-24.

Alderman, H., P.-A. Chiappori, L. Haddad, J. Hoddinott and R. Kanbur (1995): Unitary versus collective models of the household: Is it time to shift the burden of proof?, *The World Bank Research Observer*, 10 (1): 1-19.

Araar, A. and J.-Y. Duclos (2007a): Poverty and inequality components: A micro framework, Working Paper 07-35, CIRPÉE, Université Laval, Canada.

Araar, A. and J.-Y. Duclos (2007b): DASP: Distributive Analysis Stata Package, PEP, CIRPÉE and World Bank, Université Laval.

Araar, A. and J.-Y. Duclos (2006): DAD: A software for distributive analysis/ Analyse distributive, PEP-PMMA Training, Addis Ababa, June 2006, http://www.pepnet.org/fileadmin/medias/pdf/files_events/5th_ethiopia/introduction_dad.ppt., [last accessed: 2010-05-06].

Arcand, J.-L. and B. d'Hombres (2006): Testing for separation in agricultural household models and unobservable household specific effects, MPRA Paper No. 1863.

Atkinson, A.B. (1970): On the measurement of inequality, *Journal of Economic Theory*, 2 (3): 244-63.

Azam, M. and A. Shariff (2009): Changes in income inequality in rural India: Decomposing the Gini by income sources, Working Paper.

Babatunde, R.O. and M. Qaim (2009): Poverty and income inequality in rural Nigeria: The role of off-farm income diversification, paper presented at the PEGNet Conference 2009: Policies for Reducing Inequality in the Developing World, Institute of Social Studies, The Hague, 3rd-4th September 2009.

Bajpai, N. and T. Jian (1996): Reform strategies of China and India: Suggestions for future action, Discussion Paper Harvard Institute for International Development.

Baltagi, B.H. (2008): Econometric Analysis of Panel Data, 4th edition, Chichester: Wiley.

Bandourian, R., J.B. McDonald and R.S. Turley (2002): A comparison of parametric models of income distribution across countries and over time, Luxembourg Income Study Working Paper No. 305.

Bardhan, P. and C. Udry (1999): Development Microeconomics, Oxford: Oxford University Press.

Bareth, G. (2003). Möglichkeiten und Grenzen der regionalen agrarumweltrelevanten Modellierung unter Nutzung von GIS in China am Beispiel der Nordchinesischen Tiefebene. Habilitation (postdoctoral lecture qualification). Stuttgart, Germany: University of Hohenheim.

Barning, R. (2007): Economic evaluation of nitrogen application in the North China Plain, Ph.D. Thesis, University of Hohenheim.

Barro, R.J. (2001): Education and economic growth, in: Helliwell, J.F. (ed.): The contribution of human and social capital to sustained economic growth and well-being, OECD: 14-41, http://www.oecd.org/dataoecd/5/49/1825455.pdf, [last accessed: 2010-11-11].

Becker, G.S. (1965): A Theory of the allocation of time, *Economic Journal*, 75 (299): 493-517.

Benjamin, C. and A. Kimhi (2006): Farm work, off-farm work, and hired farm labour: estimating a discrete-choice model of French farm couples' labour decisions, *European Review of Agricultural Economics*, 33 (2): 149-71.

Benjamin, D. (1992): Household composition, labor markets, and labor demand: Testing for separation in agricultural household models, *Econometrica*, 60 (2): 287-322.

Benjamin, D., L. Brandt, J. Giles and S. Wang (2007): Inequality and poverty in China during reform, PMMA Working Paper 2007-07, Poverty and Economic Policy Research Network.

Benjamin, D. and L. Brandt (2002): Property rights, labour markets, and efficiency in a transition economy: The case of rural China, *Canadian Journal of Economics*, 35 (4): 689-716.

Benjamin, D. and L. Brandt (1999): Markets and inequality in rural China: Parallels with the past, *American Economic Review* (Papers and Proceedings), 85 (2): 292-5.

Benjamin, D. and L. Brandt (1997): Land, factor markets, and inequality in rural China: Historical evidence, *Explorations in Economic History*, 34: 460-94.

Benjamin, D., L. Brandt, and J. Giles (2005): The evolution of income inequality in rural China, *Economic Development and Cultural Change*, 53 (4): 769-824.

Berggren, N. and N. Karlson (2003): Constitutionalism, division of power and transaction costs, *Public Choice*, 117: 99-124.

Bernstein, H. and T.J. Byres (2001): From peasant studies to agrarian change, *Journal of Agrarian Change*, 1 (1): 1-56.

Bhattacharyya, A. and E. Parker (1999): Labor productivity and migration in Chinese agriculture: A stochastic frontier approach, *China Economic Review*, 10: 59-74.

Bigsten, A. and J. Levin (2000): Growth, income distribution, and poverty: A review, Working Paper in Economics No. 32, Department of Economics, Göteborg University.

Blundell, R. and T. MaCurdy (1999): Labor supply: A review of alternative approaches, in: Ashenfelter, O. and D. Card (eds.): Handbook of Labor Economics, Vol. 3, Amsterdam et al.: Elsevier.

Böber, C. (2009): Survey in Hebei and Shandong province, 12th-22nd of April 2009.

Böber, C. and M. Zeller (2009): Overuse of agricultural inputs and awareness of environmental consequences – The case of Hebei province, PR of China, Paper presented at the Tropentag 2009, Biophysical and Socio-Economic Frame Conditions for the Sustainable Management of Natural Resources, October 6-8, 2009, Hamburg/ Germany.

Böber, C. (2008): Survey in Hebei province, 4th-13th of July 2008.

Bollman, R.D. (1991): Efficiency aspects of part-time farming, in: Hallberg, M., J. Findeis and D. Lass (eds.): Multiple Job-Holding Among Farm Families, Ames: Iowa State University Press: 112-39.

Bowlus, A.J. and T. Sicular (2003): Moving toward markets? Labor allocation in rural China, *Journal of Development Economics*, 71: 567-83.

Brandt, L. and C. A. Holz (2006): Spatial price differences in China: Estimates and implications, *Economic Development and Cultural Change*, 55 (1): 43-86.

Brandt, L. and C. A. Holz (2005): Provincial-level basket values (price levels) for 1984-2004, Excel spreadsheet, http://ihome.ust.hk/~socholz/Spatial Deflators/CPI-and-basket-values-1984-2004-26Nov05.xls, [last accessed: 2009-03-11].

Brandt, L and B. Sands (1990): Beyond Malthus and Ricardo – Economic growth, land concentration and income distribution in early 20th-Century rural China, *Journal of Economic History*, 50 (4): 807-27.

Brosig, S., T. Glauben, T. Herzfeld and X. Wang (2009): Persistence of full- and part-time farming in Southern China, *China Economic Review*, 20: 360-71.

Brosig, S., T. Glauben, T. Herzfeld, S. Rozelle and X. Wang (2007): The dynamics of Chinese rural households' participation in labor markets, *Agricultural Economics*, 37: 167-78.

Brüderl, J. (2010): Applied regression analysis using Stata, http://www2.sowi.uni-mannheim.de/lsssm/veranst/AppliedRegression.pdf, [last accessed: 2010-03-17].

Buchenrieder, G. (2001): Theoretical concepts of institution sequencing and timing: How applicable are they to the rural transformation process?, in: Buchenrieder, G. (ed.): Rural institutions sequencing and timing in transition economies, Weikersheim: Margraf: 1-25.

Buschena, D., V. Smith and H. Di (2005): Policy reform and farmers' wheat allocation in rural China: A case study, *The Australian Journal of Agricultural and Resource Economics*, 49: 143-58.

Cameron, A.C. and P.K. Trivedi (2009): Microeconometrics using Stata, College Station, Texas: Stata Press.

Carter, C.A. and J. Zhu (2009): Trade liberalization and agricultural terms of trade in China: Price scissors revisited, Contributed paper prepared for presentation at the International Association of Agricultural Economists Conference, Beijing, China, August 16th-22nd, 2009.

Carter, C.A., J. Chen and B. Chu (1999): Agricultural productivity growth in China: Farm level versus national measurement, Working Paper No. 99-001, Department of Agricultural and Resource Economics, University of California Davis.

Carter, M.R. and Y. Yao (2002): Local versus global separabiltiy in agricultural household models: The factor price equalization effect of land transfer rights, *American Journal of Agricultural Economics*, 84 (3): 702-15.

Chan, A. and J. Unger (1982): The hidden economy of Rural China, *Pacific Affairs*, 55 (3): 452-71.

Chan, K.W. and W. Buckingham (2008): Is China abolishing the hukou system?, *The China Quarterly*, doi:10.1017/S0305741008000787.

Chan, S. and A.H. Stevens (2001): Job loss and employment patterns of older workers, *Journal of Labor Economics*, 19 (2): 484-521.

Chang, H. and Y. Zhang (2010): China overhauls agricultural subsidies, http://english.caijing.com.cn/2009-09-22/110257864.html, [last accessed: 2010-04-17].

Chaplin, H., S. Davidova and M. Gorton (2003): Agricultural adjustment and the diversification of farm households in central Europe, Contributed paper selected for presentation at the 25th International Conference of Agricultural Economists, August 16th-22nd, 2003, Durban, South Africa.

Chau, T.W., H. Li, P.W. Liu and J. Zhang (2007): Testing the collective model of household labor supply: Evidence from China, *China Economic Review*, 18: 389-402.

Chen, A.Z., W. Huffman and S. Rozelle (2004): Migration and local off-farm working in rural China, Paper prepared for presentation at the American Agricultural Economics Association Annual Meeting, Denver, USA., August 1st-3rd, 2004.

Chen, A.Z., W. Huffman and S. Rozelle (2003): Technical efficiency of Chinese grain production: A stochastic production frontier approach, Paper prepared for presentation at the American Agricultural Economics Association Annual Meeting, Montreal, Canada, July 27th-30th, 2007.

Chen, L. (2006): Grain market liberalization and deregulation in China: The mediating role of markets for farm household in Jiangxi Province, Ph.D. Thesis, Wageningen University.

Chen, S. and M. Ravallion (2004): Welfare impacts of China's accession to the World Trade Organization, *The World Bank Economic Review*, 18 (1): 29-57.

Chen, S. and M. Ravallion (1996): Data in transition: Assessing rural living standards in Southern China, *China Economic Review*, 7 (1): 23-56.

Chiappori, P.-A. (1988): Rational household labor supply, *Econometrica*, 56 (1): 63-90.

China Business World.com (CBW) (2010): Hebei Province, http://www.cbw.com/general/gintro/hebei.html, [last accessed: 2010-05-06].

Chin, G.T. (2005): Securing a rural land market: Political-economic determinants of institutional change in China's agriculture sector, *Asian Perspective*, 29 (4): 209-44.

Chipman, J. (1985): The theory and measurement of income distribution, in: Basmann, R.L. and G. Rhodes, Jr. (eds.): Advances in econometrics, Greenwich, CT: JAI Press: 135-65.

Chow, G. (2006): Are Chinese official statistics reliable?, *CESifo Economic Studies*, 52 (2): 396-414.

Cleves, M.A., W.W. Gould and R.G. Gutierrez (2002): An Introduction to survival analysis using Stata, College Station, Texas: Stat Press.

Coase, R.H. (1960): The problem of social cost, The Journal of Law and Economics, 3: 1-44, reprinted in Coase, R.H. (1988): The firm, the market, and the law, Chicago and London: The University of Chicago Press.

Conceição, P., J.K. Galbraith and P. Bradford (2001): The Theil index in sequences of nested and hierarchic grouping structures: Implications for the measurement of inequality through time, with data aggregated at different levels of industrial classification, *Eastern Economic Journal*, 27 (4): 491-514.

Corsi, A. and J.L. Findeis (2000): True state dependence and heterogeneity in off-farm labour participation, *European Review of Agricultural Economics*, 27 (2): 127-51.

Coutu, A.J. (1957): Planning of total resource use in low-income and part-time farms, *Journal of Farm Economics*, 39 (5), Proceedings of the Annual Meeting of the American Farm Economic Association: 1350-9.

Cox, N. (2007): RE: st: Shapiro Wilk: data interpretation, http://www.stata.com/statalist/archive/2007-02/msg01003.html, [last accessed: 2010-03-09].

Croll, E. (1994): From Heaven to Earth, London and New York: Routledge.

Croll, E. (1981): The politics of marriage in contemporary China, Cambridge: Cambridge University Press.

Dasgupta, P., A.K. Sen and D. Starrett (1973): Notes on the measurement of inequality, *Journal of Economic Theory*, 6: 180-7.

Davis, D. (1989): Chinese social welfare: Policies and outcomes, *The China Quarterly*, 119: 577-97.

Davis, J. (2002): Land reform initiatives in China, in: Peters, G. (ed.): Proceedings of the XXIV International Conference of Agricultural Economists, Aldershot: Ashgate: 383-98.

Deaton, A. (1997): The analysis of household surveys: A microeconometric approach to development policy, Baltimore: John Hopkins University Press.

de Brauw, A. (2003): Are women taking over the farm in China? Working Paper, Economics Department at Williams College, Williamstown.

de Brauw, A., J. Huang, S. Rozelle, L. Zhang and Y. Zhang (2002): The evolution of China's rural labor markets during the reforms, *Journal of Comparative Economics*, 30: 329-53.

de Janvry, A. and E. Sadoulet (2003): Progress in the modeling of rural households' behavior under market failures, http://are.berkeley.edu/~sadoulet/papers/HH-Thorbecke.pdf, [last accessed: 2010-06-12].

de Janvry, A. and E. Sadoulet (2001): Income strategies among rural households in Mexico: The role of off-farm activities, *World Development*, 29 (3): 467-80.

de Janvry, A., E. Sadoulet and N. Zhu (2005): The role of non-farm incomes in reducing rural poverty and inequality in China, Working Paper, University of California, Berkeley.

De la Mothe, J. and D. Foray (2001): Knowledge management in the innovation process, Boston: Kluwer.

Deolalikar, A.B. and W.P.M. Vijerberg (1987): A test of the heterogeneity of family and hired labour in Asian agriculture, *Oxford Bulletin of Economics and Statistics*, 49 (3): 291-305.

Deutsch, J. and J. Silber (2004): Measuring the impact of various income sources on the link between inequality and development: Implications for the Kuznets Curve, *Review of Development Economics*, 8 (1): 110-27.

Dewatripont, M. and G. Roland (1992): The Virtues of Gradualism and Legitimacy in the Transition to Market Economy, *The Economic Journal*, 102: 291-300.

Dollar, D. (2007): Poverty, inequality and social disparities during China's economic reform, World Bank Policy Research Working Paper 4253.

Donaldson, D. and J.A. Weymark (1980): A single-parameter generalization of the Gini indices of inequality, *Journal of Economic Theory*, 22: 67-86.

Duclos, J.-Y., A. Araar and J. Giles (2008): Chronic and transient poverty: Measurement and estimation, with evidence from China, CIRPÉE, Université Laval, Canada, (Final version due to personal communication with J.-Y. Duclos).

Duclos, J-Y. (2002): Poverty and equity: Theory and estimation, Département d'économique and CRÉFA, Université Laval, Canada, Preliminary version, http://www.pep-nct.org/fileadmin/medias/pdf/I-Poverty-equity-duc los.pdf, [last accessed: 2010-05-12].

ERS (2010): China's provinces, United States Department of Agriculture, Economic Research Service, http://www.ers.usda.gov/Data/China/Provinces .aspx, [last accessed: 2010-02-22].

Estudillo, J.P. (1997): Income inequality in the Philippines, 1961-91, *The Developing Economies*, 35 (1): 68-95.

Eucken, W. (2004): Grundsätze der Wirtschaftspolitik, 7th edition, Tübingen: Mohr, Siebeck.

Fafchamps, M. and A.R. Quisumbing (1999): Human capital, productivity, and labor allocation in rural Pakistan, *The Journal of Human Resources*, 34 (2): 369-406.

Fan, S. (2007): Sustainable agricultural and rural development strategies in China: New challenges and opportunities, Presentation made at the 6th block seminar of the first phase of the International Research Training Group (IRTG), Beijing, China, March 28th, 2007.

Fan, S. (1990): Effects of technological change and institutional reform on production growth in Chinese agriculture, *American Journal of Agricultural Economics*, 73 (2): 265-75.

Fan, S., L. Zhang and X. Zhang (2004): Reforms, investment, and poverty in rural China, *Economic Development and Cultural Change*, 52 (2): 395-421.

Fang, C. and J.C. Beghin (2000): Food self-sufficiency, comparative advantage, and agricultural trade: A policy analysis matrix for Chinese agriculture, Working Paper 99-WP 223, Center for Agricultural and Rural Development and Department of Economics Iowa State University Ames, Iowa 50011-1070.

Food and Agriculture Organization of the United Nations (FAO) (2010): Land Resources in 2008, FAOSTAT, http://faostat.fao.org/site/377/default.aspx [last accessed: 2010-09-09].

Feng, S. and N. Heerink (2008): Are farm households' land renting and migration decisions inter-related in rural China?, NJAS Wageningen, *Journal of Life Sciences*, 55: 345-62.

Findeis, J.L. and D.A. Lass (1994): Labor decisions by agricultural households: Interrelationships between off-farm labor supply and hired labor demand, PRI Working Paper 94-08, University Park.

Foster, J., J. Greer and E. Thorbecke (1984): A class of decomposable poverty measures, *Econometrica*, 52 (3): 761-6.

Friedman, M. (1971): A theory of the consumption function, 6. Printing, Princeton: Princeton University Press.

Fuller, A.M. (1991): Multiple job-holding among farm families in Canada, in: Hallberg, M., J. Findeis and D. Lass (eds.): Multiple job-holding among farm families, Ames: Iowa State University Press: 31-44.

Gale, F., B. Lohmar and F. Tuan (2005): China's new farm subsidies, Electronic Outlook Report for the Economic Research Service, United States Department of Agriculture, WRS-05-01.

Gebauer, R.H. (1996): Mikroökonomische Arbeitsangebotsmodelle – agrarökonomische und –politische Implikationen, in: Hagedorn, K. (ed.): Institutioneller Wandel und Politische Ökonomie von Landwirtschaft und Agrarpolitik, Festschrift zum 65. Geburtstag von Günther Schmitt, Frankfurt and New York: Campus: 429-43.

Glauben, T., T. Herzfeld and X. Wang (2008): Labor market participation of Chinese agricultural households: Empirical evidence from Zhejiang Province, *Food Policy*, 33 (4): 329-40.

Glauben, T., T. Herzfeld and X. Wang (2005): Labor market participation of Chinese agricultural households, Paper prepared for the presentation at the 11th Congress of the EAAE (European Association of Agricultural Economists), 'The Future of Rural Europe in the Global Agri-Food System' , Copenhagen, Denmark, August 24th-27th, 2005.

Glauben, T., H. Tietje and C. Weiss (2006): Agriculture on the move: Exploring regional differences in farm exit rates in western Germany, *Jahrbuch für Regionalwissenschaft*, 26: 103-18.

Goldin, C. (1994): The U-shaped female labor force function in economic development and economic history, Workin Paper No. 4707, National Bureau of Economic Research, Cambridge, MA.

Gould, B.W. and W.E. Saupe (1989): Off-farm labor market entry and exit, *American Journal of Agricultural Economics*, 71 (4): 960-9.

Gregory, P.R. and R.C. Stuart (2001): Russian and Soviet economic performance and structure, 7th ed. Boston et al.: Addison Wesley.

Grilli, L. and C. Rampichini (2007): A multinomial logit model for the analysis of graduates' skills, *Statistical Methods and Applications*, 16 (3): 381-93.

Haan, P. (2004): Discrete choice labor supply: Conditional logit vs. random coefficient models, DIW Discussion Papers No. 394, German Institute for Economic Research.

Halliday, T.J. (2010): Intra-household labor supply, migration, and subsistence constraints in a risky environment: Evidence from rural El Salvador, IZA Discussion Paper, No. 4903.

Hanf, C.-H. (1996): Beziehungen zwischen Haushalt und Betrieb in der Landwirtschaft, in: Hagedorn, K. (ed.): Institutioneller Wandel und Politische Ökonomie von Landwirtschaft und Agrarpolitik, Festschrift zum 65. Geburtstag von Günther Schmitt, Frankfurt and New York: Campus: 47-66.

Happe, K. (2004): Agricultural policies and farm structures: Agent-based modeling and application to EU-policy reform, edited by Institute of Agricultural Development in Central and Eastern Europe (IAMO), http://www.iamo.de/dok/sr_vol30.pdf [last accessed: 2010-09-15].

Harris, J.R. and M.P. Todaro (1970): Migration, unemployment and development: A two-sector analysis, *The American Economic Review*, 60 (1): 126-142.

Hartford, K. (1985): Socialist agriculture is dead; Long live socialist agriculture!, Organizational transformation in rural China, in: Perry, E.J. and C. Wong (eds.): The political economy of reform in Post-Mao China, Cambridge (MA) and London: Harvard University Press: 31-61.

Harsanyi, J.C. (1955): Cardinal welfare, individualistic ethics, and interpersonal comparisons of utility, *The Journal of Political Economy*, 63 (4): 309-21.

Haughton, J. and S.R. Khandker (2009): Handbook of poverty and inequality, Washington, D.C.: The World Bank.

Heady, E.O. (1963): Marginal rates of substitution between technology, land and labor, *Journal of Farm Economics*, 45 (1): 137-45.

Hebel, J. (2004): Social welfare in rural China, in: Ho, P., J. Eyferth and E.B. Vermeer (eds.) (2004): Rural development in transitional China, London: Frank Cass: 224-251.

Heerink, N., F. Qu, M. Kuiper, X. Shi and S. Tan (2007): Policy reforms, rice production and sustainable land use in China: A macro–micro analysis, *Agricultural Systems*, 94: 784-800.

Hertel, T.W., F. Zhai and Z. Wang (2004): Implications of WTO accession for poverty in China, in: Bhattasali, D, S. Li and W. Martin (eds.): China and the WTO: Accession, policy reform, and poverty reduction strategies, Washington D.C.: The World Bank.

Hilbe, J.M. (2009): Logistic Regression Models, Boca Raton: Taylor and Francis.

Hildreth, R.J. (1991): Policy issues and research needs, in: Hallberg, M., J. Findeis and D. Lass (eds.): Multiple job-holding among farm families, Ames: Iowa State University Press: 335-8.

Hodgson, G.M. (2007): Meanings of methodological individualism, *Journal of Economic Methodology*, 14 (2): 211-26.

Hu, W. (1997): Household land tenure reform in China: its impact on farming land use and agro-environment, *Land Use Policy*, 14 (3):175-86.

Huang, J., X. Wang, H. Zhi, Z. Huang and S. Rozelle (2011): Subsidies and distortions in China's agriculture: Evidence from producer-level data, The Australian Journal of Agricultural and Resource Economics, 55: 59-71.

Hussain, A. (2004): Coping with and adapting to job losses and declines in farm earnings in China, in: Bhattasali, D., S. Li and W. Martin (eds.): China and the WTO: Accession, policy reform, and poverty reduction strategies, Washington D.C.: The World Bank.

Ilahi, N. (2000): The intra-household allocation of time and tasks: What have we learnt from the empirical literature, Policy Research Report on Gender and Development, Working Paper Series No. 13, The World Bank.

IRTG (2010): Project structure and linkages between groups and subprojects, Personal communication.

Jacoby, H.G., G. Lu and S. Rozelle (2002): Hazards of expropriation: Tenure insecurity and investments in rural China, *American Economic Review*, 92: 1420-47.

Jalan, J. and M. Ravallion (2000): Is transient poverty different? – Evidence from rural China, *Journal of Development Studies*, 36 (6): 82-99.

Jalan, J. and M. Ravallion (1999): Are the poor less well insured? Evidence on vulnerability to income risk in rural China, *Journal of Development Economics*, 58: 61-81.

Jalan, J. and M. Ravallion (1998): Transient poverty in postreform rural China, *Journal of Comparative Economics*, 26 (2): 338-57.

Jenkins, S.P. (2008): Essex Summer School course 'Survival Analysis', http://www.iser.essex.ac.uk/iser/teaching/module-ec968, [last accessed: 2009-11-02].

Jenkins, S.P. (1997): Discrete time proportional hazards regression, *Stata Technical Bulletin*, 39: 22-32.

Jenkins, S.P. (1995a): Accounting for inequality trends: Decomposition analyses for the UK, 1971-86, *Economica*, 62: 29-63.

Jenkins, S.P. (1995b): Easy estimation methods for discrete-time duration models, *Oxford Bulletin of Economics and Statistics*, 57: 129-37.

Jia, X. (2010): Personal communication, 2010-07-15.

Jia, X. (2008): Credit rationing and institutional constraint: Evidence from rural China, Ph.D. Thesis, University of Hohenheim.

Jia, X. and A. Fock (2007): Thirty Years of Agricultural Transition in China (1977–2007) and the 'New Rural Campaign', paper prepared for presentation at the 106th seminar of the European Association of Agricultural Economists (EAAE), Pro-poor development in low income countries: Food, agriculture, trade, and environment, 25th-27th October 2007 – Montpellier, France.

Johnston, B.F. and J.W. Mellor (1961): The role of agriculture in economic development, *The American Economic Review*, 51 (4): 566-93.

Kakwani, N.C. (1980): Income inequality and poverty: Methods of estimation and policy applications, New York et al.: Oxford University Press.

Kalbfleisch, J. D. and R.L. Prentice (1980): The statistical analysis of failure time data, New York: Wiley.

Karplus, V.J. and X.W. Deng (2008): Agricultural biotechnology in China: Origins and prospects, Berlin et al.: Springer.

Kennedy, J.J. (2007): From the tax-for-fee reform to the abolition of agricultural taxes: The impact on township governments in North-west China, *The China Quarterly*, 189: 43-59.

Key, N., E. Sadoulet and A. de Janvry (2000): Transaction costs and agricultural household supply response, *American Journal of Agricultural Economics*, 82 (2): 245-59.

Kimhi, A. (2009): Demand for on-farm permanent hired labour on family holdings: A comment, *European Review of Agricultural Economics*, 36 (3): 447-52.

Kimhi, A. (2007): Regression-based inequality decomposition: A critical review and application to farm-household income data, Discussion Paper No. 16.07, The Department of Agricultural Economics and Management, The Hebrew University of Jerusalem.

Kimhi, A. (2000): Is part-time farming really a step in the way out of agriculture?, *American Journal of Agricultural Economics*, 82: 38-48.

Kimhi, A. (1994): Optimal timing of farm transferal from parent to child, *American Journal of Agricultural Economics*, 76: 228-36.

Kirschke, D., M. Odening, A. Häger and O. Mußhoff (2007): Strukturwandel im Agrarsektor, Humboldt-Spektrum 1/2007: 24-31.

Kleiber, C. (2005): The Lorenz curve in economics and econometrics, Invited paper, presented at the Gini-Lorenz Centennial Conference, Sienna, May 23rd-26th, 2005.

Knight, F. (1921): Risk, uncertainty and profit, Originally published: Boston: Houghton Mifflin, available at: http://www.econlib.org/library/Knight/knRUP.html, [last accessed: 2010-07-23].

Knight, J. and L. Song (2005): Towards a labour market in China, Oxford et al.: Oxford University Press.

Knight, J. and L.Y. Yueh (2004): Job mobility of residents and migrants in urban China, *Journal of Comparative Economics*, 32: 637-60.

Knight, J. and L.Y. Yueh (2002): The role of social capital in the labour market in China, Discussion Paper No. 121, Department of Economics, University of Oxford.

Krug, B. (1990): Theoretische Grundlagen des Reformprozesses in der VR China: Wirtschaftspolitischer Konzeptionswandel als Reflex politisch-ökonomischen Umdenkens, in: Cassel, D. (ed.): Wirtschaftssysteme im Umbruch, München: Vahlen: 276-93.

Krugman, P.R. and M. Obstfeld (2004): Internationale Wirtschaft: Theorie und Politik der Außenwirtschaft, 6. Auflage, München et al.: Pearson Education.

Kuiper, M.H. (2005): Village modeling – A Chinese recipe for blending general equilibrium and household modeling, Ph.D. Thesis, Wageningen University.

Kung, J.K. (2002): Off-farm labor markets and the emergence of land rental markets in rural China, *Journal of Comparative Economics*, 30: 395-414.

Kurosaki, T. (2003): Measurement of chronic and transient poverty: Theory and application to Pakistan, Discussion Paper Series A No. 436, The Institute of Economic Research, Hitotsubashi University, Kunitchi, Tokyo, Japan.

Lee, J.E. (1965): Allocating farm resources between farm and nonfarm uses, *Journal of Farm Economics*, 47 (1): 83-92.

Li, S., P. Wang and X. Yue (2007): The causes of chronic and transient poverty and their implications for poverty reduction policy in rural China, PMMA Working Paper 2007-12, Poverty and Economic Policy (PEP) Research Network.

Lien, G., O. Flaten, A.M. Jervell, M. Ebbesvik, M. Koesling, and P.S. Valle (2006): Management and risk characteristics of part-time and full-time farmers in Norway, *Review of Agricultural Economics*, 28: 111-131.

Lin, G.C.S. (2009): Developing China: Land, politics and social conditions, Abingdon and New York: Routledge.

Lin, G.C.S., and P. Ho (2003): China's land resources and land-use change: Insights from the 1996 land survey, *Land Use Policy*, 20 (2): 87-107.

Lin, J.Y. (1997): Institutional reforms and dynamics of agricultural growth in China, *Food Policy*, 22 (3): 201-12.

Lin, J.Y. (1988): The household responsibility system in China's agricultural reform: A theoretical and empirical study, *Economic Development and Cultural Change*, 36 (3): 199-224.

Lin, J.Y. (1987): Household farm, cooperative farm, and efficiency: Evidence from rural de-collectivization in China, Working Paper No: 533, New Haven, Conn: Yale University, Economic Growth Center, cited by: Fan, S. (1990): Effects of technological change and institutional reform on production growth in Chinese agriculture, *American Journal of Agricultural Economics*, 73 (2): 265-75.

Liu, X. and T. Sicular (2008): Non-agricultural employment determinants and income inequality decomposition, EPRI Working Paper, 2008-6.

Lohmar, B. (1999): Land tenure insecurity and labor allocation in rural China, Paper presented at the 1999 Annual Meeting of the American Agricultural Economics Association, Nashville, TN, USA.

Lohmar, B., Z. Zhang, and A. Somwaru (2001): Land rental market development and agricultural production in China. Paper presented at the 2001 Annual Meeting of the American Agricultural Economics Association, Chicago, IL, USA.

Lopez, R.E. (1984): Estimating labor supply and production decisions of self-employed farm producers, *European Economic Review*, 24: 61-82.

Lubell, H. (1947): Effects of redistribution of income on consumers' expenditures, *The American Economic Review*, 37 (1): 157-70.

Luo, R., Y. Shi, L. Zhang, C. Liu, S. Rozelle and B. Sharbono (2009): Malnutrition in China's rural boarding schools: the case of primary schools in Shaanxi Province, *Asia Pacific Journal of Education*, 29 (4): 481-501.

Manski, C.F. (2000): Economic analysis of social interactions, *The Journal of Economic Perspectives*, 14 (3): 115-36.

Maurer-Fazio, M., J.W. Hughes and D. Zhang (2005): Economic reform and changing patterns of labor force participation in urban and rural China, William Davidson Institute Working Paper No. 787.

McConnell, D.J. and J.L. Dillon (1997): Farm management for Asia: A systems approach, Rome: Food and Agriculture Organization of the United Nations.

McGuire, W., B. Fleisher and I. Sheldon (2007): Off-farm employment opportunities and educational attainment in rural China, paper presented at an IATRC (International Agricultural Trade Research Consortium), International Symposium, July 8th-9th, 2007, Beijing, China.

McMillan, J. and B. Naughton (1992): How to reform a planned economy: Lessons from China, *Oxford Review of Economic Policy*, 8 (1): 130-43.

Milanovic, B. (2002): Do we tend to overestimate poverty gaps?, The impact of equivalency scales on the calculation of the poverty gap, *Applied Economics Letters*, 9: 69-72.

Meng, X., R. Gregory and Y. Wang (2005): Poverty, inequality, and growth in urban China, *Journal of Comparative Economics*, 33: 710-29.

Ministry of Agriculture of the People's Republic of China (MoA) (2010): The Law of the People's Republic of China on Land Contract in Rural Areas, http://english.agri.gov.cn/ga/plar/200906/t20090623_1103.htm, [last accessed: 2010-05-05].

Motonishi, T. (2003): Why has income inequality in Thailand increased? An analysis using 1975-1998 surveys, ERD Working Paper No. 43.

Mueller, D.C. (2003): Public Choice III, Cambridge et al.: Cambridge University Press.

Mundell, R.A. (1961): A Theory of optimum currency areas, *The American Economic Review*, 51 (4): 657-65.

Muyanga, M. (2008): Household vulnerability to transient and chronic poverty: Evidence from Rural Kenia, paper presented at The Ninth Annual Global Development Conference "Security for Development: Confronting Threats to Survival and Safety" of the Global Development Network, 29th of January to 5th of February 2008, Brisbane Australia.

Nakajima, C. (1986): Subjective equilibrium theory of the farm household. Amsterdam et al.: Elsevier.

National Bureau of Statistics of China (NBS) (various years): China Statistical Yearbook, http://www.stats.gov.cn/english/statisticaldata/yearlydata/, [last accessed: 2010-02-22].

National Development Reform Commission of the People's Republic of China, Department of Climate Change (2010): Land Administration Law of the People's Republic of China, http://www.ccchina.gov.cn/en/NewsInfo.asp?NewsId=5383, [last accessed: 2010-05-05].

Ness, P. van and S. Raichur (1989): Dilemmas of social development: An analysis of strategic lines in China, 1949-1981, in: Ness, P. van (ed.): Market reforms in socialist societies, comparing China and Hungary, Boulder and London: Lynne Rienner Publishers: 143-69.

Nevell, D. (2000): Using aggregated cumulative hazard plots to visualize failure data, *Quality and Reliability Engineering International*, 16: 209-19.

Newbery, D. (1970): A theorem on the measurement of inequality, *Journal of Economic Theory*, 2: 264-6.

North, D.C. (1994): Institutional change: A framework of analysis, Economic History 9412001, EconWPA, revised 1994-12-14.

North, D.C. (1990): Institutions, institutional change and economic performance, Cambridge et al.: Cambridge University Press.

OECD (1995): Adjustment in OECD agriculture: Issues and policy responses, Paris: Organization for Economic Cooperation and Development (OECD).

Pang, L., A. de Brauw and S. Rozelle (2004): Working until dropping: Employment behavior of the elderly in rural China, Working Paper No. 201, Williamstown, MA, USA: Williams College.

Park, H.M. (2008): Univariate analysis and normality test using SAS, Stata, and SPSS, University Information Technology Services Center for Statistical and Mathematical Computing, Indiana University, http://www.indiana.edu / ~statmath/stat/all/normality/normality.pdf, [last accessed: 2010-03-10].

peopledaily (2010): China's comprehensive agricultural mechanization level to exceed 48.8% in 2009, http://english.peopledaily.com.cn/90001/90778/ 98505/ 6848923.html, [last accessed: 2010-04-17].

Phimister, E. and D. Roberts (2006): The effect of off-farm work on the intensity of agricultural production, *Environmental and Resource Economics*, 34: 493-515.

Pingali, P.L. (1997): From subsistence to commercial production systems: The Transformation of Asian agriculture, American Journal of Agricultural Economics, 79 (2): 628-34.

Piore, M.J. (2004): Qualitative research: Does it fit in economics?, Paper prepared for presentation at the conference on "Do Facts Matter in Elaborating Theories? Cross Perspectives from Economics, Management, Political Science and Sociology," at CRG-Ecole Polytechnique, Paris, in October of 2002, revised version available at: http://econ-www.mit.edu/files/1125, [last accessed: 2010-11-02].

Piotrowski, S. (2009): Land property rights and natural resource use: An analysis of household behavior in rural China, Frankfurt am Main et al.: Peter Lang.

Polachek, S.W. (1981): Occupation self-selection: A human capital approach to sex differences in occupational structure, *The Review of Economics and Statistics*, 63 (1): 60-9.

Pope, J., D. Annandale and A. Morrison-Saunders (2004): Conceptualising sustainability assessment, Environmental Impact Assessment Review, 24: 595-616.

Putterman, L. (1990): Effort, productivity and incentive in a 1970s Chinese People's Commune, *Journal of Comparative Economics*, 14 (1): 88-104.

Putterman, L. and M. DiGiorgio (1985): Choice and efficiency in a model of democratic semi-collective agriculture, *Oxford Economic Papers*, 37: 1-21.

Qian, Y. (2003): How Reform Worked in China, in: Rodrik, D. (ed.): In search of prosperity: Analytic narratives on economic growth, Princeton University Press: 297-333.

Qian, Y. (2000): The institutional foundations of market transition in the People's Republic of China, ADB Institute Working Paper, 9.

Ravallion, M. and S. Chen (2007): China's (uneven) progress against poverty, *Journal of Development Economics*, 82: 1-42.

Rawski, E.S. (1972): Agricultural change and the peasant economy of South China, Cambridge, MA: Harvard University Press.

Reardon, T., K. Stamoulis, A. Balisacan, M.-E. Cruz, J. Berdegué and B. Banks (1998): Rural nonfarm incomes in developing countries, in: FAO: The state of food and agriculture, 1998, Rome: FAO, Part III, http://www.fao.org/ docrep/w9500e/w9500e12.htm, [last accessed: 2010-04-26].

Rese, M. (2000): Logistische Regression, in: Backhaus, K., B. Erichson, W. Plinke and R. Weiber (eds.): Multivariate Analysemethoden: Eine Anwendungsorientierte Einführung, 9th edition, p. 104-44, Berlin et al.: Springer.

Reyes, C.M. (2003): A Study on chronic and transient poverty, MIMAP Research Paper No. 58, Micro Impacts of Macroeconomic Adjustment Policies Project.

Rigg, J. (2006): Land, farming, livelihoods, and poverty: Rethinking the links in the Rural South, *World Development*, 34 (1): 180-202.

Roll, C.R. (1980): The distribution of rural incomes in China, New York: Garland.

Rosenzweig, M.R. (1980): Neoclassical theory and the optimizing peasant: An econometric analysis of market family labor supply in a developing country, *The Quarterly Journal of Economics*, 94 (1): 31-55.

Rosenzweig, M.R. and O. Stark (1989): Consumption smoothing, migration, and marriage: Evidence from rural India, *The Journal of Political Economy*, 97 (4): 905-26.

Rosenzweig, M.R. and K.I. Wolpin (1985): Specific experience, household structure and intergenerational transfers: Farm family land and labor arrangements in developing countries, *The Quarterly Journal of Economics*, 100 (supplement): 961-87.

Rothschild, M. and J.E. Stiglitz (1973): Some further results on the measurement of inequality, Journal of Economic Theory, 6: 188-204.

Rozelle, S. (1994): Rural industrialization and increasing inequality: Emerging patterns in China's reforming economy, *Journal of Comparative Economics*, 19: 362-91.

Rozelle, S., X.-Y. Dong, L. Zhang and A. Manson (2002): Gender wage gaps in post-reform rural China, World Bank Working Paper.

Rozelle, S., C. Pray and J. Huang (1997): Agricultural research policy in China: Testing the limits of commercialization-led reform, *Comparative Economic Studies*, 39 (2): 37-71.

Rumbaur, C. (2008): Regionale Risikoabschätzung der Nitratauswaschung in der Nordchinesischen Tiefebene in Abhängigkeit von der Nutzungsintensität, Ph.D. Thesis, Technische Universität Bergakademie Freiberg.

Sachs, J.D. and W.T. Woo (1997): Understanding China's economic performance, Working Paper 5933, National Bureau of Economic Research (NBER), Cambridge MA.

Sanders, R. (2000): Prospects for sustainable development in the Chinese countryside, The political economy of Chinese ecological agriculture, Aldershot: Ashgate Publishers.

Sandrey, R. and H. Edinger (2009): The relevance of Chinese agricultural technologies for African smallholder farmers: Agricultural technology research in China, Report prepared for the African Agricultural Technology Foundation, Centre for Chinese Studies, University of Stellenbosch.

Sarkisian, N. (2010): Sociology 704: Topics in Multivariate Statistics, http://www.sarkisian.net/sc740/mlogit.pdf, [last accessed: 2010-04-15].

Scrimshaw, S.C.M. (1990): Combining quantitative and qualitative methods in the study of intra-household resource allocation, in: Rogers, B.L. and N.P. Schlossman (eds.) (1990): Intra-household Resource Allocation: Issues and methods for development policy and planning, Tokyo: The United Nations University Press.

Schüller, A. (2002): Theorie des wirtschaftlichen Systemvergleichs – Ausgangspunkte, Weiterentwicklung und Perspektiven, in: Gutman, G., H. Hamel, H. Leipold, A. Schüller, H.J. Thieme (eds.): Marburger Studien zur Ordnungsökonomik, Schriften zu Ordnungsfragen der Wirtschaft, 70, Stuttgart: Lucius & Lucius: 2-32.

Schultz, T.P. (1990): Testing the Neoclassical model of family labor supply and fertility, *The Journal of Human Resources*, 25 (4): 599-634.

Schultz, T.W. (1964): Transforming traditional agriculture, New Haven: Yale University Press.

Schumpeter, J. (1909): On the concept of social value, *The Quarterly Journal of Economics*, 23 (2): 213-32.

Schwarze, S. and M. Zeller (2005): Income diversification of rural households in Central Sulawesi, Indonesia, *Quarterly Journal of International Agriculture*, 44 (1): 61-73.

Sen, A.K. (1986): Poverty and famines: An essay on entitlement and deprivation, Reprint, Oxford: Clarendon Press.

Sen, A.K. (1966): Labour allocation in a cooperative enterprise, *The Review of Economic Studies*, 33 (4): 361-71.

Sen, A.K. (1962): An aspect of Indian agriculture, *Economics Weekly*, 14, Annual Number: 243-6.

Shi, X., N. Heerink and F. Qu (2007): Choices between different off-farm employment sub-categories: An empirical analysis for Jiangxi Province, China, *China Economic Review*, 18: 438–55.

Shorrocks, A.F. (1999): Decomposition procedures for distributional analysis: A unified framework based on the shapely value, http://www.komkon.org /~tacik/ science/shapley.pdf, [last accessed: 2010-05-04].

Shorrocks, A.F. (1984): Inequality decomposition by population subgroups, *Econometrica*, 52 (6): 1369-85.

Shorrocks, A.F. (1983): The impact of income components on the distribution of family incomes, *Quarterly Journal of Economics*, 98 (2): 311-26.

Shorrocks, A.F. (1982): Inequality decomposition by factor components, *Econometrica*, 50: 193-211.

Sicular, T. and Y. Zhao (2004): Earnings and labor mobility in rural China; Implications for China's accession to the WTO, in: Bhattasali, D, S. Li and W. Martin (eds.): China and the WTO: Accession, policy reform, and poverty reduction strategies, Washington D.C.: The World Bank.

Šik, O. (1968): Plan und Markt im Sozialismus, Wien: Molden.

Sikei, G., M.O. Odhiambo and J. Olwande (2009): Labour allocation patterns of rural households to agriculture and forest activities in Kakamega district, Western Kenya, Contributed Paper prepared for presentation at the International Association of Agricultural Economists Conference, Beijing, China, August 16th-22nd, 2009.

Singh, I., L. Squire and J. Strauss (1986): A survey of agricultural household models: Recent findings and policy implications, *The World Bank Economic Review*, 1 (1): 149-79.

Skinner, M.W., R.G. Kuhn and A.E. Joseph (2001): Agricultural land protection in China: a case study of local governance in Zhejiang Province, *Land Use Policy*, 18 (4): 329-40.

Solot, I.B. (2006): The Chinese agricultural policy trilemma, *Perspectives*, 7 (1): 36-46.

Son, H.H. (2006): Assessing the pro-poorness of government fiscal policy in Thailand, International Poverty Centre, United Nations Development Programme, Working Paper No. 15.

Son, H.H. and N. Kakwani (2004): Economic growth and poverty reduction: Initial conditions matter, International Poverty Centre, United Nations Development Programme, Working Paper No. 2.

Spiertz, H. and O. Oenema (2004): Resource use efficiency and management of nutrients in agricultural systems; in: Römheld, V., R. Doluschitz, F. Zhang, R. Jayakumar, and M. Wolff (eds.): Promoting environmentally-friendly agricultural production in China: Resource management for sustainable intensive agriculture systems, Beijing, China: Tsinghua University Press.

Stephan, G. and M. Ahlheim (1996): Ökonomische Ökologie, Berlin et al.: Springer.

Suh, C.-H. (1985): Interdependence between off-farm employment and land-use intensity among small farms in Korea, *Journal of Rural Development,* 8 (1): 35-50.

Sumner, D.A. and E. Frazao (1989): Wage rates in a poor rural area with emphasis on the impact of farm and nonfarm experience, *Economic Development and Cultural Change*, 37 (4): 709-18.

Swinnen, J.F.M. (2009): Reforms, globalization and endogenous agricultural systems, Paper presented at the 111 EAAE-IAAE Seminar 'Small Farms: decline or persistence' University of Kent, Canterbury, UK, 26th-27th June 2009.

Swinnen, J.F.M. and S. Rozelle (2006): From Marx and Mao to the market, New York: Oxford University Press.

Theeuwes, J. (1981): Family labour force participation: Multinomial logit estimates, *Applied Economics*, 13 (4): 481-98.

Tinbergen, J. (1975): Income distribution: Analysis and policies, Amsterdam et al.: North-Holland Publishers et al..

Tsang, S. (1996): Against 'big bang' in economic transition: normative and positive arguments, *Cambridge Journal of Economics*, 20: 183-93.

Tschajanow, A.W. (1923): Die Lehre von der bäuerlichen Wirtschaft: Versuch einer Theorie der Familienwirtschaft im Landbau, Berlin: Parey.

Tuan, F., A. Somwaru and X. Diao (2000): Rural labor migration, characteristics, and employment pattern: A study based on China's agricultural census, TMD Discussion Paper No. 36, Trade and Macroeconomics Division, Washington, D.C.: The International Food Policy Research Institute.

Uchida, E., S. Rozelle and J. Xu (2007): Conservation, liquidity constraints and off-farm labor: Impact of the Grain for Green Program on rural households in China, Selected Paper prepared for presentation at the American Agricultural Economics Association Annual Meeting, Portland, OR, July 29th-August 1st, 2007.

United Nations Development Program (UNDP) (2008). China human development report 2007-2008: Basic public services benefiting 1.3 Billion Chinese. Beijing: China Translation and Publishing Corporation.

Varis, O. and P. Vakkilainen (2001): China's 8 challenges to water resource management in the first quarter of the 21st century, *Geomorphology*, 41: 93-104.

von Urff, W. (1982): Die Rolle der Landwirtschaft in der Entwicklung, in: von Blanckenburg, P. (ed.): Handbuch der Landwirtschaft und Ernährung in den Entwicklungsländern, Stuttgart: Ulmer: 19-37.

Wales, T.J. and A.D. Woodland (1976): Estimation of household utiltiy functions and labor supply responses, International Economic Review, 17 (2): 397-410.

Wan, G. H. (2002): Regression-based inequality decomposition: Pitfalls and a solution procedure, UNU WIDER Discussion Paper, No. 2002/101.

Wan, G.H. and Z.Y. Zhou (2005): Income inequality in rural China: Regression-based decomposition using household data, *Review of Development Economics*, 9 (1): 107-20.

Wan, G.H. and E. Cheng (2001): Effects of land fragmentation and returns to scale in the Chinese farming sector, *Applied Economics*, 33 (2): 183-94.

Wang, T. (2004): China: Sources of real exchange rate fluctuations, IMF Working Paper 04/18.

Wang, X. (2007): Labor market behavior of Chinese rural households during transition, Ph.D. Thesis, Studies on the Agricultural and Food Sector in Central and Eastern Europe, edited by the Leibniz Institute of Agricultural Development in Central and Eastern Europe (IAMO), Halle (Saale).

Watkins, J.W.N. (1952): The principle of methodological individualism, *British Journal for the Philosophy of Science*, 3 (2): 186-9.

Weiss, C.R. (1999): Farm growth and survival: Econometric evidence for individual farms in upper Austria, *American Journal of Agricultural Economics*, 81: 103-16.

Weiss, C.R. (1997): Do they come back again?, The symmetry and reversibility of off-farm employment, *European Review of Agricultural Economics*, 24: 65-84.

Wooldridge, J.M. (2002): Econometric analysis of cross section and panel data, Cambridge, Massachusetts: MIT Press.

World Development Report (WDR) (2008): Agriculture for development, Washington D.C.: The World Bank.

Wu, H.X. and X. Meng (1997): Do Chinese farmers reinvest in grain production?, *China Economic Review*, 7 (2): 123-34.

Yang, D.T. (1997): Education and off-farm work, *Economic Development and Cultural Change*, 45 (3): 613-32.

Yang, D.T. and H. Zhou (1999): Rural-urban disparity and sectoral labour allocation in China, *Journal of Development Studies*, 35 (3): 105-33.

Yotopoulos, P.A. and L.J. Lau (1974): On modeling the agricultural sector in developing economies, *Journal of Development Economics*, 1: 105-27.

Yu, L., R. Luo and L. Zhang (2007): Decomposing income inequality and policy implications in rural China, *China and World Economy*, 15 (2): 44-58.

Yu, W. and H.G. Jensen (2009): China's agricultural policy transition: Impacts of recent reforms and future scenarios, *Journal of Agricultural Economics*, 61 (2): 343-68.

Zeller, M., G. Schrieder, J. von Braun and F. Heidhues (1997): Rural finance for food security for the poor: Implications for policy and research, Food Policy Review No. 4, Washington, D.C.: The International Food Policy Research Institute.

Zhang, L. (2010): Boost subsidies to save China's farms, http://www.china.org.cn/ opinion/2010-03/11/content_19588079.htm, [last accessed: 2010-04-17].

Zhang, L., J. Wang, J. Huang and S. Rozelle (2008): Development of groundwater markets in China: A glimpse into progress to date, *World Development*, 36 (4): 706-26.

Zhang, L., J. Huang and S. Rozelle (2002): Employment, emerging labor markets, and the role of education in rural China, *China Economic Review*, 13: 313-28.

Zhang, T. and H.-F. Zou (1998): Fiscal decentralization, public spending, and economic growth, *Journal of Public Economics*, 67: 221-40.

Zhang, X. and S. Fan (2004): Public investment and regional inequality in rural China, *Agricultural Economics*, 30: 89-100.

Zhang, X., T.D. Mount and R.N. Boisvert (2004): Industrialization, urbanization and land use in China, *Journal of Chinese Economic and Business Studies*, 2 (3): 207-24.

Zhao, R., X. Chen, F. Zhang, H. Zhang, J. Schroder and V. Römheld (2006): Fertilization and nitrogen balance in a wheat–maize rotation system in North China, *Agronomy Journal*, 98 (4): 938-945.

Zhao, Y. and G.J. Wen (1999): Land holding and social security in rural China, *Homo Oeconomicus*, 16 (2): 157-76.

Zhen, L. and J.K. Routray (2003): Operational indicators for measuring agricultural sustainability in developing countries, *Environmental Management*, 32 (1): 34-46.

Zhen, L. and J.K Routray (2002): Groundwater resource use practices and implications for sustainable agricultural development in the North China Plain: A case study in Ningjin county of Shandong province, PR China, *Water Resources Development*, 18 (4): 581-93.

Zhen, L. and M. Zoebisch (2006): Resource use in agricultural sustainability: Risks and consequences of intensive cropping in China, *Journal of Agricultural and Rural Development in the Tropics and Subtropics*, Supplement 86.

Zhou, Z.-Y., and W.-M. Tian (2005): Grains in China - Foodgrain, feedgrain and world trade. Hants, UK: Ashgate.

Zhou, Z.-Y., D.A. Sumner and H. Lee (2001): Part-time farming trends in China: A comparison with the Japanese and Korean experience, *Comparative Economic Studies*, 38 (3): 99-132.

Zhu, L. (1991): Rural reform and peasant income in China: The impact of China's post-mao rural reforms in selected regions, Houndsmills et al.: Macmillan.

Zhu, L. and Z. Jiang (1995): "Yigong-Daizhen" in China: A new experience with labor-intensive public works in poor areas, in: von Braun, J. (ed.) (1995): Employment for poverty reduction and food security, Washington D.C.: International Food Policy Research Institute.

Appendix A

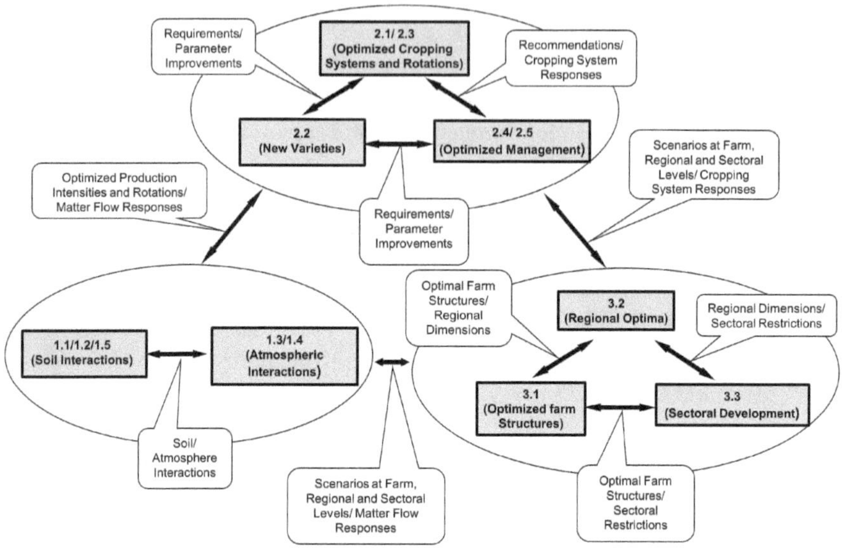

Source: Adapted from IRTG (2010).

Figure 12: The International Research Training Group: Sustainable Resource Use in North China; Structure and information flows

Source: Adapted from ERS (2010).

Figure 13: Map of the People's Republic of China

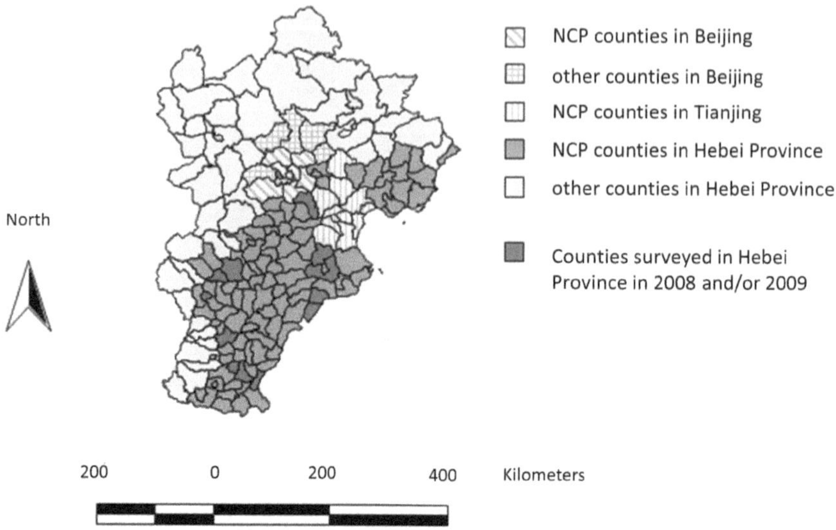

Source: Adapted from Bareth (2003).

Figure 14: Map of Hebei province and counties of Hebei belonging to the North China Plain

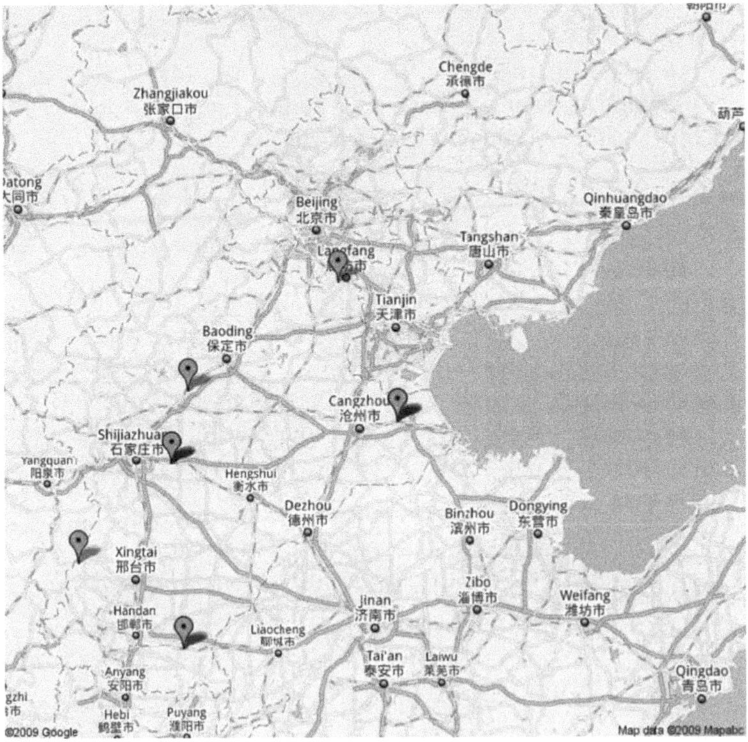

Source: Village location based on village names provided with the RCRE data set and on google.maps, http://maps.google.de/.

Figure 15: Map of villages 1-6 of the RCRE survey

Appendix B

Table 22 presents the summary statistics for interaction terms between the village variables and the time dummies used in chapter 7.1.2.

Table 22: Location and time interaction terms used in separability models and respective summary statistics

	Variable	Mean	Std. Dev.	Min.	Max.
V1*D_1995 (1 if V1=1&D_1995=1, 0 otherwise)	V1_D_1995	0.024	0.152	0	1
V1*D_1996 (1 if V1=1&D_1996=1, 0 otherwise)	V1_D_1996	0.024	0.152	0	1
V1*D_1998 (1 if V1=1&D_1998=1, 0 otherwise)	V1_D_1998	0.023	0.150	0	1
V1*D_1999 (1 if V1=1&D_1999=1, 0 otherwise)	V1_D_1999	0.024	0.152	0	1
V1*D_2000 (1 if V1=1&D_2000=1, 0 otherwise)	V1_D_2000	0.024	0.152	0	1
V1*D_2001 (1 if V1=1&D_2001=1, 0 otherwise)	V1_D_2001	0.024	0.152	0	1
V1*D_2002 (1 if V1=1&D_2002=1, 0 otherwise)	V1_D_2002	0.024	0.152	0	1
V2*D_1995 (1 if V2=1&D_1995=1, 0 otherwise)	V2_D_1995	0.021	0.144	0	1
V2*D_1996 (1 if V2=1&D_1996=1, 0 otherwise)	V2_D_1996	0.021	0.144	0	1
V2*D_1998 (1 if V2=1&D_1998=1, 0 otherwise)	V2_D_1998	0.021	0.144	0	1
V2*D_1999 (1 if V2=1&D_1999=1, 0 otherwise)	V2_D_1999	0.021	0.144	0	1
V2*D_2000 (1 if V2=1&D_2000=1, 0 otherwise)	V2_D_2000	0.021	0.144	0	1
V2*D_2001 (1 if V2=1&D_2001=1, 0 otherwise)	V2_D_2001	0.021	0.144	0	1
V2*D_2002 (1 if V2=1&D_2002=1, 0 otherwise)	V2_D_2002	0.021	0.144	0	1
V3*D_1995 (1 if V3=1&D_1995=1, 0 otherwise)	V3_D_1995	0.021	0.142	0	1
V3*D_1996 (1 if V3=1&D_1996=1, 0 otherwise)	V3_D_1996	0.020	0.139	0	1
V3*D_1998 (1 if V3=1&D_1998=1, 0 otherwise)	V3_D_1998	0.018	0.134	0	1
V3*D_1999 (1 if V3=1&D_1999=1, 0 otherwise)	V3_D_1999	0.022	0.148	0	1
V3*D_2000 (1 if V3=1&D_2000=1, 0 otherwise)	V3_D_2000	0.022	0.147	0	1
V3*D_2001 (1 if V3=1&D_2001=1, 0 otherwise)	V3_D_2001	0.022	0.147	0	1
V3*D_2002 (1 if V3=1&D_2002=1, 0 otherwise)	V3_D_2002	0.022	0.147	0	1
V4*D_1995 (1 if V4=1&D_1995=1, 0 otherwise)	V4_D_1995	0.014	0.118	0	1
V4*D_1996 (1 if V4=1&D_1996=1, 0 otherwise)	V4_D_1996	0.014	0.118	0	1
V4*D_1998 (1 if V4=1&D_1998=1, 0 otherwise)	V4_D_1998	0.014	0.118	0	1

Table 22 continued					
V4*D_1999 (1 if V4=1&D_1999=1, 0 otherwise)	V4_D_1999	0.014	0.118	0	1
V4*D_2000 (1 if V4=1&D_2000=1, 0 otherwise)	V4_D_2000	0.014	0.118	0	1
V4*D_2001 (1 if V4=1&D_2001=1, 0 otherwise)	V4_D_2001	0.014	0.118	0	1
V4*D_2002 (1 if V4=1&D_2002=1, 0 otherwise)	V4_D_2002	0.014	0.118	0	1
V5*D_1995 (1 if V5=1&D_1995=1, 0 otherwise)	V5_D_1995	0.033	0.178	0	1
V5*D_1996 (1 if V5=1&D_1996=1, 0 otherwise)	V5_D_1996	0.033	0.179	0	1
V5*D_1998 (1 if V5=1&D_1998=1, 0 otherwise)	V5_D_1998	0.034	0.175	0	1
V5*D_1999 (1 if V5=1&D_1999=1, 0 otherwise)	V5_D_1999	0.033	0.179	0	1
V5*D_2000 (1 if V5=1&D_2000=1, 0 otherwise)	V5_D_2000	0.033	0.179	0	1
V5*D_2001 (1 if V5=1&D_2001=1, 0 otherwise)	V5_D_2001	0.033	0.179	0	1
V5*D_2002 (1 if V5=1&D_2002=1, 0 otherwise)	V5_D_2002	0.032	0.177	0	1
V6*D_1995 (1 if V6=1&D_1995=1, 0 otherwise)	V6_D_1995	0.031	0.173	0	1
V6*D_1996 (1 if V6=1&D_1996=1, 0 otherwise)	V6_D_1996	0.031	0.173	0	1
V6*D_1997 (1 if V6=1&D_1997=1, 0 otherwise)	V6_D_1997	0.031	0.173	0	1
V6*D_1998 (1 if V6=1&D_1998=1, 0 otherwise)	V6_D_1998	0.031	0.173	0	1
V6*D_1999 (1 if V6=1&D_1999=1, 0 otherwise)	V6_D_1999	0.031	0.173	0	1
V6*D_2000 (1 if V6=1&D_2000=1, 0 otherwise)	V6_D_2000	0.031	0.173	0	1
V6*D_2001 (1 if V6=1&D_2001=1, 0 otherwise)	V6_D_2001	0.031	0.173	0	1
V6*D_2002 (1 if V6=1&D_2002=1, 0 otherwise)	V6_D_2002	0.031	0.173	0	1

Source: Own computations based on RCRE survey data for Hebei 1995-2002.

Appendix C

In this part the distribution of the covariates used in the analysis of the farm structure persistence (chapter 7.3) is discussed.

The Shapiro Wilk test is applied to test for normality distribution of the explanatory variables in hazard rate estimations. This test is appropriate to test for normal distribution of continuous and nominal variables. A test statistic close to 1 would indicate normality (Park, 2008).

The respective test hypotheses are:

H_0: The covariate i is normally distributed; i = {HSIZE, EDUS, LAND LIVES}

H_1: The covariate i is not normally distributed;

Table 23: Results Shapiro Wilk test

Variable	Observations	z	Prob > z	H_0
HSIZE	4832	11.667	0.0000	rejected
EDUS	4706	6.174	0.0000	rejected
LAND	4832	12.775	0.0000	rejected
LIVES	4832	19.872	0.0000	rejected

Source: Own computations based on the RCRE data for Hebei, 1995-2002.

But the Shapiro Wilk test can also be misleading and has to be interpreted with caution (Cox, 2007). In addition plotting the observations in histograms reveals that they are not following the pattern of a normal distribution (*Figure 16*).

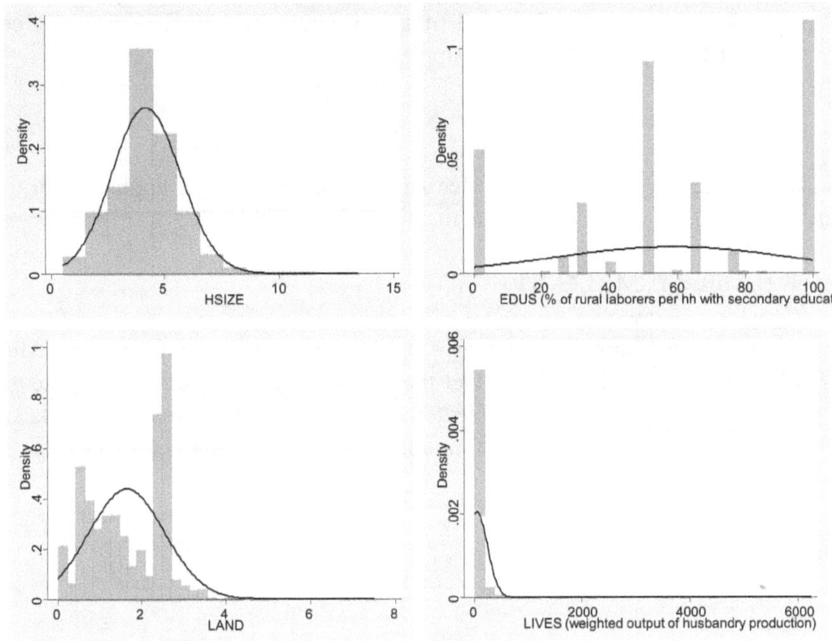

Source: Own computations based on RCRE survey data for Hebei 1995-2002.

Figure 16: Distribution plots

For categorical or binomial variables such as the 1/0 variables EMPLOY, MIGRANT, and PARTY a Chi-square goodness of fit test could be applied to test if the observations are consistent with a specified distribution. Because the distributional pattern of these dichotomous variables is of less interest here it will not be discussed further.

Because most of the independent variables are not normally distributed a non-parametric test has to be applied to test if the mean values of the respective covariates differ between the two samples full-time farm households and part-time farm households.

Regarding the comparison of the respective means for the covariates in the full- and part-time farm the Two-sample Wilcoxon rank-sum (Mann-Whitney) test is applied for the continuous and nominal variables with:

H_0: mean for covariate *i* in full-time sub sample equal to mean for covariate in part-time sub sample;

H_1: mean for covariate i in full-time sub sample not equal to mean for co-variate i in part-time sub sample;

i= {HSIZE, EDUS, LAND, LIVES}

For the dummy variables the Median Two-Sample test is applied with the same hypothesis as above but for the means of the covariates.

i= {EMPLOY, MIGRANT; PARTY}

The significance level is set at $\alpha = 0.05$. If the p-value is equal or smaller than 0.05 then the null-hypothesis that the means of the respective covariate are the same for both samples can be rejected (at 5% error probability). The tests are performed in Stata using the -ranksum- and -median- commands respectively.

Table 24: Comparison of mean values for full-time and part-time sub sample

Variable	Mann-Whitney		
	z	p	H_0
HSIZE	12.939	0.000	rejected
EDUS	-0.883	0.377	not rejected
LAND	-7.141	0.000	rejected
LIVES	2.916	0.004	rejected
	Median Two Sample		
	χ^2 (continuity corrected)	p	H_0
EMPLOY	0.5510	0.458	not rejected
MIGRANT	491.4936	0.000	rejected
PARTY	33.5460	0.000	rejected

Source: Own computations based on the RCRE data for Hebei, 1995-2002.

Appendix D

To prevent endogeneity problems stemming form the use of observed agricultural income in the regression of labor market participation choices in a first step a linear model is estimated and the resulting predicted values for agricultural income are inputted in the multinomial logit estimation. The linear model is estimated using OLS and treating all observations as cross-section data set. The natural logarithm of household's agricultural income as the dependent variable is deflated with 1990 being the base year.

Following Glauben et al. (2008) a set of explanatory variables as below in *Table 25* will be used for the estimation of observed income of the rural households in Hebei in 1990 prices.[19] The available amount of agricultural land is considered as exogenous to household's labor market participation decision because land in rural China is distributed administratively and household members that work in non-farm in-village jobs or (for some time) leave the village for migrant work still keep their land use rights (de Janvry et al., 2005).

Table 25: First step estimation of agricultural income – Variables, and estimation results

Variable	Coefficient		Robust Std. Errors	t	P>t
Total amount of labor days devoted to agricultural household business (planting + husbandry + fishery + forestry)	0.001	***	0.000	32.18	0.000
Share of female labor force on rural labor force	0.124	***	0.023	5.29	0.000
Share of laborer graduated from elementary school	0.143	***	0.023	6.23	0.000
Share of laborer graduated from secondary school	0.234	***	0.023	10.32	0.000
Share of laborer graduated from high school and above	0.276	***	0.029	9.44	0.000
Share of laborer with special skills	-0.011		0.031	-0.36	0.720
Dummy variable if the hh is active in planting	0.983	***	0.062	15.89	0.000
Dummy variable if the hh is active in forestry	0.157	***	0.031	5.09	0.000
Dummy variable if the hh is active in fishing	0.187	***	0.069	2.73	0.006

19 Thomas Herzfeld and Xiaobing Wang kindly provided the results of their first step regression in the paper of Glauben et al. (2008). Their support is highly appreciated.

Table 25 continued					
Dummy variable if the hh is active in orchard production	0.183	***	0.020	9.09	0.000
Number of permanent residents	0.047	***	0.005	9.57	0.000
Total amount of arable, orchard and forestry land	0.039	***	0.002	17.50	0.000
Dummy for Village 2	-0.255	***	0.035	-7.39	0.000
Dummy for Village 3	0.222	***	0.019	11.75	0.000
Dummy for Village 4	0.010		0.020	0-49	0.623
Dummy for Village 5	0.367	***	0.021	17.38	0.000
Dummy for Village 6	-0.294	***	0.021	-13.72	0.000
D_1987	0.260	***	0.025	10.44	0.000
D_1988	0.526	***	0.025	20.90	0.000
D_1989	0.876	***	0.025	35.09	0.000
D_1990	0.956	***	0.025	38.70	0.000
D_1991	0.916	***	0.025	36.57	0.000
D_1993	1.288	***	0.026	50.52	0.000
D_1995	2.525	***	0.025	99.16	0.000
D_1996	2.614	***	0.026	101.70	0.000
D_1998	2.658	***	0.026	103.01	0.000
D_1999	2.283	***	0.026	88.42	0.000
D_2000	2.438	***	0.026	94.66	0.000
D_2001	2.373	***	0.026	91.27	0.000
D_2002	2.295	***	0.026	88.03	0.000
Constant	4.640	***	0.067	69.23	0.000
Observations	8,260	R^2	0.843		
F (30, 8229)	1474.2 3				

Notes: The dummies for husbandry, village 1 and 1986 are the omitted categories.
***: significant at 1% level of error probability,
**: significant at 5% level of error probability,
*: significant at 10% level of error probability.

Source: Own computations based on RCRE survey data for Hebei 1986-2002.

Based on this regression the per capita values of the predicted logged agricultural household income are used as one of the explanatory variables in the multinomial logit estimation.

HOHENHEIMER VOLKSWIRTSCHAFTLICHE SCHRIFTEN

Band 1 Walter Deffaa: Anonymisierte Befragungen mit zufallsverschlüsselten Antworten. Die Randomized-Response-Technik (RRT). Methodische Grundlagen, Modelle und Anwendungen. 1982.

Band 2 Thomas Michael Baum: Staatsverschuldung und Stabilisierungspolitik in der Demokratie. Zur neoinstitutionalistischen Kritik der keynesianischen Fiskalpolitik. 1982.

Band 3 Klaus Schröter: Die wettbewerbspolitische Behandlung der leitungsgebundenen Energiewirtschaft. Dargestellt am Beispiel der Fernwärmewirtschaft der Bundesrepublik Deutschland. 1986.

Band 4 Hugo Mann: Theorie und Politik der Steuerreform in der Demokratie. 1987.

Band 5 Max Christoph Wewel: Intervallarithmetische Dependenzanalyse in der Ökonometrie. Ein konjekturaler Ansatz. 1987.

Band 6 Heinrich Pascher: Die U.S.-amerikanische Deregulation Policy im Luftverkehrs- und Bankenbereich. 1987.

Band 7 Harald Lob: Die Entwicklung der französischen Wettbewerbspolitik bis zur Verordnung Nr. 86-1243 vom 01. Dezember 1986. Eine exemplarische Untersuchung der Erfassung der Behinderungsstrategie auf der Grundlage des Konzepts eines wirksamen Wettbewerbs. 1988.

Band 8 Ulrich Kirschner: Die Erfassung der Nachfragemacht von Handelsunternehmen. Eine Analyse der ökonomischen Beurteilungskriterien und der wettbewerbsrechtlichen Instrumente im Bereich der Verhaltenskontrolle.1988.

Band 9 Friedhelm Herb: Marktwirtschaftliche Innovationspolitik. 1988.

Band 10 Claus Schnabel: Zur ökonomischen Analyse der Gewerkschaften in der Bundesrepublik Deutschland. Theoretische und empirische Untersuchungen von Mitgliederentwicklung, Verhalten und Einfluß auf wirtschaftliche Größen. 1989.

Band 11 Jan B. Rittaler: Industrial Concentration and the Chicago School of Antitrust Analysis. A Critical Evaluation on the Basis of Effective Competition. 1989.

Band 12 Thomas Märtz: Interessengruppen und Gruppeninteressen in der Demokratie. Zur Theorie des Rent-Seeking. 1990.

Band 13 Andreas Maurer: Statistische Verfahren zur Ermittlung von oligopolistischen Strukturen. 1990.

Band 14 Peter Mendler: Zur ökonomischen und politisch-institutionellen Analyse öffentlicher Kredithilfen. 1992.

Band 15 Heinrich J. Engelke: Die Interpretation der Rundfunkfreiheit des Grundgesetzes: Eine Analyse aus ökonomischer Sicht. 1992.

Band 16 Thomas Fischer: Staat, Recht und Verfassung im Denken von Walter Eucken. Zu den staats- und rechtstheoretischen Grundlagen einer wirtschaftsordnungspolitischen Konzeption. 1993.

Band 17 Stefan Elßer: Innovationswettbewerb. Determinanten und Unternehmensverhalten. 1993.

Band 18 Reinhard Scharff: Regionalpolitik und regionale Entwicklungspotentiale. Eine kritische Analyse. 1993.

Band 19 Karin Beckmann: Probleme der Regionalpolitik im Zuge der Vollendung des Europäischen Binnenmarktes. Eine ökonomische Analyse. 1995.

Band 20 Bernd Nolte: Engpaßfaktoren der Innovation und Innovationsinfrastruktur. Eine theoretische und empirische Analyse für ländliche Wirtschaftsräume in Baden-Württemberg. 1996.

Band 21 Klaus-Rainer Brintzinger: Die Nationalökonomie an den Universitäten Freiburg, Heidelberg und Tübingen 1918 - 1945. Eine institutionenhistorische, vergleichende Studie der wirtschaftswissenschaftlichen Fakultäten und Abteilungen südwestdeutscher Universitäten. 1996.

Band 22 Steffen Binder: Die Idee der Konsumentensouveränität in der Wettbewerbstheorie. Teleokratische vs. nomokratische Auffassung. 1996.

Band 23 Alexander Burger: Deregulierungspotentiale in der Gesetzlichen Rentenversicherung. Reformnotwendigkeiten versus Reformmöglichkeiten. 1996.

Band 24 Burkhard Scherer: Regionale Entwicklungspolitik. Konzeption einer dezentralisierten und integrierten Regionalpolitik. 1997.

Band 25 Frauke Wolf: Lorenzkurvendisparität. Neuere Entwicklungen, Erweiterungen und Anwendungen. 1997.

Band 26 Hans Pitlik: Politische Ökonomie des Föderalismus. Föderative Kompetenzverteilung im Lichte der konstitutionellen Ökonomik. 1997.

Band 27 Stephan Seiter: Der Beitrag Nicholas Kaldors zur Neuen Wachstumstheorie. Eine vergleichende Studie vor dem Hintergrund der Debatte über den Verdoorn-Zusammenhang. 1997.

Band 28 André Schmidt: Ordnungspolitische Perspektiven der europäischen Integration im Spannungsfeld von Wettbewerbs- und Industriepolitik. 1998.

Band 29 Bernd Blessin: Innovations- und Umweltmanagement in kleinen und mittleren Unternehmen. Eine theoretische und empirische Analyse. 1998.

Band 30 Oliver Letzgus: Die Ökonomie internationalen Umweltschutzes. 1999.

Band 31 Claudia Hafner: Systemwettbewerb versus Harmonisierung in Europa. Am Beispiel des Arbeitsmarktes. 1999.

Band 32 Jürgen Kulle: Ökonomie der Musikindustrie. Eine Analyse der körperlichen und unkörperlichen Musikverwertung mit Hilfe von Tonträgern und Netzen. 1998.

Band 33 Michael Ganske: Intertemporale Aspekte von Staatsverschuldung und Außenhandel. 1999.

Band 34 Margit Ströbele: Die Deregulierungswirkungen der europäischen Integration. Das Beispiel der Sondermärkte. 1999.

Band 35 Marion Benesch: Devisenmarktinterventionen in Theorie und Praxis. Eine umfassende Analyse ihrer Zielsetzungen, Wirkungsweisen und wirtschaftspolitischen Bedeutung. 1999.

Band 36 Torsten Gruber: Unterschiedliche geldpolitische Transmissionsmechanismen und Stabilitätskulturen als mögliche Ursachen geldpolitischer Spannungen in der Europäischen Währungsunion. 2000.

Band 37 Bertram Melzig-Thiel: Arbeit in der Informationsgesellschaft. Chancen und Risiken neuer Informations- und Kommunikationstechnologien für die Beschäftigung. 2000.

Band 38 Annette Fritz: Die Entsorgungswirtschaft im Spannungsfeld zwischen Abfallpolitik und Kartellrecht. Eine industrieökonomische Branchenstudie. 2001.

Band 39 Harald Strotmann: Arbeitsplatzdynamik in der baden-württembergischen Industrie. Eine Analyse mit amtlichen Betriebspaneldaten. 2002.

Band 40 Dietrich Benner: Qualitätsungewißheit bei Gütern mit Vertrauenseigenschaften. Entwicklung und Anwendung eines entscheidungstheoretisch fundierten Analyserahmens. 2002.

Band 41 Jürgen M. Schechler: Sozialkapital und Netzwerkökonomik. 2002.

Band 42 Kay-Uwe May: Haushaltskonsolidierung durch Ausgabekürzungen. Restriktionen und Strategien. 2002.

Band 43 Peter Kühnl: Der Wechselkurs als Zwischenziel der Geldpolitik im Aufholprozess. Die monetärkeynesianische Entwicklungsstrategie der Berliner Schule vor dem Hintergrund der makroökonomischen Entwicklung ausgewählter Länder Mittel- und Osteuropas. 2003.

Band 44 Steffen Wirth: Nichtparametrische Analyse von Bildungsertragsraten. Neuere Entwicklungen und Anwendungen. 2003.

Band 45 Bernhard Holwegler: Innovation, Diffusion und Beschäftigung. Die ökonomische Theorie der Technologiediffusion und ihr Beitrag zur Erklärung technologischer Arbeitslosigkeit. 2003.

Band 46 Guntram R. M. Hepperle: Zukunftsorientierte Industriepolitik. Möglichkeiten und Grenzen. 2004.

Band 47 Udo Vullhorst: Stabilisierungspolitik bei supranationaler Geldpolitik und nationaler Fiskalpolitik. Eine spieltheoretische Betrachung. 2004.

Band 48 Matthias Rösch: Die Bedeutung von Investivlöhnen und Gewinnbeteiligungen für Einkommensverteilung und Beschäftigung. 2004.

Band 49 Michael Bubik: Erfolgskriterien für Unternehmenszusammenschlüsse. Eine theoretische und exemplarische Analyse. 2005.

Band 50 Jörg Weltin: Internationale Unternehmensbesteuerung. Allokation der Besteuerungsrechte unter veränderten Rahmenbedingungen. 2005.

Band 51 Susanne Reichart: Zum Konvergenzprozess der mittel- und osteuropäischen EU-Beitrittsländer. 2005.

Band 52 Daniel Hartmann: Geldpolitik und Beschäftigung. Die geldpolitische Strategie der Federal Reserve: Vorbild oder Auslaufmodell? 2005.

Band 53 Marc Peter Radke: Explaining Financial Crises. A Cyclical Approach. 2005.

Band 54 Katja Hölsch: Umverteilungseffekte in Europa. Eine Analyse für ausgewählte Länder. 2006.

Band 55 Ulrike Lehr: Contingent Valuation Daten und Bayes'sche Verfahren. Ein Vorschlag zur Verbesserung von Umweltbewertung und Nutzentransfer. 2006.

Band 56 Jutta Maute: Hyperinflation, Currency Board, and Bust. The Case of Argentina. 2006.

Band 57 Michael Knittel: Geldpolitik und Stabilität des Bankensystems. Das Liquiditätsproblem aus Sicht der Theoriegeschichte und der gegenwärtigen Finanzmarktentwicklung. 2007.

Band 58 Oliver Frör: Rationality Concepts in Environmental Valuation. 2007.

Band 59 Jochen Gert Arend Wiegmann: Produktivitätsentwicklung in Deutschland. 2008.

Band 60 Nicola Meier: China – The New Developmental State? An Empirical Analysis of the Automotive Industry. 2009.

Band 61 Carsten H. Wander: Logistik und Wettbewerb. Zur Rolle logistischer (Re-)Organisation in einer wettbewerbsbasierten Marktwirtschaft. 2009.

Band 62 Sven Wydra: Produktions- und Beschäftigungseffekte neuer Technologien. Am Beispiel der Biotechnologie. 2010.

Band 63 Andreas Schaal: Die Relevanz von Venture Capital für Innovation und Beschäftigung. Theoretische Klärung und empirische Analyse. 2010

Band 64 Sybille Sobczak: Geldpolitik und Vermögensmärkte. Volkswirtschaftliche Bedeutung von und geldpolitische Reaktion auf Asset Price Bubbles. 2010

Band 65 Constanze Dobler: The Impact of Formal and Informal Institutions on Economic Growth. A Case Study on the MENA Region. 2011.

Band 66 Tobias Börger: Social Desirability and Environmental Valuation. 2012.

Band 67 Julian Christ: Innovative Places in Europe. Research Clustering, Co-Patenting Networks and the Growth of Regions. 2012.

Band 68 Christian Böber: China in Transition. Poverty, Income Decomposition and Labor Allocation of Agricultural Households in Hebei Province. 2012.

www.peterlang.de

FSC
www.fsc.org
MIX
Papier | Fördert
gute Waldnutzung
FSC® C083411

Kolibri 360 GmbH
Ferdinand-Jühlke-Straße 7
99095 Erfurt, Deutschland
produktsicherheit@kolibri360.de